# THIRTY PSALMISTS

# Thirty Psalmists

## *Personalities of the Psalter*

## FLEMING JAMES

Edited and with a Foreword
by
R. LANSING HICKS

The Seabury Press • New York

*First* Seabury Paperback *Edition Published 1965*

TO REBECCA, MY WIFE

# EDITOR'S FOREWORD

*Thirty Psalmists* was first published in 1938. The war began soon after its appearance, and it went out of print before 1946. In its own right, this volume had a most favorable initial reception among scholars as well as among laymen, for whom it was written. In 1941, Dr. James's second book, *Personalities of the Old Testament*, appeared and became a classroom classic. Written with the same warmth and clarity that made the latter text so popular, *Thirty Psalmists* has for a number of years been a rare item, long sought after by both students and pastors.

The original edition of this book bore the subtitle "A Study in Personalities of the Psalter as seen against the Background of Gunkel's Type-study of the Psalms." As cumbersome as the statement was, it described accurately the author's intention and pointed to his method. The finished results of Gunkel's monumental research in the Type-analysis (*Gattungskritik*) of the Psalms had just been published in Germany in 1933, and Dr. James, convinced of the immense value of this scientific method, was eager to introduce it to English-speaking readers.

Therefore, when this book appeared in 1938, it was the first major work by an American scholar to present the mature fruits of Gunkel's labor to this country; and this in itself remains one of its significant contributions to biblical studies. But Gunkel's work furnished only the background. Professor James brought to the study of these Psalmists the illumination of his own clear scholarship. Accordingly, he offers a fresh translation of all the Psalms here selected as well as his own interpretation of their rhythmic structure; in difficult areas he constantly cites the suggestions of leading British and European commentators and assesses them critically; and throughout the book he reflects what the Psalms have meant to him in his own devotional life.

The structure of Gunkel's Type-study of the Psalms was erected on two pillars, which, at their foundations, are basically related: form and cultus. This renowned German scholar had already published epoch-making form-critical investigations of the early traditions embedded in the book of Genesis, and these had also led him far into the study of Israel's cultic life. From this vantage point, he could then view Hebrew psalmody in a fresh perspective, as Dr. James's book well illustrates.

Since the 1930's the debate in Psalm studies has centered on how to use these tools more effectively and on what relationships exist between cultic institutions and the history of forms. The most massive work, for instance, since Gunkel's time has been done by Sigmund Mowinckel. And he has fused form-critical and cult-historical observations into a "cult-functional" approach, which attempts not only "to understand every surviving psalm as a real cult psalm, made for a definite cultic situation" (a position Gunkel could not hold), but in addition may provide a method for distinguishing these cult psalms from a "private psalmody" which later developed in Israel's life.[1]

Artur Weiser also shows Gunkel's formative influence. In his excellent commentary, Weiser insists that along with the history of the forms of the Psalms, we must seek to delineate "the history of the traditions manifested in them, and also the history of the Old Testament cultus as the sphere of life in which these traditions were preserved as a living force." This quest leads him back to a great "Autumnal Festival of Yahweh," celebrated by the early tribal confederacy of Israel at the New Year, which enacted ceremonially the renewal of the Sinai Covenant and guaranteed peace and salvation. This festival formed a cultic drama that supplies the *Sitz im Leben* for many of Israel's Psalms.[2]

The time, location, and specific purpose of such a seasonal festival; the role which the Davidic king played in the cultic drama; and the interpretation of the particular Psalms to be identified with it—these are major problems on which many

[1] Mowinckel, *The Psalms in Israel's Worship*, Vol. I, pp. 34f.
[2] Weiser, *The Psalms*, pp. 23ff.

modern scholars have worked.[3] Although the treatment of the "Royal Psalms" in *Thirty Psalmists* may seem far behind the vanguard of recent investigators in this area, its position favoring an early date for Royal Psalmody and its insistence upon the sacral function of the king are now widely accepted. Fleming James adopted Gunkel's method and used it (though not uncritically) in his own studies because he felt that its emphasis upon form and cult was fundamentally sound; and to this extent, time has proved him right.

Let it be perfectly clear that this Seabury edition of *Thirty Psalmists* is not being sent forth as a new book. Being convinced that the original work has abiding merit, we reissue this volume first of all to make it available to a new generation of readers. The text of the book stands essentially as Fleming James wrote it, and today's students will recognize its limitations of time and perspective.

Nevertheless, this is a new edition, not just a reprint, and we have taken the opportunity to make a considerable number of changes in both content and arrangement. From the Berkeley Divinity School Library, we had access to a copy of *Thirty Psalmists* personally annotated by the author. Thereby some changes that Dr. James himself wished to make—as few as they are—have been incorporated into this new edition.

More important for the present reader are the additions and rearrangements. In 1934, Dr. James contributed an essay on the religion of the Psalmists to a fine collection of studies which was never widely circulated in America. The substance of this chapter is now built into our final section, "Some Concluding Reflections." The present Bibliography contains items both new and old, for it attempts to serve two purposes. It retains all the titles which Dr. James used as his chief sources in writing *Thirty Psalmists,* and it offers a limited selection of works which helps to indicate the directions that Psalm studies have taken since 1938. New bibliographical material will also be found in a few revised footnotes.

In the original edition, Dr. James had used small separate

---

[3] See especially the works by A. R. Johnson, H. J. Kraus, and C. Westermann in the Bibliography.

sections in the front, and a lengthy appendix, to introduce Gunkel's work and to describe his own method. To make all this material more readily available, as well as to eliminate some duplication, we have brought it together, now somewhat reshaped and furnished with new headings, into an "Author's Introduction."

Throughout his life, Fleming James exhibited a remarkable combination of scholarship and deep piety. At the age of twenty-two, he had already received his Ph.D. in classical Greek from the University of Pennsylvania when he entered the Philadelphia Divinity School, where his father was Professor of Homiletics. He was ordained a priest in the Episcopal Church in 1902 and served for nearly twenty years in the active parish ministry, first as missionary-in-charge of the American Congregation of the Church of Our Saviour in Shanghai, and later in parishes in Philadelphia and New Jersey. Then, in 1921, Dr. James accepted appointment as Professor of Old Testament at the Berkeley Divinity School, and in 1940 became Dean of the School of Theology of the University of the South. When he retired from Sewanee in 1947, he joined the committee preparing the Revised Standard Version of the Bible and rendered distinguished service as Executive Secretary of the Old Testament section, thus devoting his last major scholarly efforts to the translation of the Bible.[4]

Students and colleagues, parishioners and friends, who knew Dr. James in person loved him for his warmth of personality, depth of scholarship, and purity of spirit. Happily these same qualities live on in the pages of his writings for a wide company of readers. May the reappearance of *Thirty Psalmists*—Fleming James's first book—serve as a fresh tribute to this generous Christian scholar.

[4] For a fuller account of Dr. James's life, work, and personality, see R. L. Hicks and R. C. Dentan (eds.), "Essays in Honor of Fleming James on His Seventy-fifth Birthday," *Anglican Theological Review*, XXXIV, 4, pp. 195ff.

# PREFACE

The author extends his thanks to the late Rector of the Church of the Holy Trinity, Philadelphia, the Rev. Howard R. Weir, and to the other members of the Committee, for appointing him the Bohlen Lecturer for 1936; to Professors Millar Burrows, George Dahl, Charles B. Hedrick, Cuthbert A. Simpson and Charles L. Taylor, Jr., for reading the manuscript and making valuable suggestions; to Mrs. Fleming James, Jr., for typing the manuscript and improving it; to Mrs. Ormonde L. Rolls for studying the manuscript and giving advice concerning it; to the Rev. Kenneth W. Cameron and several students of the Berkeley Divinity School for assistance in correcting the proofs; to Mr. Franklin E. Parker, Jr., Trustee of the Berkeley Divinity School, for introducing the manuscript to the publishers; to the staff of Messrs. G. P. Putnam's Sons for their courtesy, patience and cordial interest in bringing out this book; and to the many others whose encouragement and help have contributed to its production.

The citations from the American Standard Edition of the Revised Bible are made with permission of the copyright owner, the International Council of Religious Education.

# CONTENTS

# AUTHOR'S INTRODUCTION

## The Value of Studying the Psalmists

IN ALL ages the Psalms have been to Bible readers the very heart of the Old Testament, even vying with the Gospels themselves for first place in the affections of God's people. They have been used by Christian leaders alike in times of trial and in seasons of joy to sustain, inspire, comfort, and delight the religious heart. They have been employed both in public worship and in private devotion. Their cadences still possess a power to find us as perhaps no other parts of the Bible can.

What is the reason for this pre-eminence and enduring worth? Is it not that in the Psalmists we have the classic expression of the life of the soul with God? They lived with God in an intense, absorbing way that was all their own and were able somehow to put that life into words that are absolute and final. These two things taken together make what we call a classic. The determinative feature of the classic is that it does not wear out. The more it is used the fresher, the more compelling it grows.

What more rewarding task then could be undertaken by the Christian than to seek a clearer understanding, a more intimate knowledge of these men? And that is what this book proposes for itself. Its aim is to select a number of the Psalmists and listen to what they tell us of themselves. It is their *self-revelation* that will interest us. What has each to say of God as he finds Him, of himself in his life with God, of man and man's life in the light of God? And in asking this we shall not have in mind—except incidentally—any application of what we learn to our own lives. Our eyes will be turned away from ourselves to the Psalmists.

In these treatments of the Psalmists, the author has used his own translation of the Hebrew text. In it he has endeavored to make the reader *feel* the Hebrew, so far as that is possible. He has therefore kept where he could the order of the Hebrew words and has rendered them with a literalness that may often seem bald. He has also followed the *Hebrew numbering* of the verses, which is usually higher by one than the English.

The form of the divine name (Yahweh) which was probably used by the ancient Israelites, and is current in most scholarly writing today, has been retained. There is no need to explain here that the pronunciation "Jehovah" arose out of a mistake. If, however, the reader finds that the word "Yahweh" distracts him, let him adopt the Jewish practice, which has prevailed for more than two thousand years, and substitute "The Lord."

To mark the stresses recurring in the poetry of the Psalter, the author has employed an acute accent ('). Hebrew poetry has no meter, in the sense of a measured scheme of syllables, but is characterized by a strongly marked *rhythm*. This rhythm is created by the beats which fall upon the important words of a verse, conforming roughly to a certain pattern. If, in reading, the accented syllables of the translation be stressed, some idea (however inadequate) of the rhythm of the original may be obtained.

Another feature of Hebrew poetry is its division of a verse into sections, usually into halves; and this has been indicated by a space introduced into the line. The fact that the *numbered* verses do not invariably correspond to the verse arrangement of the translation need not surprise the reader, for this numbering was introduced in comparatively modern times, when the ancient versification was no longer understood correctly. For two centuries, however, such understanding has grown, and during the last generation, modern research has brought it to a point where there is general agreement as to principles, though the details are often differently worked out.[1] The present writer,

---

[1] For an excellent present-day summary of the principles of ancient Hebrew poetry, see the articles, in *The Interpreter's Dictionary of the Bible*, by Gottwald on "Poetry, Hebrew" (especially its bibliography) and by Hempel on "Psalms" (pp. 944-947); see also Mowinckel, *The Psalms*

in his division of verses and assignment of stress, has endeavored to follow one or more modern translators and has refrained from innovations of his own.

In a number of passages the reader will notice an *asterisk* (\*) affixed to a word or a sentence. This indicates that the translation is not rendering the exact text of the Hebrew Bible (called the Massoretic text), but is following some emendation. Emendations are occasionally necessary because the Hebrew text has been in places imperfectly preserved, sometimes so imperfectly that it makes no sense or is even quite untranslatable. In such places it frequently differs from the ancient versions, showing that the writers of these versions either had before them a different text from ours, or found themselves unable to make much out of the passage. Modern commentators have been apt to emend our Hebrew text very freely, some of them carrying the practice so far as to give to a verse, or even to a series of verses, a sense quite different from that of the present Hebrew words. The author has endeavored to retain the Massoretic text where that is at all possible. Often, therefore, the Hebrew text reappears in his translation in a form that may strike the reader as uncouth; but such uncouthness may be nearer to what the Psalmist himself wrote than the neat alterations of some modern scholars.

Where emendations have seemed necessary, the author has in the main avoided conjectural corrections by modern scholars and, if possible, has followed one or more of the chief ancient versions. These are three in number: (*a*) the Greek translation of the Hebrew Bible, commonly called the Septuagint (LXX, c.200 B.C.); (*b*) the early Christian translation into Syriac (the Peshitta, second century A.D.); and (*c*) Jerome's translation into Latin from the Hebrew (c.400 A.D.).[2] These often preserve a better reading than the Massoretic text; and in the case of textual uncertainties, they show us how the difficulties were met by leading ancient translators.

---

*in Israel's Worship,* Ch. XIX. For ancient Hebrew music, see Werner's articles on "Music" and "Musical Instruments" in the *Dictionary,* and Mowinckel, *op. cit.,* Ch. XIV. (Ed.)

[2] Not the Vulgate, which in the case of the Psalms is translated from the Septuagint.

## The Problem of Classifying the Psalms

As soon as we speak of making a selection from among the Psalmists, we are at once confronted with the question: On what principle shall we select? There are one hundred and fifty Psalms; and after making allowance for the possibility that a single poet may occasionally be the Author of two or more of them, we still are confronted in the Psalter with a company of a hundred or more persons, each of whom has sung in his own way of God and His dealings with men. Can they be divided into groups, that we may take one or more from each group? We are therefore almost compelled to classify the Psalms in some fashion.

In the past the Psalms have been classified in various ways. An obvious grouping for practical needs would be to divide them according to the *situations in which they would be appropriate*. The present writer has still in an old Prayer Book a list of Psalms which he made to guide his choice of reading in pastoral calls: Psalms for the sick-room, for the time of trouble or of burdened conscience, Psalms of thanksgiving for deliverance, and the like. Such a division, however, is too subjective to be scientific; and, moreover, it is ruled out for the present study by the very aim we have set: not to consider ourselves but the Psalmists.

Other methods divide the Psalms according to the *soul-moods they express* (Psalms of Sad, Joyful, and Restful Moods);[3] according to *topics* (Psalms of adoration, reflection, thanksgiving; Psalms concerning Yahweh's universal reign, or concerning the King, or in celebration of worship);[4] or according to the *nature of their contents* (Prayers, Praises, Petitions, Confessions, Intercessions, Deprecations, Instructions, Meditations).[5]

These examples of division according to various principles might easily be multiplied. They all have some value, but according to the exponents of the now prevailing view, they fall short of scientific accuracy.[6]

[3] Baethgen, *Die Psalmen,* 3rd Ed., p. iv.
[4] McFayden, *The Psalms in Modern Speech,* pp. 246f.
[5] Barnes, *The Psalms* (Westminster Commentary), pp. xvff.
[6] It is only fair to add that strictly scientific accuracy in classification is really not obtainable by any one, and that Gunkel's own classification is not proof against all objections.

This prevailing view is set forth principally by Hermann Gunkel in his *Einleitung in die Psalmen,* which he did not live to finish, the completed work being published by his friend Joachim Begrich, whom he selected for that task before his death in March, 1932. Stated simply, it starts from the premise that at first every sacred poem in Israel's religion was composed to be sung as an accompaniment of a ritual act. In other words, the Psalms *took their rise from the various occasions of Israel's worship.*[7] Since these occasions were of different sorts, such as the feast, the thank-offering, the sin-offering, the public fast, etc., the Psalms composed for them would fall into natural groups according to the ritual acts they accompanied.

Now let us follow in more detail the development of Gunkel's Type-study of the Psalms as he himself describes it in his masterful Introduction.[8]

*Why the Psalms are difficult to understand.* Here then is Gunkel's argument. The Psalms, though familiar enough to Bible readers, are not easy to understand. Many things combine to make this so: the absence in Hebrew of words giving the logical connection between sentences; the vagueness of the expressions used, so that one often cannot tell exactly what is meant; the way in which passion leads to exaggerated language whose literal significance can only be guessed at; the impossibility of knowing whether the Hebrew tenses refer to past, present, or future; the laconic brevity of style; the absence of trustworthy tradition as to authors, dates and occasions of writing; the poor condition of the text; and the fact that, on the whole, the Psalms have no recognizable internal arrangement.

Now since it is an unbreakable principle of science that nothing can be understood without its connection, our proper task in studying these difficult Psalms is to rediscover the relations and connections between them.

To do this we must use not only the Psalter itself but all the poetic material of ancient Israel as it survives in the rest of the

---

[7] Peters saw this, but did not use it as a principle of classification.
[8] *Einleitung,* pp. 1-31.

Bible and the Apocrypha. We must go yet further and include in our survey the poems of ancient Babylonia, Assyria, and Egypt, the discovery of which was "the most significant event for the study of the Psalms that took place in the 19th century, . . . especially since they antedate the Biblical poems by centuries, yes, in part by millennia." Into this immense and complicated material, we must try to bring light and order by establishing the Types into which it falls. For this reason the study of Types is no hobby which can be pursued or abandoned at pleasure, but a basic work without which one cannot arrive at any certainty in all the rest, the solid ground on which everything further must rise.

Gunkel's task, then, as he conceives it, is to assemble in an ordered way a number of quite self-evident things recurring in this mass of material—things, indeed, which have not up to this time been sufficiently appreciated—and on this basis to seek an explanation of the Psalter.

In primitive peoples, poetry springs out of the various occasions of life; women meet the victorious hero with a triumph-song; over the bier of the dead is raised the moving elegy; or the prophet, perhaps in the forecourt of the sanctuary, rolls the thunder of his voice upon the assembled congregation. Abundant examples of this in ancient literature show us that the Types of a primitive body of writing must be distinguished according to the different occasions of life out of which they have arisen.

*The place of the Psalms in Israel's worship.* Out of what occasions, then, did the Psalms come into being? What, to use Gunkel's phrase, was their "seat in life" (*Sitz im Leben*)? He answers that it was the *public worship of Israel.* Several things justify us in adopting this hypothesis: Later Judaism actually did employ them in worship, as is seen from the title given the Psalter in Hebrew—*tehillîm,* meaning "praises." Again, the Babylonian Psalms were obviously connected with specific transactions of divine worship, and this would incline us to think the same of the Israelitish Psalms. Then, too, the Psalms have been used in worship by both Synagogue and Church up to the present. Evidently they are fitted in themselves for such use.

This hypothesis is confirmed by the strict way in which most of them adhere to a given form, so that we often have difficulty in distinguishing one from another. Akin to this is the fashion in which they avoid anything that would fasten them to a particular occasion. Names, for instance, do not occur in the Psalter, although in other poems, such as David's lament over the death of Saul and Jonathan, names are freely used (II Sam. 1:19ff.). This absence of particulars is indeed surprising, and it can only be explained by the supposition that these Psalms are not in their original essence the outpourings of personal religion, but belong to something transcending the individual, to public worship. Therefore, the Psalms (concludes Gunkel) are, according to their most ancient origin, forms of worship, or at least they take their rise from such forms. This is corroborated by the fact that the Babylonian poems exhibit in yet stronger measure the same adherence to form.

This conclusion must not alarm us nor make us think that there is no personal, individual element in the Psalms. Quite the contrary, as we have seen. But it does bring home to us the necessity of understanding the various forms which recur in the Psalter. Only so can we measure the greatness of the Psalmists who used these forms freely and showed surprising ability to depart from them in order to utter their own heart-accents.

To obtain such understanding we must sink ourselves in the most ancient worship of Israel, and especially pay attention to those very occasions on which words were spoken or poems sung. Now there is abundant evidence that acts of worship were accompanied by words. Take only one instance, the priestly blessing. In Lev. 9:22, we are told that Aaron "lifted up his hands toward the people and blessed them." That was the *act*. The *words* of blessing are given in Num. 6:23ff.:

> Yahweh bless thee, and keep thee:
> Yahweh make his face to shine upon thee, and be
> gracious unto thee:
> Yahweh lift up his countenance upon thee, and give
> thee peace.

This combination of act and word was even more pronounced in Babylonian worship, and indeed prevailed generally over the ancient world. It survives today in the Christian sacraments where *word* and *sign* go together.

Another thing that repeats itself universally is that the words thus used were not left to the prompting of the moment, but were held fast in a form and so handed down from generation to generation. And this form was apt to be rhythmically constructed—that is, to be poetry. This was especially true of words intended to be used in the worship of a larger circle, such as a congregation or a sacred choir; for only in some artistic fashion can a number of people give orderly expression to their thought. An excellent example of this Gunkel considers to be the words uttered in the transactions pertaining to the Ark:

> And it came to pass, when the ark set forward, that
>     Moses said,
>   Rise up, O Yahweh, and let thine enemies be scat-
>       tered;
>   And let them that hate thee flee before thee.
> And when it rested, he said,
>   Return, O Yahweh, unto the ten thousands of thou-
>       sands of Israel (Num. 10:35f.).

From Psalm 24 a kindred transaction may legitimately be inferred. For a season Yahweh has been absent from his sanctuary; but now the procession bearing the ark in its midst arrives at the portals gray with age, and the chant is raised:

> Lift up your heads, O ye gates;
> And be ye lifted up, ye everlasting doors:
> And the King of glory will come in (Ps. 24:7f.).

It is not often indeed that the Old Testament gives plain examples of act and word going together; but it is not difficult for us, when it describes acts of worship, to imagine the accompanying words and vice versa. The Law and the Historical Books furnish us with a number of scattered hints that enable us to do this, and in the Psalms themselves we get frequent allusions to acts of worship which we may well suppose accompanied their recital.

For example, we hear in the Law of a Thank-offering, and we connect with it the "Thanksgiving-songs" of the Psalter, which bear the same name (*tôdā*), and not infrequently speak of the offerings which were brought at the same time as the Psalm was sung. We can get a more exact idea of the place of the Thanksgiving-song in the worship service from the allusions in such Psalms, which speak perhaps of the lifting up of a "cup of salvation" (Ps. 116:13) or presuppose the dance of the festal congregation around the altar (Ps. 118:27). Jeremiah speaks of "them that bring sacrifices of thanksgiving into the house of Yahweh" and say,

> Give thanks unto Yahweh of hosts, for Yahweh is good,
> For his loving kindness endureth forever (Jer. 33:11);

a refrain that is repeated also in the Psalter. The personal situation of the man who brought such a thank-offering is depicted in Elihu's words to Job (Job 33:19ff.), and all sorts of allusions in the Psalms fit in with this portrayal. By putting together these passages and others of the same kind, we can get a vivid picture of the act or transaction of worship which belonged to these songs.

The original Psalm, then, consisted of words composed to be recited or sung when an act of worship was being carried out. Later, as we have seen, gifted individuals shook themselves free from such connection with public worship and used the forms current in worship as a vehicle for expressing the most inward and personal experiences with God—although even they retained much of the original ways of speaking that had sprung from worship.

To repeat what has already been said, if one is to arrange these worship-Psalms according to their inner nature, one can do so only by arranging them according to the acts of worship to which they belong. In carrying out this principle, Gunkel lays down several conditions which must be strictly observed if one Type is to be distinguished from another with accuracy.

*Characteristics distinguishing the Types.* First, only such Psalms may be classed together as belong to a definite occasion of worship or at least originate from it.

Secondly, such kindred Psalms must exhibit a common treasure of ideas and moods.

A third element that is necessary without exception is that all the individual parts belonging to a Psalm of a given Type must be connected by their common forms of expression (*Formensprache*). For each Type has its own forms, or ways of uttering thought, and these are constantly reappearing in the Psalms of that Type. This leads Gunkel to lay special stress on such forms; and in our brief descriptions of each Type, we have tried at least to enumerate the chief elements of the forms that distinguish its several parts.

Finally, within each Type there must be distinguished the motifs that compose it; that is, the smaller parts into which it naturally falls. We say *naturally*, for Gunkel claims that the parts which he thus distinguished are plainly there; that he is not marking divisions he has invented or arbitrarily created, but pointing out the breaks that are actually given by the meaning of the Psalm and indicated by the form. These are:

(1) *The Introduction.* This is especially easy to identify, for it is the place where (in modern as well as ancient writings) form controls most strongly. As we begin a fairy-story with "Once upon a time" and a letter with "Dear So and so," the Psalmist was almost certain to indicate the kind of a poem he was composing by its opening words. If a Hymn, he would summon to praise; if a Lament, he would cry out for mercy, etc.

(2) *The Conclusion.* After the Introduction this is most likely to exhibit the Type, for it frequently corresponds with the Introduction even in form.

(3) *The Main Part* of the Psalm, lying between them. This must in turn be resolved into its individual parts or motifs. These are apt to follow a more or less plain law in their form and content, though their order varies with the particular Author.

Using this method, Gunkel divides the Psalms into the following Types (*Gattungen*): Hymns, Songs of Yahweh's Enthronement, Laments of the People, Royal Psalms, Laments of the Individual, Minor Types, Prophetic Psalms, and Wisdom Poetry.[9]

*The role of the individual in the Psalms.* We must now take up the question of the *individual element* in the majority of the Psalms. Gunkel's principle seems to exclude individual self-expression, at any rate in the early stages. "It was not the individual saint," he says, "who sang the first Psalms in order to pour out his most personal self before God"; it was rather the priests who "composed them and kept them at the sanctuary in order to use them on suitable occasions" (p. 19). Such Psalms would naturally abound in allusions to the acts of worship. But he goes on, "there are other poems, which in the Psalter constitute the actual majority, in which there appears nothing or very little of such allusions, which on the contrary have come forth in much more personal fashion and from out of the religious life of the individual saint. It would appear to us a very great mistake if one should overlook all this purely personal element and do as perhaps S. Mowinckel has done in his *Psalmenstudien*—interpret the Psalms in their entirety as 'cult poems.' On the contrary, we shall be compelled to bring into special prominence, because of its peculiar significance for religion, whatever departs from the Type used at that time in worship."

Gunkel, therefore, is far from denying the personal element in the majority of the Psalms. On the contrary, he tries to bring it out as the most valuable part of the Psalter; and no one who has used his commentary will say that he has failed to do this. He is particularly severe upon the view once so widely advocated—that the speaker in the Type of Psalms called "Laments" is the congregation, not any individual. While admitting that such a personification of the congregation or the nation occurs unmistakably now and then in Hebrew poetry, he declares that outside of these few passages "the interpretation of

[9] These Types are described in some detail at the beginning of each new section in the body of this book. Cross-references, listing each section and the part of the Gunkel-Begrich *Einleitung* from which it is taken, are given in the appendix. (Ed.)

the 'I' as the poet himself is so natural, yes, fundamentally so self-evident that a sound judgment will regard a deviation from this view as a tasteless error and will with all its might guard itself against committing it." (p. 174)

While the individual then at first counted for little in Psalm-making, he more and more made himself master of the Types and used them to express his own personal religious life. And this inevitably had an effect upon the Types themselves. "With the entry of the individual great poet into history, it is conceded that the Types themselves experienced all sorts of alterations. The most important of these is that the various Types became mingled—in contrast to the oldest Types, which, having their firm place in divine worship and a definite effect before their eyes which they wished to produce (an effect supplied them by their very place in worship), proceeded in a traditional circle of ideas and in firmly stamped forms, thus remaining completely pure and simple."

*The growth of new forms.* One of the forms created by a more advanced age was the "Liturgy," in which fragments of various Types were arranged antiphonally. In this artistic form the poet had a wonderful instrument which never failed him, wherewith he could depict the manifold moods of a generation now come into spiritual riches and could attain the most astounding results.

Another new form arrived at was what might in the strict sense be called "Mixed Psalms" (*Mischungen*). Here, portions of kindred Types, such as Hymn and Thanksgiving, were joined; or, for startling effect, portions of very different Types, like the Lament and the Hymn, were put side by side: the latter device being very common in the Babylonian poems.

Finally the process degenerated into a complete absence of form. A surprising example of this is Psalm 119.

Departures from the original Types of Psalms arose likewise from the influence of the Prophets. The Prophets had created their own Types, whereby they predicted the future and proclaimed the will of God; and the Psalmists learned to use these. The most significant effect of the Prophets upon the Psalmists was to turn them from the outward worship to the composition of Psalms that looked away from every external rite and were no longer fitted for public worship. At the same time the prodigious individualism of the Prophets returned, and the soul entered alone before God. Thus there came into being the peculiar treasure of the Psalter, its "spiritual" poetry, as the Germans call it, meaning thereby poems that exhibit the peculiarly personal life (p. 18). And yet, Gunkel warns us, we must not overlook the fact that even in this spiritual poetry, the forms of the Types—principally those of the Laments and Thanksgivings of the Individual—remain on the whole the same.

One of the outstanding scholars who accepts Gunkel's theory of classification does, to be sure, deny that such "spiritual," or individual, poems exist in the Psalter. Mowinckel, in his *Psalmenstudien*, claims that he is following out Gunkel's view to its logical conclusion when he maintains that all the Psalms are cult-poems in which the individual life of the soul with God does not appear. Gunkel takes issue with him sharply on this point. In historical investigation, he declares, not everything that is logical is therefore right. Mowinckel goes much too far. His fundamental error seems to lie in this, that he underestimates the spiritual elevation of the Psalmists and has on the whole too primitive a conception of Israel's spiritual life in general and of that of the Psalmists in particular. It is necessary to realize Gunkel's deep appreciation of the personal, individual element in the Psalms, for it bears directly upon any application of his method of classification to the present study of the Personalities of the Psalter.

As time went on another strain of Israel's religious life made its influence felt in the composition of Psalms. This was the so-called Wisdom Poetry, of which we have examples in the Book of Proverbs, Ecclesiastes, and Job. Its mood was reflective rather than passionate. It looked on God and human life calmly and aimed to point out to men the considerations impelling one to conform to the moral order of the world. Originally, it had nothing to do with the environment out of which the Psalms sprang, that is, the worship of the sanctuary. It was proclaimed not by priests, but by the elders, and its home was the city-gate or the market-place, where throngs went about their daily business. But it did more and more penetrate the Psalms, either producing special compositions of its own, called by Gunkel "Wisdom Poems," or making its way into the lyrical Types of Psalms and finally decomposing these completely.

*Some benefits from Type-study.* Gunkel finds that by assembling out of various Psalms the portions which contain the same motif of the same Type, one is greatly aided in understanding the Psalms. He is helped, for instance, to see the meaning of difficult passages by comparing them with kindred places in other Psalms; he is thus guided in emending the text where necessary (a guidance which, it must be confessed, Gunkel follows with great freedom!); he sees better where the natural divisions fall and how the Author intended to organize his poem; and he gains a criterion by which to estimate all attempts to combine or divide Psalms—a pastime so frequently and often wantonly indulged in by commentators, generally without sufficient data.

A final benefit derived from this study, and the most important, is that by such grouping of the entire material according to Types and motifs, we acquire the power to arrange the whole multiform world of religion that expresses itself in the Psalms according to its own nature. We find that the Types of Psalms correspond to types of religion which it is possible to recognize. By this method we may take a more indigenous approach to the religious thought-world of the Psalmists.[10]

## OUR METHOD HERE

We shall first divide the Psalmists to be considered into groups corresponding to Gunkel's Types. Thus we shall begin with the writers of Hymns. Before passing to our own comments upon those we select, we shall in a brief introductory

[10] See Gunkel's article on "The Religion of the Psalms" in his book *What Remains of the Old Testament* (trans. by A. K. Dallas), pp. 69-114, and the section "Some Concluding Reflections" in this present volume. (Ed.)

section give the main points that Gunkel brings out regarding this particular Type of Psalm. This will include his view as to the place in worship occupied by the Hymns, proceeding to a short description of the characteristics exhibited by the Hymns themselves. So we shall get a more detailed background for our study of the Psalmists who wrote them. The same will be done for each of the other Types.

It must not be expected, however, that our idea of these writers will be profoundly influenced or altered by the study of the Types of Psalms. It is only here and there indeed that we shall have occasion to allude to the Type. For this Type-study makes no claim to explain everything. It is not, to use the words of Löhr, with which Gunkel agrees, the key that will infallibly unlock all doors to the understanding of the Psalter. Therefore, if the reader be disinclined to inquire further into such Type-study, he may omit all, or as much as he desires, of the sections describing the Types, and devote his attention to the treatments of the Psalmists themselves. Its chief service is to put a given Psalm in its setting and to throw some general light upon its component parts and the forms of expression and the ideas used in these. It furnishes in a broad way the *pattern*. But as to the individual poet who makes that inherited pattern a vehicle through which he utters his soul's experience with God, it can tell us little.

This will be the case specially with the Psalmists whom we select. For they will naturally be the men who have spoken most personally, most piercingly from their own hearts. We shall have a predilection for what Gunkel calls the "individual great poets."

It is usually impossible, as Schmidt points out, to tell whether a given Psalm was once actually written for use in worship or was ever employed in worship in the way its words would indicate. But we must remember that this makes little difference to us in our study of the personality of its Author. For even Psalms written for public worship were not constructed by a group of people but by individuals, and in them the individual expresses what he feels as a member of the worshipping group. However much he may forget his separate individuality and merge himself in the group, still it is *he* who is speaking. It is *his* words that the group take for their own. Of course mere formulae might be drawn up by a number of persons, but they would remain mere formulae giving the highest common denominator of them all. As soon as *poetry* appears, one knows there is a poet at work. Others may indeed alter his words, even improve them; but the poem is still his. Hans Schmidt is right: "Although public worship is the final origin of their composition, and therefore in these poems and prayers there sound the feelings of a multitude, still they almost always reveal that they have been composed from out the personal experience of an individual man, out of the deeps of the heart." (*Psalmen*, p. IX)

"Out of the deeps of the heart"—we may well take these words of the German commentator on the Psalms as our own confession of faith. It is out of the deeps of their hearts that the Psalmists selected will speak to us.

# THIRTY PSALMISTS

# I

## AUTHORS OF HYMNS

THE ESSENCE of the Hymn is that it praises God. In enthusiastic joy it tells of His power and goodness and wisdom and it celebrates the great things He has done, is doing now and will do for man. When we seek the occasions of sanctuary worship in which it was employed we naturally find them in the *festivals* of Israel's church year. Following the custom of the Canaanites, the Babylonians and Assyrians, the Israelites also sang Hymns of praise to their God when they came to offer sacrifice at the great annual feasts. Such an event can best be pictured in Gunkel's own words:

"On such a day the people assemble from far and near to the holy place. A feast day is indeed a genuine day of joy. The harvest has been gathered in, the land has once more its grain and wine . . . how shall the people not be jubilant and thank their gracious God? So they all come together in their best clothes and in their most exultant mood into the sanctuary which itself shines with its fairest adornment, and in which the priests also are officiating in their most solemn vestments. There the intoxicated eye sees in the multitude of those who have made their appearance the greatness of Israel. In the ancient period, where the celebration was in a royal sanctuary, it beheld also the splendor of the ruling house. There among the mighty masses of joyous people, by far the most of whom are to be seen only on such days, a rich variegated secular activity develops, such as that in the Catholic Church, where the 'mass' becomes a market. The chief features of the occasion however are the manifold sacred doings, in which the laity participate in their own fashion; they bring their gifts, perhaps those promised during the preceding year, to their God. In all this activity of divine worship and in the symbols of which every great sanctuary is full the transported heart feels the nearness of Yahweh—the celebraters of the feast 'see God.' There is also generous eating and drinking; yes, in the ancient period the danger might lie all too close at hand that the feast might end in unfortunate excess."

Since Israel was a nation highly endowed from the beginning with poetic gifts and a power of poetic appreciation it is natural that at these festivals the Hymns should have a prominent place; should indeed finally give tone to the whole occasion. The pilgrim entering the beloved gates of Jerusalem after a prosperous journey sang a Hymn in praise of the Holy City. The night before a feast was vocal with Hymns of anticipatory joy, like our own carols on Christmas Eve. Morning light was greeted with a Hymn. When day came there took place the entry of the congregation into the sanctuary amid loud singing of Hymns. And later whenever a company passing through the holy gates set foot upon the forecourt bringing their gifts with them, they fell down, bowed themselves and knelt, greeting the God here present with jubilations. When the sacrifice was offered and when the sacrificial meal was eaten, Hymns resounded. The climax of the feast was the procession of the congregation through the temple which is described in Ps. 68:25:

> The singers go before, the harp-players follow after,
> In the midst are the damsels playing on the timbrels."

The procession began at the entrance where the participators moistened their hands in the basins set for the purpose and bound themselves together by a rope in order to follow correctly the artistic figures of the leading dancer. So they proceeded around the altar, by which they finally came to a halt in order to tie the connecting rope to its horns. From occasional references we learn that the festal procession made its circuit in dance-step. The conclusion of such a festival in later times is vividly described in Ecclesiasticus 50, where we see the high priest on the great Day of Atonement clad in glorious vestments standing high above the people on the platform surrounding the altar, in the midst of the encircling garland of priests, and pouring out the final libation.

> Then shouted the sons of Aaron,
> They sounded the trumpets of beaten work,
> They made a great noise to be heard,
> For a remembrance before the Most High.
> Then all the people together hasted,
> And fell down upon the earth on their faces
> To worship their Lord, the Almighty, God Most High.
> The singers also praised him with their voices;
> In the whole house was there made sweet melody.
> And the people besought the Lord Most High,
> In prayer before him that is merciful,
> Till the worship of the Lord should be ended;
> And so they accomplished his service.
> Then went he down, and lifted up his hands
> Over the whole congregation of the children of Israel,
> To give blessing unto the Lord with his lips,
> And to glory in his name.
> And he bowed himself down in worship the second time,
> To declare the blessing from the Most High (Ecclus. 50:16-21).

Such then were the festivals of Israel and such the place accorded in these to Hymns. Consider now the Hymn itself and the divisions into which it naturally falls.

It begins with an Introduction, in which the poet usually summons the congregation, or groups within it, his own soul, or yet other beings than man, to join in the praise of God.

> O come, let us sing unto Yahweh;
> Let us make a joyful noise to the rock of our salvation (Ps. 95:1).

The frequently recurring "Halleluia," which we have taken over from the Hebrew, means "Praise Yahweh"; and this, it is not too bold to say, was the "primary cell" of Hymn singing.

After the Introduction follows the Main Part of the Hymn, usually ushered in by some word or clause of transition indicating the *reason* why Yahweh should be praised. We see this in the *Venite:*

> "For Yahweh is a great God...." (Ps. 95:3)

And again in Psalm 103 where a series of participles are translated as relative clauses:

> Who forgiveth all thine iniquities;
> Who healeth all thy diseases, etc.

Such a series of participles is one of the things most characteristic of the Hymn.

The Main Portion thus ushered in generally contains nothing but short sentences which express something especially praiseworthy in God, arousing the heart of the poet to enthusiasm for His greatness. These may tell God's attributes or His works or His deeds in the past on behalf of Israel. It would occupy us too long if we should attempt to give examples here: these will be had when we come to the study of the several Psalmists. God is usually spoken of in the third person, this being varied occasionally with the second person. In the Hymn God is not *prayed to* as a rule; He is only praised.

Finally comes the Conclusion, which is apt to bear the same form as the Introduction. Thus in Psalm 103 the poet ends his enumeration of God's praiseworthy qualities with a renewed summons to bless Him, addressed now to the angels, to the heavenly hosts of God's ministers, to all God's works in all places of His dominion, and coming back to himself as he began.

Such are the chief divisions of the Hymn. The forms used in them all have great vigor and persist throughout the Psalter, even penetrating other Types of Psalms, as we shall see. All of them do not occur in all Hymns but they are present in most. One other feature that must be noted is that the Introduction may be repeated one or more times in the Main Part of the Hymn, when the poet wishes to mark a new beginning. Thus in the *Venite* the Psalmist returns in verse 6 to his summons:

> O come, let us worship and bow down;
> Let us kneel before Yahweh our Maker. (Ps. 95:6)

In thus summing up what Gunkel has to say concerning the divisions, we have been compelled to mention only one or two of the *forms* employed in these divisions. Upon these Gunkel lays much stress, and rightly. But if we should attempt to enumerate them here a mere list would be barren, and a detailed treatment would take us beyond the bounds of the space possible in our brief study. We shall however compensate in some measure for this by pointing out from time to time significant forms as they occur in the several Psalms to be considered.

# I

## *1. HYMNS IN GENERAL*

The Author of Psalm 8

*How excellent is thy name in all the world!*

We come upon him standing under a moonlit sky where
the moon is not yet bright enough to obscure the stars, with
peace brooding over the world. It is a spectacle to move even
the common man, and here (as we shall see) is no common
man. As he looks and looks his heart kindles, till at last he
breaks forth into utterance:

"Yahweh!"

That is his first word. Though he has the soul of a poet and
the rapture of an artist it is not this beauty, this majesty and
splendor that carries him away. Rather, He who gives meaning
to it all. It is His Name, His Personality that is revealed there,
in that expanse stretched out not only over the Psalmist's neighborhood and country but the entire world—His Name of wideness, greatness and glory.

> 2. [1] Yahwéh, our Lórd,      how majéstic is thy Náme      in
>    áll the eárth,
>    Who hast sét * thy spléndor upon the heávens!

This man feels nothing alien in the moonlit expanse. For is
not He whose splendor is set upon it Yahweh—our Lord?
We belong to Him, we Israelites. In a sense all this is ours
for we are His. And yet it is not ours only, it is spread over
the whole earth.

[1] The verse numbering in the *translation* follows the Hebrew, and is
often slightly different from that of the English Bible. In the rest of the
text the English numbering is used, except where expressly noted.

Notice the plural that he spontaneously uses—our Lord.
Even in this moment of ecstasy the Psalmist does not isolate
himself from the church of which he is a member. High as he
may rise on the wings of his own thought, intimately as he may
speak to God, he feels himself one with his brethren, part
of a great whole. So though in the next verses he uses "I"
he returns to "our" at the close. He could have understood
how Jesus taught His disciples to pray in the plural. Notice
too that to him Yahweh is "Thou," not "He." Here he breaks
away from the usual form of the Hymn, which speaks of
God in the third person. That will not do for this Psalmist.
And again, though he feels the congregation, he does not address them. The traditional summons to praise is omitted, as
he rushes at once into the Main Part of his Hymn.

Now his thought takes a sudden and surprising turn, from
God's glory in the skies to a little child. Somehow to him the
two go together:

> 3. From the moúths of little chíldren and súcklings,    thou
>      hast foúnded stréngth    becaúse of thine énemies,
>    To cause to ceáse the énemy and the self-avénger.

Yes, the same quality of God is manifested in the silent, jew-
elled sky and in the voice of a child—His strength. There
is in a little boy, in what he says, what he is, something not
weak but strong with the strength of the universe. Of this
something Yahweh has laid the very foundation of strength.

Certainly this man is not following the crowd, who look for
strength in the fierce, the tumultuous, the violent. In nature
the wind, the lightning, the earthquake, among men the war-
rior's battle-fury, the wild rush for vengeance—these make
them feel power. But our Psalmist finds in the "sound of gentle
stillness" (I Ki. 19:12) of the moonlit night, in the sweet
patter of a child's talk something stronger than storm or
wrath. Here is Yahweh's defence against His enemies. For they
*are* His enemies who rage and slay. But they will not prevail.
This quiet joyous tender something will win, will cause them
to cease and will go on forever!

'Schmidt is tempted to think that this man must have a

little boy or girl of his own by whose bed he passed as he came out into the moonlight, whose "dear glee" yet rings in his ears. That is why he thinks of children's voices. Schmidt may be right. Certainly this Psalmist loves children, sees them deeply as God sees them, and so doing sees God and man also in their true meaning.

For the sight of the moonlit sky tends to obscure man's significance:

> 4. When I view thy heávens,    the wórk of thy fíngers,
>       the moón and the stárs which thou hast estáblished,
> 5. What is mán, that thou shouldst remémber him,
>       and the són of man, that thou shouldst vísit him?

There we moderns understand! True, our Psalmist has no knowledge of the immensity of space or of unthinkable distances computed in light-years. But his sky is vast enough to strike him with the same misgiving that we feel when we look at the stars. Can man count here?

But he has found an answer to that doubt. When he turns his eyes from the sky to man in the midst of the world he sees a plain fact which contradicts what moon and stars seem to say. It is man's uniqueness and power.

> 6. But thou hast máde him to come líttle short of Gód,
>       and with glóry and hónor didst thou crówn him.
> 7. Thou didst make him to rúle over the wórks of thy hánds,    áll hast thou sét under his feét.

Then the "all" unfolds itself in review:

> 8. Sheép, and óxen, áll of them,    and álso the beásts of the wíld.
> 9. Bírds of the heávens and físh of the seá,    pássing through the páths of the seás.

Man has dominion, honor, glory. To this extent our Psalmist would understand the modern humanists when they insist on man's value. On the other hand people with a religious outlook may well be startled by his boldness in maintaining that man falls *only a little short of God*. Christians indeed have sometimes refused to believe this of humanity in general and have interpreted the saying of the Messiah (as in Heb. 2:9).[1] But the Psalmist means just *man.*

Yet he is not a humanist for he would be astonished that the humanists should not see the *significance* of man's value. He is singing not man's praises but God's. And the reason he dwells on the glory of man is that it reveals the glory of God. "Thou hast made him rule."

And so it is to the glory of God that he returns in the great corporate refrain which concludes the Psalm:

> 10. Yahwéh, our Lórd,     how majéstic is thy náme     in
> áll the eárth!

The more we study this Psalmist the more we see that we are dealing with a man of profound insight and great freshness of thought. Two of his ideas are unusual in the Old Testament.

One is the use he makes of the little child to symbolize the deepest power of God, the force destined to prevail over all other forces. The only other Old Testament writer to do this is Isaiah (or whoever is the author of Is. 11:1-9) when he pictures a small boy leading or driving wolf and lamb, leopard and kid, young lion and calf, in peace. Perhaps our Lord had the same thought in mind when He told His disciples that they must become as little children (Mt. 18:4). At any rate, He shared the *idea,* whether He used the child as a symbol of it or no. And on the day when He entered Jerusalem in conscious fulfilment of the prophecy in Zech. 9:9 f., choosing the ass to show a King lowly yet victorious, His thoughts upon the cutting off of the chariot, the horse

---

[1] While the *Psalmist himself* is not thinking of the future Messiah there is good reason for the Christian, looking back upon the life, death and exaltation of our Lord, to see in this (and in many other passages of the Psalms) an *unconscious* foreshadowing of Christ. König calls such an unconscious foreshadowing a *typus verbalis;* that is, "an unconscious expression which found a parallel in the life of the Messiah and therefore may be looked upon as woven into the spiritual history of Israel by its invisible Leader (God)." *Die Psalmen,* p. 154. Possibly this is the idea brought out by the writer of 2 Peter 1:20f. It is very different from what Herkenne calls *direct* Messianic prediction, meaning *conscious* foretelling of the Messiah by the Psalmist.

and the battle bow, upon the speaking of peace to the nations
—it was quite in harmony with His mood to accept the
hosannas of children and to justify doing so by the words of
this Psalmist: "Yea, did ye never read, Out of the mouths
of babes and sucklings thou hast perfected praise?" (Mt.
21:16).[1]

The other idea which we find unusual is that man's godlike-
ness and dominion over the animals manifest God's glory. Of
course the Old Testament is full of the thought of man praising God, but that is different. Man's littleness, transitoriness,
weakness are also used to set off by contrast God's greatness,
eternity, power—which is quite contrary to this idea. Man's wisdom is indeed spoken of as a gift to God, which might by implication glorify the Giver. On the whole, however, the Old Testament writers are shy of the thought of man's excellence. The
Prophets, following the philosophy of the great writer of the
J document of the Pentateuch,[2] sternly warn man away from
anything like pride in his own strength and accomplishments.
Only the Priestly Writers in their account of Creation (Gen.
1:26 ff) boldly exult in his power as honoring God. Our
Psalmist dares to take from the same ancient tradition as they
this startling thought and to peal it out unafraid.

Johannes Hempel has pointed out that yet two other ideas
find expression in this poem. They are the concepts which,
he declares, go ever hand in hand through the religious development of Israel: man's distance (*Abstand*) from God and
man's unitedness (*Verbundenheit*) with God. "Nowhere therefore," he says, "does the character of Israelitish piety stand
out so plainly as in 'the lofty praise of God in Psalm 8, truly
the most beautiful creation that the religious literature of all
times has produced in this Type' (Wundt)." For this reason
he can find no passage more fitting with which to conclude his
noble book on "God and Man in the Old Testament" than
the word of our Psalmist:

[1] The reading here ("praise") is that of the Septuagint, which the
Greek-speaking evangelist probably substituted for the Hebrew text
("strength") that our Lord must have used.

[2] In the story of the tower of Babel. Gen. 11:1 ff.

> "What is man, that thou shouldst remember him?...
> Thou hast made him to come little short of God...." [1]

Our Psalmist has given us an undying Hymn, using traditional Hymn forms with the utmost freedom to express his own great thoughts of God and man. When it came to be rendered in public worship the first and last verses with their plural pronoun may well have been sung by a choir, while a priest chanted the rest. So personal is it however that we can hardly picture it as being *composed* for public worship, and Gunkel himself regards such an idea as unlikely.

[1] *Gott und Mensch im Alten Testament,* Stuttgart, 1936, p. 297. We must remember, of course, that the Hebrew word which we have translated God (Elohîm) does not here refer to Yahweh, but to those lesser superhuman beings with whom Israelitish thought peopled the transcendent world. "To the highest God man is not indeed to be compared, but to the lower Elohîm beings—the ancient translations say 'the angels'—he is similar" (Gunkel).

## *The heavens declare the glory of God*

It is today almost universally agreed that Psalm 19 is not a unit. It falls into two manifest divisions, the first of which, (vv.1-6), celebrates the glory of God in the skies, the second, (vv.7-14), His revelation in the Law. The reasons for separating the two portions are briefly their difference in subject, tone and meter. Just how they came to be joined in a single Psalm is unknown to us. Barnes may be right in supposing that the writer of verses 7-14 prefixed an ancient nature-psalm to his own praise of the Law, and we shall speak of that possibility when we come to consider verses 7-14. For our present purpose however we shall treat verses 1-6 as quite independent.

Again it is agreed that 1-6 is very old as Israelitish Psalms go. Along with this feeling for its antiquity runs a high estimate of its poetic quality. "The poem," says Gunkel, "belongs to the loftiest creations of the Old Testament and surpasses many Hymns by its primitive power and pristine beauty." Kittel calls it "one of the most powerful lyrical poems of ancient Israel."

What now can be gleaned from it as to the man who composed it? Like the writer of Psalm 8 he meditates on the heavens, but he does not confine his thoughts to the night sky (Bertholet). Indeed, it is not the moon and stars but the sun that dazzles his soul. We like to think of him, as we did of the writer of Psalm 8, standing out under the open expanse perhaps just when the shadows of night are giving place to the piercing glory of the rising sun. Like a true Hebrew of old he somehow feels that each day, each night has its own individuality. He sees them in their unwearied succession, hears night chanting unto night across the intervening days, the days chanting likewise across to their oncoming brothers. It is like the antiphonal seraph-song that Isaiah heard

in his vision of the Lord (Is. 6:3). Doubtless he has in his
mind the widely-spread antique notion that the heavenly bodies
in their revolving utter ravishing music, though man cannot
distinguish it. And now, what are they chanting?

2. The heávens are télling the glóry of Gód,    and the wórk
   of his hánds decláres the fírmament;
3. Dáy unto dáy poúrs out speéch,    and níght unto níght
   shóws knówledge.
4. There is nó speéch and nó wórds,    nót heárd is their
   voíce.
5. Into áll the eárth has gone fórth their voíce,*    and to
   the énds of the wórld their wórds.

What a picture! Small wonder that it inspired Addison to
compose his evening hymn "The spacious firmament on high"
—though how far even the stately English falls below the
original!

Glory! cry the days and nights, but not their own; it is
the glory of God. When this man, like the Author of Psalm 8,
looks up transported into the skies it is God that he sees and
hears. For with his inner ear he *can* hear the words which
are yet no words. Like him again he feels the wideness of the
sky, the universal sweep of its proclamation, soundless yet
plain to the ends of the world.

And now, perhaps as the sun rises, he turns to the blazing
disc and sees there also—God.

For the sún he pláced a tént in thém;
6. And *it* like a brídegroom comes fórth from its bridal
   cánopy,    it exúlts like a héro to rún its coúrse.
7. From the énd of the heávens is its going fórth,    and its
   círcling unto the énds of them;
   And there is nóthing híd from its héat.

Possibly the Psalmist has here taken over a still more ancient
hymn to the sun itself, but if so he has wholly transformed it.
The splendor, freshness, vigor, speed of the sun, its inescapable
heat, are but manifestations of the Power that made it and
set its tent in the heavens. How much more is God!

For all the resemblances between this man and the Author
of Psalm 8, we can see a difference. The contrast here is not
as there between the heavens and man, but between the heavens
and God.

How keenly we feel that contrast today! For us the heavens are telling *some* glory, but what? Is it their own only? That is the answer of naturalism. It makes the "steeps of space" "inhuman," it leaves man alone in the midst of vastnesses and splendors that are alien to his deepest nature. There is no more desolate message than that which the stars utter—if they proclaim only themselves. But if they do not; if behind them, through them, is Something More, Something that gives meaning to them, that answers our own hearts, or rather that our own hearts answer, then indeed do the heavens declare the glory of God.

And so this man of old, with his onleaping rhythm and his exultant faith, joins with the writer of Psalm 8 to fling us a challenge; and at the same time in his certainty he comforts and sustains us.

It is a Hymn that he has composed yet not in the usual forms of a Hymn, for like Psalm 8 it lacks the summons to praise, it has no Conclusion, and the way in which it employs the thought of God's creative and sustaining power is quite individual. Certainly here is a man who moves as a master among traditional forms, using or discarding them at will.

*The law of the* LORD *is an undefiled law*

This Psalmist, like the two preceding, is uttering a meditation. While the first part of his poem is a Hymn, in that it praises, it contains no summons to praise. Instead, he breaks at once into his Main Portion. Here, as was the case in the other two Psalms, his first word reveals what occupies his thoughts: The Law of Yahweh! He must tell of the Law, but notice that (as Barnes points out) the truly emphatic word is the second, *Yahweh*. For to him the Law reveals the heart of his God, and in praising it he is praising God.

What then does he mean by this word Law which he enriches with many synonyms in the ensuing verses? Certainly he is speaking of much or most or all of what is contained in the first five books of the Old Testament; and in particular of the actual laws and ordinances contained therein. He means then a manuscript, a parchment, a *book*. Let us face the fact! He is going to talk of religion nourished on a book, rather than on the living words of men of God! Some scholars seem to regard this as a tragic declension from the older religion which *perhaps* did pretty much without books. Let us admit that in passing from verses 1-6 we have, as Schmidt says, come indoors; the four walls of a room surround us, and we see a face bent over a written roll.

And let it be admitted also that the Law of which he tells contains large blocks of ritual prescriptions, such as dietary laws, laws as to clean and unclean, as to the kinds of sacrifice and the keeping of the various festivals. But let it be remembered that it likewise has within it the Ten Commandments and the social precepts of the Book of the Covenant, the Holiness Code and Deuteronomy; precepts as to the treatment of the poor, the debtor, the foreigner, the widow and orphan, the slave, parents, wives, neighbors; precepts as to justice in the courts, and the beautiful Deuteronomic portrayals of devotion to God—great utterances, many of which the modern Christian cannot read without enthusiasm saddened by a sense of personal and corporate shortcoming. For such things, said the Law, Yahweh cares! Even its ritual laws must be read against this background: they show the way to do honor to *this kind of God*. And so when our Lord summed up the Law He declared its basic command to be that of love.

It is of this Law that our Psalmist speaks. And he does so evidently as one who has lived in and with the Law. As Kittel says, his Psalm comes forth from experience.

> 8. The láw of Yahwéh is pérfect,   restóring the soúl,
>    The téstimony of Yahwéh is súre,   making wíse the símple,
> 9. The órdinances of Yahwéh are ríght,   making glád the heárt,
>    The commándment of Yahwéh is púre,   líghtening the eýes,
> 10. The feár of Yahwéh is cleán,   endúring for éver,
>    The júdgments of Yahwéh are trué,   they are júst, all togéther. . . .

Reflect a moment on these adjectives with which he describes the Law (for all the nouns he uses are synonyms for the Law): *Complete:* perfect, without blemish. That expresses the satisfaction which the mind feels in the absolute, the utter ideal. *Sure:* dependable, always to be trusted, never leaving one in the lurch. *Right:* straight—again satisfying the ideal. *Pure:* selected, sifted, clean, clear. The word is used of the sun in the Song of Songs. *Clean:* the same idea from the side of worship. *True:* an idea akin to trustworthy—what one can believe utterly. We see what this man loves! We see how the delight he takes in having everything and everyone "clean" for divine worship is of a piece with his passion for having physical pureness and freshness about him; and the Law reminds him of both. We see how he longs for the ideal, the true, the dependable, and finds it in God's Law.

Then consider what the Law does for him. It revives his failing strength, it gives him, the uninstructed, an understanding of life, it delights his heart, it quickens his perception, it

satisfies his craving for that which endures amid the changes
and chances of the world, it always rings true.

No wonder then that he finds these judgments of Yahweh
good!

> 11. They are more desírable than góld,     and than múch fine
>      góld;
>      And they are sweéter than hóney,     and the hóney of
>      the cómb.

And there is a yet further benefit from them:

> 12. Moreóver thy sérvant is wárned by thém;     in keéping
>      them the rewárd is greát.

He does not tell what kind of reward he means. Is it prosperity which the Wise Men of Proverbs so constantly promise?
Or is it something more spiritual? Probably it partakes of
both. He has found that along with the happiness of being
obedient to God there came to him outward blessings which
like a true Israelite he has interpreted as signs of God's favor.
But one cannot therefore charge him with being materially
minded for the whole Psalm shows that his heart is not primarily on things, but on God.

And now suddenly the tone of his Psalm changes; from
being a Hymn it takes on the aspect of another great Type
which we shall consider later—the Lament of an Individual.
He concludes with self-distrust and aspiration:

> 13. Érrors whó can discérn?     From hídden faults acquít
>      me.
> 14. Álso from presúmptuous [1] (deeds) [2] hold báck thy sérv-
>      ant;     let them nót rúle over me.
>
>      Thén shall I be pérfect, and I shall be ínnocent     from
>      greát transgréssion.

That is the prayer of a humble-minded man. Errors are
lesser sins which might easily escape his notice. For their
forgiveness he can only throw himself on the mercy of God.
Then there are the flagrant sins, deeds of passion, of the

---

[1] Mowinckel thinks that in v.14 the Psalmist prays for protection against
demons who tempt man into mortal sin. *Psalmenstudien* I, p. 72.

[2] Or "men."

"high hand." What he needs in dealing with these is not dis-
cernment but self-control. Yet he knows he is weak, he must
rely on God's firm hand to keep him from them.

Then comes his aspiration, expressed in the form of expectation: to be perfect and "empty" of serious wickedness.
Some commentators (Gunkel, Staerk, etc.) do not like this
verse. It shows, they think, that the Psalmist feels one really
can be perfect, can keep the Law completely. In fact Kittel
goes so far as to speak of his "happy self-satisfaction." Schmidt
is sure that "the deep seriousness of the eternal dissatisfaction
(*Ungenügens*), the consuming hunger after righteousness, has
never touched the soul of this poet." Nor do they approve
the way in which he distinguishes small from great sins, as if
all sins were not fundamentally alike! He overlooks also the
fact that sin is primarily subjective not objective, and lies
in the man himself (Gunkel).

All this may be true; and yet it is certainly possible to
regard the Psalmist in quite a different light. After all, he
does not say that he is already perfect; he merely sets per-
fection as the goal which he shall attain when his prayer for
forgiveness and help is granted. Is he going any farther than
our Lord went when He said: "Ye shall be perfect as your
heavenly Father is perfect"? (Mt. 5:48). Nor can the present
writer feel that he is pleased with himself. His tone is not
at all like that of the self-congratulatory Pharisee in the
temple; he is humble and does not compare himself with
others. As for making a distinction between errors and great
transgression, why should he not? Are they after all the
same? Does our Christian recognition of the fact that all sin
proceeds from the heart, that it lies in an intention contrary to
God's will, preclude us from acknowledging that some sins
are worse than others? One wonders whether the Germans
who find fault with our Psalmist here are not a trifle biased
by their Lutheran tradition. At any rate we need not hesitate
to see in him a pure soul who serves God for love, who loves
the Law for its power to satisfy his ideal longings, who dis-
trusts himself and prays, much as we pray, not to be led into

temptation but delivered from evil. He and Jesus are not far apart.

The man who speaks thus is not primarily a student even though we may picture him bent over a book indoors. He has in him nothing of the lawyer, concerned for exact definition ("And who is my neighbor?" Lk. 10:29) or of the casuist applying the Law in perplexing cases ("Whose wife shall she be?" Mk. 12:23). He is not a legalist, if by that we mean a man who sees duty neatly contained in a series of definite prescriptions, by the carrying out of which one completely meets the demands of God. As a matter of fact the Law on its moral side mingles ideals and principles (such as "Thou shalt love thy neighbor as thyself," "Honor thy father and thy mother") with precise injunctions in a way that would render impossible any neat delimitation of duties. And the element in the Law that excites enthusiasm like that of our Psalmist is just this ideal element; one hardly grows dithyrambic over food-taboos and quarantine regulations!

He is none of these but a thinker of kindling thoughts, a poet who spontaneously clothes such thoughts in images of beauty. Perhaps Gunkel is right in saying that he has not given us a work of art. The expressions he uses regarding the Law may not be original. But he has found in his Bible the revelation of God by which he lives and he sings its praises with contagious joy.

His poem is not a Hymn throughout, as we have seen, but mixed with the prayer which belongs to another Type of Psalm. This blending and the Author's devotion to the written Law seem to point to a late date.

If as Barnes and Baethgen think it was this Psalmist who combined his own composition with the vigorous nature Hymn of verse 1-6, he displayed a sense of the congruous which strikes us when we read the two portions of the Psalm as one.[1] For with all their dissimilarities in theme, tone and meter, the two poems utter complementary truths—God's revelation

[1] König argues that the difference in theme and the change of meter do not exclude the possibility that a single poet composed the whole Psalm at one time. *Die Psalmen*, p. 106.

in the heavens and in the revealed Law. There is no incon-
sistency in imagining that the man who has learned from an
older poet to hear the music of heaven's antiphonal days and
nights should utter his kindred delight in God's perfect written revelation, and binding the two into a single Psalm should
present it in lieu of a material thank-offering to Yahweh. For
with such a presentation he closes his own poem, and perhaps
the present Psalm as it stands:

> 15. Let the wórds of my moúth bé accéptable    and the
> meditátion of my heárt in thy síght,
> Yahwéh, my róck and my redeémer.

*The voice of the* LORD *is upon the waters*

We come now to a Psalmist who, like the Authors of the
8th and 19th Psalms, sees God in nature, but unlike them
depicts not the revelation of the clear heavens but the majesty
of Yahweh in the thunderstorm. His Hymn begins with the
summons to praise that we have found missing in the other
two but instead of sounding the usual call to the congregation
and choir of the temple to pay honor to Yahweh he addresses
a sublimer, more awful chorus. Raising his eyes upward he
calls to the hosts of superhuman beings who attend the King
of Heaven:

> 1. Gíve unto Yahwéh, ye sóns of the góds,
>    Gíve unto Yahwéh glóry and stréngth;
> 2 Gíve unto Yahwéh the glóry of his náme,
>    Prostráte yourselves before Yahwéh in the véstments of
>    hóliness.

It is a mythological inheritance on which he is drawing
here—the ancient belief that Yahweh is surrounded by a multitude of divine beings not unlike Himself. But he has transformed it in true Hebrew fashion till now these gods are
simply the courtiers of the supreme Lord. They stand about
Him in His heavenly temple of which the Psalmist will presently speak, waiting to do Him service, falling down before
Him in adoration.

Now the Psalmist proceeds to the Main Part of his Hymn
in which he will tell the reasons why Yahweh is to be praised.
In the usual Hymn these group themselves about two themes,
God's mastery over nature and His gracious dealings with
Israel in history. This Psalmist, as Schmidt points out, employs only the first. Many other Psalmists do the same; but
the peculiarity of this Psalmist, the secret of the incomparable
beauty of his Psalm, is that he does not seek the greatness
of God in nature as a whole but makes it much more vivid

by selecting a single manifestation of it in the thunderstorm (Schmidt).

Suddenly the burst of praise in the heavens is drowned by a peal of thunder—the Voice of Yahweh! The storm is coming in from the Mediterranean. Another peal, and it is sweeping over the Lebanon range, breaking the giant trees, making the mountains themselves to leap about like young calves. (What oriental audacity in the image!) Peal follows peal as it goes onward into the southern desert, making the hinds to bring forth for very terror, leaving stripped forests in its path.[1]

The Voice of Yahweh! Such the Psalmist, taught by a more primitive age, believes it to be. And in the Hebrew original the very sound of the words is a peal of thunder followed by a crash. *Qôl Yahwéh*—there you hear it. And in order to get something of that peal and crash into our minds, let us retain the Hebrew words in our translation:

3. *Qô'l Yahwéh* upon the wáters!    The Gód of glóry thún-
    ders!
    Yahwéh upon greát wáters!
4. *Qô'l Yahwéh* in pówer!    *Qô'l Yahwéh* in májesty!
5. *Qô'l Yahwéh* is breáking the cédars,
    Yes, Yahwéh breáks the cédars of Lébanon!
6. He makes * Lébanon to skíp about like a cálf,
    And Sírion[2] like a yoúng wíld-ox.
7. *Qô'l Yahwéh* is cleáving    flámes of fíre!
8. *Qô'l Yahwéh* makes the désert whírl,
    Yahwéh whírls the désert of Kádesh!
9. *Qô'l Yahwéh* is making the hínds to cálve,
    And it stríps the fórests bare.

While this deafening devastating uproar is travelling over the earth, Yahweh pealing forth His splendor in solemn terrible monotony, the Hymn of the heavenly worshippers is proceeding. Now an echo of it is heard in an interval of the storm:

And in his témple áll of it is sáying "Glóry."

Then high over the heavenly ocean above the firmament, the ocean whence pour down the torrents of the rain, Yahweh is seen.

[1] Herkenne thinks that no single storm is described by the Psalmist, but that he puts the north and the south together for literary effect.
[2] Mt. Hermon.

10. Yahwéh above the floód is seáted,
Yes, Yahwéh is seáted, kíng for éver!

And that can mean only one thing for Israel. They need not fear amid the crashing of the thunder; its power is a symbol of their power, its terror is their confidence.

11. Yahwéh will gíve stréngth to his peóple,
Yahwéh will bléss his peóple in peáce.

So, as Delitzsch said, "Glory in the highest" is the beginning, "Peace on earth" is the ending. And that shows us something of this Psalmist. All that we may know of him must be gleaned from his praises of God, for he himself remains hidden behind them. We can see that he is a sublime poet who consecrates his gift spontaneously to portraying God's glory, that he welcomes the thunderstorm unafraid because in it he hears the Voice of God; that therefore he exults in it, feels that he as a son of Israel shares in its majesty, since he too belongs to God; that amidst its tumult he catches strains of the heavenly Hymn which alone is worthy to celebrate Yahweh's greatness; that in its terror he finds peace.

His Hymn has been called the Psalm of the Seven Thunders; yet beneath it dwells a quiet joy, the joy of love and faith. From this stillness it swells forth in its mighty tumult, and into this stillness it returns.

# THE AUTHOR OF PSALM 95

## *O come, let us sing unto the* LORD

The Psalmists whom we have studied up to this moment are all men of strong individuality, and in consequence their Hymns have exhibited such freedom in the use of Hymn forms that we have not yet given our attention to any one who composed a Hymn of the usual sort. It is time that we do this. We have the choice of a number of beautiful Hymns among the Psalms following Psalm 29, but in most of them the personality of the Author is not clearly marked. Let us pass on then to the Author of a very familiar Hymn, Psalm 95, commonly called the *Venite*. Here we shall encounter a man whom we can picture from his poem. And yet he too is so individual that he continues the regular Hymn motifs through only the first part of his Psalm, breaking off at verse 8 into quite another Type than the Hymn, so that the Psalm in its totality is called by Gunkel a "Prophetic Liturgy."

His work has a special interest for us because, as we have said, it is familiar. Every time we meet together for Morning Prayer we say or sing it at the beginning of the praise portion of the office. And this is no new thing in the Church but goes back to ancient custom. "It was once, as it should be," Barnes says, "the actual beginning of a service. In the service of the Seven Hours according to the use of Sarum, which dates from a little before 1200 A.D., this Psalm is the first appointed to be sung. Saint Benedict (circ. 480-553), the founder of the Benedictine Order, directed that Psalm 95 (preceded by Psalm 3) should be said by the whole monastery together when the monks first arose from sleep. It has been included in our English Matins from 1549 onwards." We may well desire therefore to know what we can of its Author.

The opening verses, as has been said, constitute a Hymn of the usual kind (Gunkel), such as the assembled congregation renders to the honor of its God. Gunkel proceeds: "The

special occasion on which it was sung is to be seen from its
own words. When the holy procession presses through the
gate of the fore-court and catches sight of the temple, the
place of the divine presence, then the whole congregation
falls down in the dust, shouting with joy to the mighty God
who dwells among His people; and then they strike up this
song."

Such was its probable use by the Jewish church, and it is
plain that the Author himself has composed it with this use
in mind. But it is not only for the edification of others that
he writes. On the contrary he includes himself in the worshippers addressed and the thoughts he utters are those that
arise within him on such an occasion. We may imagine that
he is one of a band of pilgrims (Schmidt) who have come to
Jerusalem for a great feast and are now experiencing the joy
of taking part in a festal procession such as that described
by Gunkel in the passage just quoted.

> 1. Cóme, let us cry aloúd to Yahwéh,
>    Let us shoút to the róck of our salvátion,
> 2. Let us cóme befóre him with thanksgíving,
>    With psálms let us shoút unto hím!

That is after the manner of a regular Hymn introduction,
summoning the congregation to praise; but it shows the intensity of this man's feelings, "The Psalm opens with a crash
of words," says Barnes. Our Psalmist is no decorous modern
church-goer, quietly taking his place in a subdued genteel
congregation. Yahweh is so glorious that he cannot contain
himself: he wants to let go and have everyone else let go!
And why? Rushing into his Main Part he tells:

> 3. For a greát Gód is Yahwéh
>    And a greát kíng over áll góds!

Yahweh's uniqueness is no worn-out tale to him. In the
midst of a world where mankind throngs the temples of great
deities ruling over splendid cities and vast domains he is
ravished by the wonder of the truth that these divinities are
all *under Yahweh*. Probably he believes that they exist; [1] but

---

[1] This is the view of Oesterley. *Fresh Approach to the Psalms*, p. 213.

before Yahweh they are nothing. For Yahweh alone controls all things—the unsearched regions of the earth, the high mountains, the sea before which the Hebrew ever shrank back in fear, the endless continents and islands.

> 4. In whóse hánd are the deép places [1] of the eárth,
>    And the heíghts of the moúntains are hís;
> 5. Whóse the seá, and *hé* máde it,
>    And the dry lánd his hánds fórmed.

This is the familiar creation motif so common in the Hymns, but rendered with what freshness and jubilation!

And now as if by a new flight upward he would rush still higher he summons again to praise:

> 6. Come ín, let us fall dówn and bów ourselves,
>    Let us kneél before Yahwéh our máker.

At once he is off on the second great Hymn motif—Yahweh's care for Israel. How naturally he ties it on to the other motif of creation: our Maker.

> 7. For *hé* is our Gód
>    And wé the peóple of his pásture
>    And the flóck of his hánd.

This figure of the shepherd was familiar to a sheep-keeping people, yet for our Psalmist it has not grown stale. He sees in the thousands pouring into the temple court a flock cared for and fed by the Shepherd who is greater than they —drawing near now to that same Shepherd for He is here! How utterly the poet merges himself in the congregation, how objective he is; and yet so full of rapture that his contagion spreads to all!

Then suddenly his note changes utterly. It is as if he held up to the shouting, almost rollicking procession a warning hand. Stop! You who are giving yourselves up to this joy before God, who are casting yourselves before Him with abandonment of devotion—will you also *obey* Him? Remember the past! The Hymnist has turned Prophet.

---

[1] i.e. the places to be searched out. By transposing two letters we could read with the LXX: "far places," "ends."

Todáy—oh, that you may heár his voíce—
8. Hárden not your heárts as at Merî'bah
As in the dáy of Mássah in the wílderness,
9. Whére your fáthers témpted me,
Tríed me, yes, sáw my wórk.

This is not the happy lesson from the history of God's dealings with His people usually inculcated by the Hymnists. They
love to remind the church of Yahweh's kindness, of all the
things He has done for Israel. But as can be seen in the
Psalmists who devote whole Psalms to these ancient stories,
there is another way of looking at these same mercies.[1] How
did Israel receive them? With ingratitude and rebellion. That
is the way our Psalmist is now taking. What was the result of
Israel's stubbornness?

10. Fórty yeárs I loáthed
Thís * generátion and saíd,
A peóple erring of heárt are théy.
And théy knéw not my wáys.
11. To whóm I swáre in my wráth,
They shall not énter into my rést.

The solemn voice of prophetic admonition dies away. No
further need to point the moral! Let the joyous worshippers
think it over! They also long for Yahweh's "rest"—the refreshment He has prepared for His faithful in the wonderful
time to come. Well, there is a way to it, and only one way.

This sudden transition is so unexpected that some modern scholars have thought that what follows comes from a
differ∪nt hand. Surely our Psalmist is no Hymnist, we may say.
If he were, when he had reached the climax of the Main
Part of his Hymn he would return in the full burst of an
ecstatic Conclusion to the summons of his Introduction. That
is what the American Prayer Book makes him do in its version of the *Venite*. And if they must needs rewrite our Psalmist's Hymn, we must acknowledge that the first Prayer Book
revisers of the American Church did fairly well, seeing that
they did not have the advantage of Gunkel's Type-Study to
guide them! In revising the English Book of Common Prayer
our Church fathers went over to Psalm 96 and took from it

[1] See p. 233 ff.

two of its later verses. In so doing they could not of course know that the Author of Psalm 96 passes in verse 7 from a Hymn to a Psalm of Yahweh's Enthronement. But since such a Psalm is much like a Hymn, as we shall presently see, these fit in rather satisfactorily:

> 9. Wórship Yahwéh in the adórnment of hóliness,
>    Be in écstasy befóre him, all the eárth....
> 13. For he cómes, for he cómes to júdge the eárth.
>    He will júdge the wórld in ríghteousness
>    And the peóples with his trúth.

The Psalmist however does not intend to conclude in that way. For to his mind worship has two elements, and he wishes to express both. These two elements may for want of better terms be called the corporately mystical and the ethical. When people draw near to God they ought to feel Him. That is the mystical side of worship. It naturally leads to joy because God is what He is—so great and good. Its dominant expression is therefore the Hymn. On the other hand, just because God is good men ought in approaching Him to realize their own lack of goodness and strive to overcome it. This leads to self-examination, penitence, resolve. We have already seen how the author of Psalm 19:7-14 exhibits this second side along with the first. The two ought to go together, the first issuing in the second. Indeed, the *test* of all worship is the life that worshippers lead in the midst of men.

The great Prophets had seen the necessity of the ethical side of religion so passionately that they tended to forget the other. "What doth Yahweh require of thee, but to do justly, and to love kindness, and to walk humbly with thy God?" (Mic. 6:8). Indeed, Amos and Isaiah had gone so far as to denounce the jubilant hymnic element in worship as offensive to God, at least where right was not done to men.

> I háte, I rejéct your feásts,
> And I will not sméll in your assémblies.
> For thoúgh you bríng me whole-ófferings
> And oblátions, I will nót be pleásed,
> And the peáce-offerings of your fátlings I will not regárd.
> Take awáy from upón me the úproar of thy sóngs,

And the twánging of thy hárps I will not heár.
But let jústice róll as wáters,
And ríght as a streám that faíls not! (Amos 5: 21 ff. cf. Is.
   1:11 ff.)

Our Psalmist however loves the uproar of songs, the twang-
ing of harps, the enthusiasm, the joy. And he believes that God
loves them too. "Come let us cry aloud to Yahweh!" Yet he
knows that in the past such Hymn-singing has too often gone
along with a hardness of heart which ended in exclusion from
the divine joy. "Let that evil day," he cries, "not be repeated
in your 'Today.' For there comes a Tomorrow, when after
the wretchedness of the present God will give a rest—an
abiding place. Oh, that ye may hear His voice and enter in!"
And how deep is his perception of men's moral need! Schmidt
points out that other Psalmists who utter warnings like this
(e.g., Psalms 24, 15, 50) speak of individual sins, while our
Psalmist penetrates to the fundamental attitude of the soul—
to hearing the divine voice. It is from the Prophets that our
Psalmist has derived his stern moral demand and his eschatological hope. And he is, as Gunkel says, "all in all a worthy
successor of the Prophets."

Perhaps it is a loss that our American version of the *Venite*
obscures the fact.

# THE AUTHOR OF PSALM 103

## Praise the LORD, O my soul

In Psalm 103 another vivid personality appears. As we might expect, because of his very individuality he has not followed closely the traditional forms of the Hymn but has used them freely to create a lyric of intensely personal stamp.

From his own words in verses 3 to 5 we may infer his situation when he writes his Hymn. He has completely recovered from a desperate illness [1] in which he like a true Hebrew has seen the visitation of God for his sins. But God has pardoned all his sins. From death's door he has been brought back to health, he is young again! And now in the first glow of his recovery, before it becomes an old story, he pours forth his praise to the God who has wrought so bountifully with him.

> 1. Bléss, my soúl, Yahwéh,    and all withín me the náme
>    of his hóliness;
> 2. Bléss, my soúl, Yahwéh,    and forgét not áll his bénefits.

His Halleluia is addressed not to the congregation, but to himself; for that is what he means by his "soul." And he will have no half-measure of praise; all his parts and members must join the jubilant chorus. He will not let himself slip into the forgetfulness that he knows from experience will come all too quickly unless the mind keeps going back to the way in which Yahweh has dealt with him (Barnes).

Passing from his Introduction to his Main Part he tells what it is Yahweh has done, nay is doing, heaping participle upon participle in the true manner of Hymns:

> 3. He who párdons áll thine iníquities,    who heáls áll thy
>    sícknesses,

[1] One cannot indeed be sure of this. Perhaps, like the Author of Psalm 23, he is meditating upon his whole past experience with God. (So C. L. Taylor, in a verbally expressed opinion.) On the other hand he may have just emerged from a *spiritual* crisis. "There is underlying the Psalm, it seems to me, a decisive experience of forgiveness." (C. A. Simpson, in a letter.)

4. Who redeéms from the gráve thy life,     who crówns thee
with lovingkíndness and compássions,
5. Who sátisfies with goód thine órnament; [1] made néw like
the eágle is thy yoúth.

Yahweh has put upon his head the festal turban which a guest
wears at a banquet (Gunkel). His "ornament"—perhaps his
"bright eye and ruddy complexion of health" (Barnes)—now
enjoys the abundant feast spread before him by his God. He
feels his youth clothing him like the new feathers of the
moulted eagle.

But as his enraptured song proclaims his own gifts from
Yahweh his mind expands beyond self: what has happened to
him is but an instance of what Yahweh is ever doing:

6. A dóer of ríght is Yahwéh,     and of júdgments for áll the
oppréssed.

This leads him to think of the past of Israel and so he takes
up exultantly one of the two main themes upon which the
Hymn Writers are ever ringing the changes—Yahweh's goodness to His people. They too sinned but He has forgiven and
delivered them!

7. He made knówn his wáys to Móses,     to the sóns of
Iśrael his dóings.

And now in two brimming verses he distils the essence of
that divine revelation, first in the classic words of Yahweh's
self-manifestation to Moses (Exod. 34:6) and then in the loveliest utterances of the Prophets [Gunkel (Is. 57:15, Jer.
3:5-12)]:

8. Pítiful and grácious is Yahwéh,     lóng-súffering and
aboúnding in lovingkíndness.
9. Nót for éver will he conténd,     and nót for álways will
he keép. [2]

Then leaving Law and Prophets behind he puts it in images
fresh created from his own experience; for although he is
singing of God's goodness to Israel he includes himself. "In the
general..." says Gunkel (p. 433) "rings also his personal

---

[1] The reading here is uncertain. The LXX, followed by the Vulgate, has
"thy desire"; the Syriac, "thy body"; Jerome, "thy ornament."
[2] That is, keep His anger.

feeling, and it is just this which lifts his poem above most of the other Hymns."

> 10. Nót according to our síns has he dóne unto ús,    and nót according to our iníquities has he requíted ús
> 11. For as the héight of the heávens above the eárth— míghty[1] is his lovingkíndness upon them that feár him.
> 12. As the fárness of the eást from the wést,    he has set fár from ús our transgréssions.
> 13. As the píty of a fáther upon his chíldren,    pítiful is Yahwéh upon them that feár him.

And well may He be pitiful for alas He has reason. Here our Psalmist introduces a note of sadness which is hardly in keeping with the joy of a Hymn, belonging properly to a Lament. It echoes the Genesis story of man's creation.

> 14. For *hé* knóws our fráme,    he remémbers that wé are dúst.
> 15. Mán—like gráss his dáys;    as the flówer of the fiéld, só he flówers;
> 16. For the wínd goes óver it, and it ís not;    and its pláce knóws it no móre.

But the sadness endures only a moment. After all, there *is* something eternal!

> 17. But the lovingkíndness of Yahwéh is from everlásting to everlásting upon them that feár him,    and his jústice to chíldren's chíldren,
> 18. To them that keép his cóvenant    and to them that re- mémber his státutes, to dó them.

That is enough for our Psalmist. Like the rest of the faithful in his age he does not aspire to personal survival but contents himself with the thought of his children after him. Yahweh will never fail them, as He has never failed the generations gone by. And this eternal God *rules!*

> 19. Yahwéh in the heávens has estáblished his thróne,    and his kíngdom over áll has domínion.

The Main Part of the Hymn is ended; it is time for the Conclusion, when the poet summons once more to the praise of such a God. But this time he will not be alone. Nothing

---

[1] All the versions support the Hebrew text in this reading. Most modern scholars change one Hebrew letter and read: "high is his lovingkindness."

less than the supernal choirs of heaven and the whole of things created will suffice to do honor to the God of love.

> 20. Bléss Yahwéh, his ángels,     héroes of míght,     dóing his wórd *!
> 21. Bléss Yahwéh, áll his hósts,     his sérvants dóing his pleásure!
> 22. Bléss Yahwéh, áll his wórks,     in áll pláces of his domínion!

Then, returning as is the wont of Hymn writers to his opening call he summons also that one voice without which the music would not be complete:

> Bléss, my soúl, Yahwéh!

Now that we have reviewed the course of his Hymn we can pause to consider this Psalmist as he stands before us in his own creation. The first thing that strikes us is his *purity*. He utters no syllable of self-seeking or vindictiveness or complacency. Next his *humility*. This is seen in the modest way in which he merges his own experience in that of his people, giving chief place to general reflections rather than to his personal feelings (Gunkel); and again, in his sense of sin. Neither he nor his people can stand before God without forgiveness. There is also a *breadth* of affection and insight, the power to take a catholic view of God's relation to man. He does indeed confine what he says to Israel and even to the truly religious persons in Israel—"them that fear Him." But he does this in no narrow spirit; one feels that he would have included all men on the same basis of "fearing" God. It is because of this wideness of the man that he has been able, as Gunkel points out, to free the thoughts which he echoes from everything temporal and accidental so that they meet us in their full weight and beauty.

But who will deny that the chief thing distinguishing him is the way in which he makes the *love of God* his central theme? [1] To picture it he employs a figure which though familiar enough to us Christians is sparingly used in the Old Testament. "Like as a father...." He must have had a good father and his own

---

[1] "Scarcely any other passage of the Old Testament makes us feel the truth that 'God is love' so ardently as Psalm 103." Herkenne, p. 331.

children must also have taught him how a father feels. One cannot exhaust such a love; it is higher and broader than we can measure. And the poignant thing in it is its pity. Because God is sorry for us He forgives us. Sorry for our transitoriness. But His love goes on forever! Therefore we are not pitiable and the meaning of our life is joy. That, to quote Gunkel again, is the peculiar quality of this man's spirit: he knows all too well the depths of earthly life, yet he leaps up over them into the heights of gladness.

"The Author of this Hymn of praise," says Staerk, "is one of the religious men of the Old Covenant to whom we Christians must look up with reverence. Seldom in the Old Testament has any one spoken so truly and simply, so out of the deep of blessed experience, of God's loving nature. For that is the highest that the Psalmist knows to say of the God whom he bears deep in his heart: God is love...." Kittel adds: "What this acknowledgement means we cannot realize till we consider how strongly on the whole in the religion of the Old Testament fear of the destroying might of Yahweh predominated over trust in His goodness."

*O* LORD, *thou hast searched me out, and known me*

We come now to a man who goes farther in personal reflection concerning God than any of his fellow Psalmists. "This is a Psalm which stands by itself," says Barnes. Staerk declares that it is "original in every respect, and unique in the Psalter." [1] So individual is it that Gunkel finds it difficult to classify. "As to its Type," he says, "the Psalm is not easy to grasp. There can indeed be no doubt that its fundamental mood of reverent and wondering meditation on Yahweh's mysteries points to the Hymn." It has also, he adds, several of the Hymn forms, such as rhetorical questions; and its material likewise exhibits Hymn motifs, praise of Yahweh's wonderfulness and fearfulness, amazement at His works and thoughts, at His creation. The Introduction form "I praise thee" in v.14 is specially convincing. On the other hand, it lacks a definite Introduction at the beginning. This would not be surprising, for as we have seen other Hymnists omit the Introduction. It is the *content* which marks it as fundamentally peculiar. "For while this Type elsewhere distinguishes itself almost always by its splendid objectivity, here the 'I' of the poet comes forward strongly from beginning to end. The knowledge and power of God of which the Psalm treats are not so much the attributes with which He embraces the whole world as those with which He rules the poet himself; 'Thou' and 'I'—thus it goes through the whole poem! This new inward attitude of the Psalmist (unheard of in these very Hymns on Creation) is what has burst the form of the Type also. The poet starts with the Hymn and in content and form passes far beyond it" (Gunkel).

But let us look at the man himself. We come upon him as he meditates upon Yahweh—alone, in silence. No hint is given

---

[1] Herkenne is surely mistaken in regarding the Psalm as composite, and verses 6-16 as an interpolation by a later poet or redactor.

as to his surroundings. Barnes indeed gathers that he is on a journey, but this idea has apparently come to no one else. Nor does anything suggest that he is in the temple, still less taking part in worship. Even Schmidt, who looks on the majority of Psalms as connected with worship, describes his words as "prayer in a stillness, in which the soul and God are alone." It is most natural to picture him as at home in the midst of familiar surroundings and duties, whence he has withdrawn himself into the silence of his inner chamber to meet God.

His Psalm shows that he is a thinker. Not indeed in the Greek sense of a philosopher who strives to define in universal concepts the common-sense notions of the multitude but in the Hebrew sense of a religious man who does not accept religious truths as a matter of course but struggles to see into them, to grasp them in their meaning for life and the soul. Our Psalmist is the child of a developed age where maturer ideas of God have displaced more primitive concepts and now demand that they be carried out to their logical conclusions. The idea that engrosses him is monotheism. The leaders of Israel's religion had been virtual monotheists from an early period [1]—how early is a matter of dispute—but in the age of our Psalmist monotheism was asserting itself more impressively and its implications were forcing themselves upon thought. That is, when people *did* think. This Psalmist certainly does. And one implication of monotheism is stirring his mind—God's omniscience and omnipresence. For it is plain to him that Yahweh does indeed know all things and is in all places; but what does that *mean?* Like a true Hebrew he is not interested, as we have said, in getting a precise intellectual definition; he needs to see a truth in its manifold concrete details. It means this and this and this.

As he thus strives to grasp these complementary truths about God his imagination bursts into flame and he pours forth his overwhelming insights in picture after picture. He cannot pause in the manner of Hymn-writers to summon even his own soul

[1] That is, they had looked upon Yahweh as supreme over all nations and over the universe, as supreme in His nature and power. Other gods indeed existed, but these were so far below Yahweh that they need not be attended to.

to praise Yahweh; he cannot so much as speak of Him in the third person. It is Yahweh ... thou ... I:

1. Yahwéh, thou seárchest me and knówest (me);
2. *Thoú* knówest my sitting dówn and my standing úp,
   Thou discérnest my thoúght from afár.
3. My góing and my lying dówn thou meásurest;
   And with áll my wáys thou art famíliar.
4. For there is nót a wórd on my tóngue (but)
   Ló, Yahwéh, thou knówest áll of it.
5. Behínd and befóre thou shúttest me in,
   And láyest upón me thy hánd!
6. Too wónderful (such) knówledge fór me,
   It is hígh—I cánnot grásp it.

And now from Yahweh's omniscience he passes to His omnipresence:

7. Whére should I gó from thy spírit,
   And whére from thy fáce should I fleé?
8. If I go úp to heáven, thére art thoú,
   Or make my béd in Shéol, lo, there art thoú!
9. If I táke the wíngs of the dáwn,
   If I go to dwéll in the úttermost of the seá,
10. There álso thy hánd would leád me,
    And thy ríght hand would grásp me.
11. And if I sáy, Surely dárkness shall cóver * me,
    Then níght shall be líght aboút me—
12. Even dárkness shall not make dárk [1] from theé,
    But níght like dáy shall líghten!
    (As dárkness, so líght).

There is no getting away from Yahweh! Not even in the most impossible flights imagination can conceive, not anywhere in heaven or earth or Sheol beneath. With what emotion is he contemplating this? When he speaks of "fleeing" from Yahweh, of Yahweh's hand grasping him, one might think that he pictures himself a fugitive trying desperately to escape an angry God. This leads Kittel to the opinion that he is speaking from the viewpoint of the sinner whose concern is to elude God. "He is thinking less of the precious presence of divine grace by virtue of which the religious man is ever conscious of the nearness of the helping and redeeming God than of the presence of His power, fearsome to man. And so he apparently has himself less in mind than a godless man pursued by God's vengeance and attempting to run from Him. But the impossibility

[1] That is, conceal from thee.

of speaking in abstract concepts or expressions is so great that
here too he becomes at once personal and wholly direct and
speaks as if it were happening to himself. He thinks himself
hypothetically into the situation of such a fugitive and uses I
and Thou." This interpretation of Kittel is in part occasioned
by an emendation adopted by him and the other Germans in
v.10: "There also thy hand would *take* me (instead of *lead*
me)." This emendation is based upon the feeling that "lead"
does not fit in with the context and with the verb in the
parallel, "grasp" (Gunkel). The Syriac seems to corroborate
such a reading, for it has "grasp" instead of "lead"; but this
seems due to a confusion, for it has "lead" in the parallel
clause. The popular emendation, then, rests only on the claim
that "lead" is out of place here.

It is well to spend a little time over this reading, for upon
it depends in part the feeling-tone of the entire passage. The
Massoretic text has "lead," which is the same word as that
used in Psalm 23: "He leadeth me." The Greek and Syriac
versions retain it, the Syriac merely transposing "lead" and
"grasp." But does "lead" harmonise with "grasp," which seems
to imply force and even hostility, like our English "seize"
(an equally suitable translation of the Hebrew)? That depends
upon whether "grasp" can be used in a friendly sense. Now it
happens that in one of the classic passages of the Psalms we
find it employed in just this way. The Author of Psalm 73 says
to Yahweh:

> 23. "But I' álways am wíth thee
> Thou hast grásped my right hánd."

Surely, there is no reason why this Psalmist should not have
used the word to denote the same kindly taking hold! [1]

It appears then that he is thinking of Yahweh's presence in
a happy way. To be sure, he does speak of "fleeing" from it
but that verb can denote swift going away without the idea
of fear; as when Job says that his days flee from him (Job
9:25). He is picturing himself, how he might conceivably try

---

[1] It is used in the Syriac Gospels of Jesus' taking hold of the sick, e.g.
Mk. 1:31.

by every flight to get away from God, but not in fear. Quite
the contrary! For his realization that such escape is impossible
brings unspeakable joy—the true mood of a Hymn. And indeed this is the mood which prevails throughout his whole
Psalm whenever he is contemplating his own relation to God;
although another seemingly hostile expression occurs in v.5
"shuttest me in"—the regular term for besieging a city. The
metaphors show us only the boldness of the poet.

From God's omnipresence he now passes to His amazing
care and forethought in the creation of the Psalmist himself.
And this shows that our Psalmist represents a mature stage
of religious reflection. "An older, more childlike time," says
Gunkel, "saw God's marvels in the extraordinary; the more
developed spirit of the Psalmist finds one of the greatest marvels in his own body!"

> 13. For thoú hast posséssed my reíns,
>      Thou didst weáve me together in the wómb of my móther.
> 14. I will give thánks unto thee fór that feárfully
>      Am I wónderfully made:    wónderful thy wórks,
>      And my sóul knóws (it) exceédingly.
> 15. Not híd was my fráme from theé
>      Whén I was máde in sécret,
>      Wrought in many cólors in the under-párts of the eárth.
> 16. My émbryo thine éyes sáw,
>      And upón thy book were áll of them wrítten—
>      The dáys that were fáshioned—
>      And nót (yet was there) óne of thém!

Once more, as he passes in review the marvels of God, his
spirit cannot refrain itself:

> 17. And to mé how weíghty are thy thoúghts, O Gód!
>      How míghty are their countings úp!
> 18. Should I númber them, they are móre than the sánd!
>      I awáke—and stíll I am with theé!

That last is a striking thought, if the Massoretic reading be
right. Marvelous the unthinkable number of God's ideas and
purposes discoverable in the commonest of life's manifestations; but more marvellous yet that He stays by me through
the hours of sleep—still there when I awake! [1]

[1] The transition seems abrupt and for that reason it is popular to emend
by reading "finish" instead of "awake"—"when I come to the end of my
counting there is still God" (Gunkel, Schmidt, and, differently, Staerk).
Duhm, who retains the present reading with misgivings, interprets it:

And now there leaps suddenly from the lips of this adoring Psalmist, pondering over the ineffable mysteries of God's loving care, an outburst of animosity that takes us utterly aback:

19. Oh that thou wouldst kíll, O Gód, the wícked!
    Nay, ye mén of bloód, awáy from mé!
20. Whó rebél* agaínst thee in málice,
    Táke thy náme* in vaín.
21. Shall nót I háte, O Yahwéh, thy háters?
    And for those that rise agaínst thee shall I not have loáthing?
22. With a pérfect hátred do I háte them,
    As énemies are they to mé!

What does he mean? Why should the thought of the ungodly intrude here? And why should our Psalmist's love be turned in a flash by such a thought into blazing vindictiveness? The contrast is so violent that Schmidt breaks off our Psalm at verse 18, although somewhat inconsistently he regards vv.19-24 as a "passionate addition" written by our same Psalmist later! But however shocked our modern sensibilities may be at this intrusion of passion we must remember, as Gunkel points out, that it is a genuinely Hebraic phenomenon. The tenderer and more rapt our Psalmist's thoughts of God, the fiercer his anger at the men who reject such a God. And it is only fair to him to recognise that the ungodly against whom he cries for vengeance are not his personal foes. His sole grudge against them is that they are the enemies of God; that is why in loyalty he makes them his own.[1]

Frankly, we cannot love the trait exhibited here though it still is to be found among enthusiasts in any good cause, even God's. It reminds us how narrow is the line separating intense devotion from fanaticism. And yet there is in the Psalmist's words something that must always be present in any passionate

"When I awake I continue to occupy myself with the amazing wonders which enchained me the evening before" (so Kirkpatrick). Kittel has his own version: "Should I keep on numbering all day and all night, next morning I should still be doing the same." An expression so "pregnant," as Kittel terms it, permits varying interpretations.

[1] Herkenne, who follows Jerome and the Syriac in reading "a way of deceit" in v.24, thinks that the Psalmist is attacking some men who accuse him of hypocrisy and thereby cause a scandal among the faithful because the Psalmist is a person in authority. His animosity is therefore excusable: "this zeal is not immoral." There seems little ground for such a view.

love—an aroused militant attitude of the soul towards what offends that love which is far removed from anything like easy tolerance. In a sense we honor this man all the more because he could become so fierce.

His flare-up however is but for a moment. In his conclusion an entirely different note is dominant—that of self-distrust and aspiration:

> 23. Seárch me, O Gód, and knów my heárt,
>     Tést me, and knów my thoúghts,
> 24. And seé if there be any fálse* wáy in mé,
>     And leád me in the wáy endúring.

As was the case with the Author of Psalm 19:7-14, who concluded in much the same strain, Gunkel finds in these words an evidence of self-assurance on the part of the Psalmist: "I however (in contrast to the wicked) am a religious man and intend to be; thou, Lord, who lookest into the hidden, recognize it! See whether a 'lying word' is in my heart and lead me on the way of good, upright, peace-loving thought." Even Kittel, who praises his "true moral earnestness," seems to look on him as certain of his own piety. But surely Staerk is nearer right when he acquits him freely of all self-complacence. "He also (even as the wicked) is not perfect, but must pray God's grace that it may help him to find the right way, the way to life."

"The way to life." Is that what he means by the "way enduring"? There are several interpretations given—the ancient way of right (Barnes), the way that is right for all time (Duhm), the way of life spoken of in Proverbs, i.e. of long life (Kirkpatrick, Staerk) or (emending) the way of peace (Schlögl, Schmidt), or the way leading to life both here and in the coming Messianic kingdom (Kittel).

In view of the overwhelmingly preponderant attitude of the men of the Old Testament it is probably right to exclude from our interpretation of the phrase the thought of what we call a "hereafter," and agree with Gunkel when he says that "it is not in any case the way to everlasting happiness" that he means. Rather his thought is on the lasting quality of goodness in this life, its manner of making the end of the man who pursues it "peace" (Ps. 37:37).

At the same time it is a fact that we are dealing here with an unusual thinker. His idea of Sheol is certainly different from that of two other Psalmists who seem to regard it as a place where man has no further dealings with Yahweh (Pss. 39:13, 88:10 ff.). No, when our Psalmist makes his bed in Sheol—that bed from which one never rises (Gunkel)—he will find Yahweh there. If he really means it, if it is not simply poetic metaphor, then he is on the way to the belief in a continuance of life with God beyond the grave.[1] But this point cannot be pressed.

Kirkpatrick well sums up his significance. "The consciousness of the intimate personal relation between God and man which is characteristic of the whole Psalter reaches its climax here."

[1] Oesterley argues that the expression "when I awake I shall still be with thee," taken together with the Psalmist's conviction that Yahweh will still be with him in Sheol, and that he was formed in Sheol before birth, points beyond death. "The passage may reasonably be understood as implying that the Psalmist had, at any rate, the beginnings of a belief in life hereafter in the more exalted sense." (*Fresh Approach to the Psalms,* p. 270.) S. A. Cook seems to doubt this. (*The Old Testament,* N. Y. 1936, p. 135.)

# The Author of Psalm 146

*The* Lord *looseth men out of prison*

As the last selection from the Hymn-writers of the Psalter
we shall take a man whose production is not highly regarded
by a number of scholars. Its echoes of earlier Old Testament
passages are so continuous that to their minds it lacks originality. Even Gunkel, who finds in it at least one original
thought, declares that it is "in large part a placing together
of customary Hymn motifs and at the same time a pattern-
list of the fundamental Hymn forms." The generally apprecia-
tive Kirkpatrick has for it no word of praise. Duhm, followed
by Barnes, pronounces it a "compilation," and Staerk speaks
of its colorlessness.

The present writer however cannot agree with this estimate.
He has for years turned to it as one of the unique Psalms of
the Psalter which expresses as none other a certain great interest of the Old Testament. Of that more presently. It is certainly no mere compilation but a living poem that deserves to
be called by Schmidt a "glorious Hymn."

He feels also that it reveals the man who composed it. It is
not, as Staerk says, "too general and colorless and much too
conventionally liturgical" to be seriously regarded as arising
from personal experience. Staerk may indeed be right in refusing to connect it with any definite historical event, as Kittel
is inclined to do, for it seems to reflect no special happening.
But it is personal, as Gunkel, Kittel and Barnes recognise—
"the Hymn of an Individual" (Gunkel) who "does indeed come
forward in the temple and before the assembled congregation,
but desires to communicate to the others nothing but his own
feeling and experiences" (Kittel). It was not therefore, as
Schmidt seems to think, composed as a liturgy for antiphonal
voices; the same man speaks throughout. What our Psalmist
has really given us is a meditation of his own upon Yahweh's

ways with men, and in so doing he shows us himself and his
very pronounced bias. He begins: [1]

> 1. Praíse, my soúl, Yahwéh!
> 2. I will praíse Yahwéh while I líve,
>    I will síng unto my Gód as long as I have my béing.

Like the author of Psalm 103, he summons his own soul to
praise. And not only for the present moment; he pledges himself to the continued praise of a life-time. We now expect him
to open his Main Portion by telling why God is to be praised
but before he does so he prepares for it by pointing the tragic
contrast between God and men—even the most powerful—
when it comes to depending on them:

> 3. Do nót trúst in prínces,
>    In a son of mán, in whóm there is no hélp!
> 4. Fórth goes his breáth, he retúrns to his eárth,
>    In thát dáy pass awáy his púrposes.

That is the trouble with the prince—with any man. He
means well, no doubt; he wants to help (to save, the Hebrew
says). The Psalmist is not condemning this would-be bene-
factor, nor warning against his possible deceit. He may well be
a man of fidelity. And because he is in a position to do a
great deal one naturally tries to get his aid and feels secure
when it is promised. But after all he is of the earth and soon
or late he must return to it. (The Psalmist is remembering the
solemn words of the ancient Genesis story: Gen. 3:19.) Unex-
pectedly he dies and at once his plans are a thing of the past—
the plans for you on which you hoped.[2] But there is a hope
that will not disappoint.[3] The Psalmist now passes to a form
that is used in the Hymns as an indirect way of praising God,
the beatitude:

> 5. Bléssed he whose hélp * is the Gód of Jácob,
>    Whose hópe is upon Yahwéh his Gód—

---

[1] The "Halleluia" at the beginning and end are probably not part of the
original Psalm and are omitted here.

[2] This is the thought of the Psalmist which Gunkel considers original.

[3] Cook understands the Psalmist to mean that he who has Yahweh as
his help will not die as do other men. (*Old Testament*, p. 140.) This seems
to be reading into the text a meaning that is not clearly there.

Then come four participles, in the manner of Hymn-writers, telling why God is such a help. The first brings in the familiar motif of His power manifested in creation, the rest celebrate His moral dealings with men:

> 6. Who máde heáven and eárth,
> The seá and áll that is ín them,
> Who keéps trúth for éver;
> 7. Who perfórms júdgment for the oppréssed,
> Who gíves breád to the húngry.

And now the Psalmist, borne on the tide of enthusiasm, breaks off from the participles into five great pealing utterances in the indicative, each of which begins with the supreme Name that is the subject of them all. Here too he is using a traditional Hymn form.

> Yahwéh loóses the prísoners,
> 8. Yahwéh ópens (the eyes of) the blínd,
> Yahwéh raíses the bowed dówn,
> Yahwéh lóves the ríghteous,
> 9. Yahwéh guárds the álien,
> The fátherless and wídow he restóres,
> But the wáy of the wícked he makes croóked.

It is easy to see where this man's heart is. The thing for which he is concerned is the hard lot of the poor and friendless, of all upon whom the hand of society lies heavy, who are forgotten or oppressed by man. The blind also, and they who suffer from physical affliction, share in his pity. And when he thinks of Yahweh it is of a Being who cares for these unhappy people, whose chief activity is to defend and restore them. To his mind that is the great thing in Yahweh which is to be praised by the singer of Hymns—not His splendor written upon the heavens (though he touches on this), not His creative might, not His control over nature and history, or His deliverances of His people in the past, not His dealings with the soul in the domain of personal religion, but His helping of the poor. It is because Yahweh is such a God that his own praises will never be silent.

And with the dream of a world made better for the poor people his faith leaps upward in a final cry of triumph:

> 10. Kíng shall Yahwéh be for éver,
> Thy Gód, O Zíon, to generátion on generátion!

Yes, Yahweh shall be King, on and on! His purposes continue—His purposes for the poor—and His Kingdom shall come, His will be done on earth. For this reason He is a God to be looked to, a God in whom to set one's hope. That is, if one be himself poor.

And such the Psalmist feels himself to be, if we read his mind aright. He is not looking at the lot of the poor from the outside but sharing it. Not that he makes much of his own suffering or rejoices in the coming divine deliverance as a personal gain. No breath of self-seeking can be sensed in his whole poem. But it is plain that he believes in the poor; they are the righteous whom Yahweh loves (v.8). They are in fact his own people. And in his Hymn he is speaking to them.

It is this bias that gives him a special place among the Psalmists. For strange to say, most of them do not exhibit it in any marked degree. It palpitates indeed in the Law and the Prophets, and our Psalmist has drawn on these freely for his phrases and ideas, thus incurring the reproach of being a mere compiler. But when we come to the Psalter we often look in vain for a prevailing note of social righteousness. Not that the Psalmists are unsympathetic to it; [1] indeed they now and then sound it in passing. But with the exception of the Authors of Psalms 72 and 82 and this Psalmist it is not dominant in their thoughts, does not occupy the center of their attention.

The distinction of our Psalmist lies in the fact that when he thinks of God he at once thinks of His succoring the defenseless. Scholars are not agreed as to what is the central theme of his poem. Kittel finds it in the warning not to trust in man; Gunkel in the beatitude concerning him whose confidence is in Yahweh. It is remarkable that neither of them sees that his real interest lies in the social activity of Yahweh and that he devotes his chief attention to this. That is why he alone among the Hymnists has given us a Hymn of social justice.

[1] As Oesterley has pointed out, they often speak of the righteousness and justice of Yahweh. (*Fresh Approach to the Psalms,* p. 223ff.) Now and then a Psalmist will explicitly assert Yahweh's care for the poor and the oppressed (as in Pss. 9, 10, 14, 94, 102, 113).

## 2. "SONGS OF ZION"

Among the Hymns of the Psalter we come upon several which have a theme somewhat different from that of the usual Hymn in that they speak especially of Jerusalem as the City of God and praise Him by praising His chosen abode. So distinct are these Hymns that Gunkel sets them by themselves as a peculiar variety, calling them by the name which is preserved for us in Ps. 137:3, "Songs of Zion." They depart a little in form from the usual Hymn since they generally lack a proper Introduction. Other distinguishing features are the way in which they address the holy place (Pss. 87:3, 122:2 f., 6 ff.) and in particular call down blessings upon it (122:6 ff.).

These Songs of Zion are filled with prophetic content, for we understand Pss. 46, 48 and 76 as *predictive*. In this development of the Type the Psalmists had been preceded by the Prophets who uttered praises of the glorified Jerusalem of the future (Is. 26:1; 27:2-5; Jer. 31:23; cf. Is. 61:10 f.).

"It is not difficult," says Gunkel, "to understand how it was just these songs in praise of the sanctuary that had eschatological content, for ever since Isaiah Zion had played a chief rôle in the Prophets' proclaiming of the future: *here* should the great transaction come to pass whereby Yahweh manifests Himself as the Lord of all peoples, and this *'here'* echoes triumphantly in those poems: *'here'* trembling seizes the Kings (Ps. 48:6), *'here'* He breaks the quiver and the bow (Ps. 76:3)."

Such is the view of Gunkel, which is shared by Staerk and

Kittel. It is opposed to the hitherto prevailing interpretation, for scholars have been inclined to see in these Songs of Zion allusions to historic events, such as the signal deliverance of Jerusalem from Sennacherib or the victories of the Maccabees. A fair case can be made out for this historical interpretation but the present writer feels that it fails to do justice to the supernatural tone of the allusions; they are too grandiose to fit into any picture of sober historic reality. The reader senses that he is in a world of shakings and catastrophes too mighty to belong to the present or the past. Only the future can contain them—the future when God will intervene to wind up history and make a new earth.

A third view must be mentioned as clashing with Gunkel's. Mowinckel denies that there are any eschatological Psalms in the Psalter. He interprets the pictures of Zion's victory as prompted by the celebration of Yahweh's Enthronement festival, concerning which we shall speak presently. Schmidt follows him in part but recognises the Advent hope of the Prophets as forming the background of the Songs of Zion. Mowinckel's objections to Gunkel's view are (in the opinion of the present writer) convincingly answered in the latter's *Einleitung in die Psalmen,* p. 81 f. We shall accordingly adopt the eschatological interpretation in our treatment of the Authors of the Songs of Zion.

These Songs, according to Gunkel's theory, must have arisen from out the public worship of Israel but he has nothing specific to say as to the occasion in which they found their "seat in life," except that it must have been a time when the glory of Jerusalem was celebrated. Any of the great national feasts, such as were described at the beginning of this section, may well have called forth enthusiastic thoughts about Zion, especially among the pilgrims setting foot within its gates (Ps. 122:2) after a long journey from Gentile regions.

Consider now a few of the men who wrote such Songs.

# THE AUTHOR OF PSALM 46

*God is in the midst of her, therefore shall she not be
removed*

A word first as to the Type of this Psalm. It is, as Gunkel
confesses, difficult to classify. It is like the Hymns in that it
celebrates Yahweh's praise, but on the other hand it is far
removed from them in that it utters the personal feelings of
the writer and those for whom he speaks. "One can hardly
say 'we will not fear' in a Hymn." Again, Yahweh is introduced as speaking, which is a feature of Prophecy. It derives
from the Prophets also its imagery of the tumbling earth and
the engulfing waters, of the river making glad the city of God,
of Yahweh's help before the break of day, of the eternal peace
—indeed, its whole eschatological expectation. Taking account
of all these elements Gunkel decides to call it an Eschatological Hymn or more exactly, an Eschatological Song of Zion.

Consider now the man and his poem.

It is a time of trouble for Israel. Not perhaps of the spec-
tacular sort which gets into histories but only some heavier
pressing down of its age-long burden upon the feeble community of later days. Fear stalks abroad, grisly foreboding of
coming woes haunts men. Perhaps an invasion looms on the
horizon or portents in nature rouse uneasiness. People are
going about with depressed, harassed expression; gloom pervades the nation. And now in the midst of the anxiety the
Feast (whatever it is) arrives.

At least one man in Israel rises to the challenge thus presented to the people's faith. He belongs to that succession of
Israel's leaders who from Moses onwards have known how to
face dismay with an uprush of belief in God. Suddenly amid
the quailing he puts the trumpet to his lips and blows it clear
and loud.

God! That is his first word—we have seen other Psalmists
also begin with it. Why should we fear when we have *God?*

Borne on the tide of that thought he sweeps forward in "long rolling verses" (Staerk), bringing in once more the "sea of faith."

2. Gód is to ús a réfuge and stréngth,    a hélp in troúbles
found exceédingly!
3. Thérefore we will not feár at the chánging of the eárth,
at the sháking of the moúntains into the heárt of the
seás!
4. They roár, they foám—its wáters; quáke do the
moúntains at its príde.

It is a picture of the final collapse of the world.[1] Everything on which man has built crumbles, even the solid ground itself. Once more the dreadful waters—the Israelites always feared the sea—come on to submerge the earth, and the mountains cringe before them. What are our little troubles to these! And then at the climax of breathless horror peals forth a great cry:

Yahwéh of hósts is wíth us.    a high tówer to ús is
the Gód of Jácob![2]

Yes, and into that tower we can climb and be safe—even when mountains fail us. For the God who is higher than high is here—with us, in Jerusalem. And now with bewildering swiftness the scene changes. The roaring floods, the reeling hills drop below us and we see a different water, in the form that to the Israelite was perhaps the loveliest thing on earth:

5. A ríver! Its chánnels make glád the city of Gód,
The Most Hígh has sánctified * his dwélling.
6. Gód is in the mídst of her, she shall not be sháken,
Hélp her shall Gód at the túrning of the mórning.

He is thinking doubtless of the promise of the Prophet: "At eventide, behold, terror; and before the morning they are not" (Is. 17:14).

Again the image has shifted and an onslaught of raging enemies is before his mind. The enemy is not any definite nation

---

[1] "The Psalmist is here referring to the fearsome 'woes' which are to precede the advent of the Messiah, according to the traditional Jewish teaching." (Oesterley, *Fresh Approach to the Psalms*, p. 194.) It is not clear whether Oesterley attributes such a meaning to the Psalmist himself, or only to tradition.

[2] It is generally agreed that the refrain should be inserted after v.4, at the end of the first stanza.

but the portentous gathering of the peoples foretold of the end.[1] On they come and lo, at the height of their battle-fury Yahweh thunders, the ground under them dissolves.

> 7. The peóples roár, the kíngdoms sháke...  ....He gives
>    fórth his voíce, the eárth mélts....
> 8. Yahwéh of hósts is wíth us,   a high tówer to ús is the
>    Gód of Jácob!

How the refrain crashes in—like the burst of a full orchestra, triumphant, overwhelming.

It is over! The clear morning light rests upon the finished deed of God. Destruction, yes; but *what* destruction! His faithful are summoned to look at it.

> 9. Come seé the wórks of Yahwéh,   what desolátions he
>    has sét in the eárth!
> 10. He makes báttles to ceáse to the énd of the eárth!
>     The bów he breáks and he cuts in súnder the speár,
>     The wágons he búrns with fíre.

Not the corpses of Israel's enemies, as Ezekiel beheld them strewn over the mountains, but the ruined arms of war—no more battles anywhere! In the midst of the stillness our Psalmist hears the Voice of Yahweh speaking to the invading hordes who can fight no longer:

> 11. Let bé and knów that I' am Gód!
>     I will be exálted in the peóples, I will be exálted
>     in the eárth!

Vain was your fury! One cannot fight against God. And so with Yahweh lifted high above all nations, acknowledged as God by the whole earth, the refrain peals out once more:

> 12. Yahwéh of hósts is wíth us,   a high tówer to ús is
>     the Gód of Jácob!

Two things are evident concerning the man who could forge a glowing Hymn like this in the chill hour of foreboding. One is his faith. That is what the Germans love to dwell upon, for their tradition makes much of faith; and this Hymn has a

---

[1] The older interpretation, that the Psalmist is speaking not of the great future but of a recent deliverance of Jerusalem from invasion, is upheld by Löhr (*Psalmenstudien*, p. 31 f.), Baethgen, König and Herkenne. This deliverance is usually identified with the retirement of Sennacherib in 701 B.C. Mowinckel, who regards this as a Psalm of Yahweh's enthronization, also discards the eschatological interpretation (*Psalmenstudien* II, p. 15).

special place in their hearts because it suggested to Martin Luther the theme of his own sublime Hymn: *Ein feste Burg ist unser Gott*. "If we can call I Corinthians 13 the Hohelied of Love, we can with the same right call this Psalm the Hohelied of Faith." So says Kittel. He notes how several commentators in writing on this Psalm recall Horace's words describing the lofty courage of Augustus:

> Si fráctus íllabátur órbis,
> I'mpavidúm feriént ruínae.    (Odes, I, 3) [1]

But he points out how Horace's hero has only Stoic intrepidity to oppose to the falling world while the Psalmist mounts above it on the wings of trust; for here we see illumined the contrast between two views of the universe, philosophy and faith. "It is the most glorious Hymn of faith," says Staerk, "that ever was sung." Nor should we lose sight of the fact that the Psalmist's faith in Yahweh is bound up with Jerusalem. He does not indeed praise the city, as do other writers of Songs of Zion; but he sets it in the very center of his picture of a world subdued by God. And because he belongs to this Jerusalem he is not alone as was Horace's hero, but one of a great company of the faithful. In that company he merges himself; we will not fear. . . . Yahweh of hosts is with *us*. In this he is a true Hymnist, and a Prophet also. One is reminded of Isaiah's selfless cry, "Immanuel," God is with us (Is. 8:10).

The second thing that strikes the reader is the Psalmist's vision of universal peace. Barnes seems to stand alone among recent commentators in rejecting such an interpretation of his words. According to him all that our Psalmist means is:

"He exterminateth (hostile) armies throughout the land. There is no reference to the abolition of war: the Psalm refers only to the destruction of a powerful enemy host." The Germans however all translate:

"He restrains wars (or war) to the end of the earth." Such seems to be the meaning of the Hebrew and it is confirmed by the dependence in other ways of our Psalmist upon

---

[1] If the world should break and collapse
Untrembling will the ruins strike him.

the Prophets; for we know that at least two great thinkers among the Prophets had predicted Yahweh's rule over a warless world (Is. 2:2 ff., Mic. 4:1 ff.; cf. Is. 11:6 ff., Zech. 9:9 f.).

The Psalmist then declares that in the great time to come God will bring war to an end. In so doing he manifests his *faith;* but at first sight there seems to be a question as to whether he also exhibits *love.* For it is possible that the cessation of war may be regarded by him from a narrowly national point of view. He *may* mean only that Israel's enemies are rendered powerless. But if his vision is wider; if he intends Yahweh's words at the close of the Hymn to be addressed to the invading armies; and if they contain a strain of hope and invitation along with their stern rebuke—then the Psalmist sounds a universal note, and a universal note always comes from a loving heart. We have taken such a view in our interpretation. If it is correct, he stands out with the two or possibly three Prophets we have just mentioned as a bold predicter that God will end war with love. The fact that after more than two thousand years their vision still remains unfulfilled does not stamp it as an illusion.

With him and his fellows we ought also to put that other Psalmist who believed that by virtue of what comes from the mouths of little children God will perfect strength and cause to cease—the same word that this Psalmist uses—the enemy and the self-avenger (Ps. 8:2).

# THE AUTHOR OF PSALM 84

*O how amiable are thy dwellings!*

We have had something to say of pilgrims going up to the great feasts at Jerusalem and we have pictured them entering Yahweh's house with joy at the end of their journey. But now for the first time we shall come face to face with a man who is passing through that experience and hear him tell what it means to him. That is, if the usual interpretation of Psalm 84 is correct; for most recent commentators regard it as a pilgrim Psalm.[1] Barnes indeed differs from the view of the majority in thinking that the author of the Psalm is an anointed person— a king or high priest—who for some reason can not himself make his way to the temple but sees in his mind's eye the happy companies of his fellow-Israelites consummating their pilgrimage. Barnes may be right, but even so it is a *pilgrim's* feelings that are uttered, though it be only in imagination. Another recent view which departs from the usual opinion to some degree is that of Schmidt, who looks on the Psalm as a Liturgy of which only certain verses are rendered by pilgrims (2-5, 11-12), the other verses being the responses of priests. This conception of the Psalm robs it of its personal spontaneity, and rests upon no manifest indications in the text. It is better therefore to disregard it, as well as the theory sponsored by Barnes, and to treat the Psalm as the outpouring of a pilgrim's emotions on arriving at Jerusalem.

Of its Type Gunkel has this to say: "This unique Psalm, so delicate in its feeling, contains the forms of the Hymn. To these belong the lines at the close (v.12) in which Yahweh's name is the subject and the beatitudes praising the truly religious—an indirect way of praising God Himself. But there comes out much more strongly in the poem the glorifying of the sanctuary." That is why he calls it a Song of Zion.

Our Psalmist then is a Pilgrim whose "feet are standing"

[1] Herkenne holds that it is not a pilgrim Psalm, but expresses the homesickness of a Levite for the temple.

within the gates of Jerusalem (Ps. 122:2). He seems to be a man who lives in fairly comfortable circumstances among Gentiles, perhaps in an Aramaic-speaking city (Kittel), whither even before the Exile Israelites went to better their fortunes. For he belongs to the Pre-Exilic Period, as his mention of the king shows. After deliberation he has made up his mind to undertake the long journey to Jerusalem. The "highways are in his heart." With all his success in a foreign land he is not happy there, for his home, his "nest," is to be found only in the temple of God.

And now he is here! Perhaps he is entering with the great procession into the forecourt of the sanctuary; or he may just be catching sight of the temple for the first time as he reaches the crest of the mount of Olives. Rapture seizes upon him, his transports of joy almost overcome him.

2. Hów lóvely thy dwéllings, Yahwéh of hósts!
3. My soúl lóngs, yea, faínts for the coúrts of Yahwéh,
My heárt and my flésh shout for jóy to the líving Gód!

Far has he wandered, like a swallow seeking a home, and now he has found it. Perhaps his eyes are upon a mother-bird darting home to her nest in the stone-work of the sanctuary, where religious awe protects her brood from the marauder (Gunkel).

4. Yea, the bírd has foúnd a hoúse, and the swállow a nést for hersélf
Whére she láys her yoúng—
Thý áltars, Yahwéh of hósts, my kíng and my Gód!

Then his thought passes from the happy birds to the far happier men whose continual employment is in the service of the temple:

5. Bléssed they who dwéll in thy hoúse! for éver they praíse thee!

Happy also the pilgrim who dares to make the journey home; who conscious of the dangers and hardships and his own weakness decides to throw himself upon Yahweh's protection on the road:

6. Bléssed the mán whose stréngth is in theé, the highways in their heárt!

7. Pássing through the válley of weéping [1]    they máke it a
    place of spríngs,
   Yea, the early raín clóthes it with bléssings.
8. They gó from stréngth to stréngth—The God of góds
    will be seén in Zíon.

Such his journey has seemed to him. The terrible parched
ways he dreaded so much proved through God's kindness to
have abundant water. The fall of the early rain had clothed
the wastes with verdure. It was like Paradise (Gunkel). Instead of the exhaustion he anticipated a new vigor poured
through him, increasing as he went on. And to the gladness of
such travel was added ever that greater rapture of hope: he
would see God in Zion! And now he and his companions stand
before the sanctuary, they are seeing God!

Face to face with Yahweh he falls to prayer. But not for
himself is his supplication:

9. Yahwéh, Gód of hósts,    heár my práyer,
    Give eár, O Gód of Jácob!
10. Behóld, O Gód our shiéld,    and loók upon the fáce
     of thine anoínted.

To this man Jerusalem is everything and the guardian of
Jerusalem is the king. The king represents the nation and in
his peace his people shall have peace. We need not suppose,
as does Schmidt, that the mention of the king shows some
connection of the feast with the royal office. Nor need we
with Gunkel and Duhm remove the prayer as an interruption
to the thought of the Psalmist.

Now he returns to his chief thought—the happiness of stay-
ing continually in the temple. The very beggar who haunts
the entrance to the sanctuary eking out his existence with the
alms of the worshippers, having no shelter from sun or rain
(Barnes), is more to be envied than the Israelite living in
comfort among the heathen:

11. For bétter a dáy in thy coúrts    than a thóusand.    I
     should choóse
    To stand at the thréshold in the hoúse of my Gód    rather
     than to dwéll in the ténts of wíckedness.

[1] Altering the Hebrew word slightly to make it conform to the ancient
versions.

Surely one basking in the light of Yahweh, hiding under His protection as one can in His house, would enjoy a continual stream of prosperity.

> 12. For a sún and shiéld is Yahwéh Gód;      he gíves fávor and hónor,
> Yahwéh does not hóld back goód      for them that wálk úprightly.

There speaks a true disciple of the Wise Men, to whose mind devotion to God and outward success go hand in hand. The Psalmist accepts the retribution dogma as a matter of course. Why should a man not reap what he sows and why should not God reward His faithful servants with good things? And so, carried away by the joy that he pictures, and the wonder of the great Name of Him from whom all flows, he turns once more to God, in whose presence he stands at last, and breaks forth into a final beatitude:

> 13. Yahwéh of hósts,      bléssed the mán that trústs in theé!

As we consider his Song of Zion we cannot fail to see that this man is distinguished above all the Psalmists we have hitherto studied by one thing—his love of the temple and its worship. He cannot speak of it without rapture and his dearest wish would be to pass his life within its precincts praising God continually as do the members of the temple clergy and choir. And the reason of his delight in the sanctuary is that he there comes face to face with God—the living God. What he longs and faints for is the presence of Yahweh, as it can be had, he believes, in only one place in all the earth.

His devotion to God is very pure. He does indeed speak of the favor and honor and good things which come from God when one lives near Him, but his mind is plainly on something that transcends these—the companionship of God. One can see this by the way in which he is ever passing from the third person to the second. It seems as if he could not talk *about* God for more than a moment without breaking through to talk *to* Him.

He delights to live with God and that is why he loves the temple. In his Psalm there is a noticeable silence regarding the rites of worship. Not a word of the whole stately round of sacrifices. He speaks only of *praising* God. And yet his Psalm is drenched in the dew of worship.

He does not indeed stand alone in this. Other Psalmists have in different ways given tongue to the joy of the sanctuary and one or two of them will later come before us. But perhaps none of them have quite attained to the classic finality which characterises the work of this Psalmist. His Psalm will remain forever the supreme Psalm of the Sanctuary.

*I was glad when they said unto me, We will go into the
house of the* LORD

Before bringing to a close our brief selection of Authors of
Songs of Zion we shall consider another man who was also a
pilgrim. Like the Author of Psalm 84 he utters the emotions and
thoughts which came to him when on pilgrimage but he does
so quite differently. He too strikes a very personal note, so
that we must not see in his Psalm a general pilgrim song but
a record of his own inner experience.

To him the city of Jerusalem is an object of passionate
love, and he has given us a Psalm that may be called a Song
of Zion with even more justice than the two we have just
studied. It will be seen how the name of Jerusalem rings
through it like a refrain.

He has come to the Holy City with a caravan of fellow-
pilgrims from his own neighborhood. Unlike the Author of
Psalm 84 he has nothing to tell of the journey. All his thought
is concentrated on the ecstatic moment when he stands at last
within the gates of Jerusalem. Perhaps he is looking back on
that moment from the quiet of his own home (Kirkpatrick),
or he is just arriving at the city (Kittel), or just leaving it
(Staerk, Schmidt). In any case his memory goes back to the
happy day when some of his neighbors (apparently) came to
him with the proposal that he join them in a pilgrimage to the
temple. Evidently he lived some distance away and such a
journey was by no means a routine matter. They perhaps did
not realise what their words meant to him, how they went
straight down to the deepest spring of love in his heart, causing
it to gush forth in joy.

> 1. I was glád when they saíd to mé,     "To the hoúse of
>    Yahwéh let us gó."

What followed that invitation—the bustle of preparation,
the days and nights on the road, the hardships, the companion-

ships—all are passed over. Everything is concentrated on the
overwhelming fact of arrival:

> 2. Stánding áre our féet     in thy gátes, Jerúsalem! [1]

And as it comes over him what this city means—has meant in
the glorious past—will mean in days to come—he breaks out
in exultant praises:

> 3. Jerúsalem! that is buílt as a cíty     that is joíned for
>    itsélf togéther!
> 4. Whíther go úp the tríbes,     the tríbes of Yáh,
>    (As a) téstimony to I'srael,     to give thánks to the
>    náme of Yahwéh.

It is plain what thought the city arouses in him: its solid unity
—emblematic of the unity of the nation which expresses itself
there in the converging upon it (the Israelite always said "the
going up to it") of all the scattered clans of Yahweh from all
the world.[2]

From the religious significance of Jerusalem he turns to the
political. What mighty memories of the kings of old live on
in it!

> 5. For thére were sét thrónes for júdgment—thrónes for     —
>    the hoúse of Dávid.

Yes, it was David who chose Jerusalem and established his
house there in all its majesty. And he left there a tradition of
justice—for the Hebrew word "judgment" which our Psalmist
uses always has an ethical overtone. He looks back on David's
line as not only glorious monarchs but also true dispensers of
justice.

---

[1] Herkenne reminds us that a similar rapture is felt by modern pilgrims
to Palestine when for the first time they catch sight of the holy city.

[2] The expression used in the present Hebrew text is a difficult one and
it is fashionable to emend it thus:
"Jerusalem that is rebuilt without gaps or breaches" (Schmidt, Staerk,
Moffatt).
But such a change goes against the ancient versions and turns the idea
of Israel's unity into that of mere physical restoration. Gunkel keeps the
former when he reads:
"Jerusalem is built as a city whose family comes together in her."
Surely we ought not to cancel out this great conception of unity. And
notice that the unity of which the city is an embodiment really rests in
God, for the tribes which go up thither are the tribes of Yahweh, and it
is to the "house of Yahweh" that they ascend.

It is of the past that he is speaking. Staerk indeed thinks the verse has hope in it as well as memory—hope of the splendor of the David-Messiah yet to come—and that it is this hope which helps to bind into one the scattered tribes converging on Jerusalem. But a sober reading of the Hebrew hardly seems to warrant such a belief, attractive though it may be. On the other hand the Psalmist does not project any *gloom* into the past, as Schmidt imagines when he would read between the lines a remembrance not only of the fame and splendor of the ancient royal city, but also of its places of execution and its prisons. It is not the "shuddering of its great history" that our Psalmist would recall, but the noble precedent of equity established there by David.

Transported by his enthusiasm he turns to his fellow-pilgrims and calls on them to join him in greeting:

> 6. Práy for the wélfare of Jerúsalem! [1]    May they have quíet
>    that lóve thee!
> 7. May there bé wélfare in thy rámparts,    quíet in thy stróng-
>    holds!

And now his love surges out towards all "the tribes of Yah," the immense congregation of the faithful, who love Jerusalem, and come up to her. He belongs to them, they to him.

> 8. For the sáke of my bréthren and my compánions    I will
>    sáy, Prospérity be withín thee!

Then his thought returns to that sacred place with which he began—the temple of God, which is the center of the city and its fellowship.

> 9. For the sáke of the hoúse of Yahwéh our Gód    I will
>    seék goód for theé.

Such are his words, translated as literally as possible. But the English can never render the refrain that keeps beating through them, a refrain supplied by the last two syllables of the name Jerusalem.[2] Correctly or not, the Hebrew identified these syllables with the common word *shalôm*, which is com-

---

[1] This may well mean, "Salute Jerusalem" (ARV mg), since the salutation in common use seems to have been *"Shalôm"*.

[2] In our Psalmist's day it was pronounced Yerushalēm, not Yerushalayim as now pointed. (Ges. Kautzsch, *Hebrew Grammar*, 88c).

monly rendered "peace" though it really signifies "complete-
ness" and therefore includes also the idea of soundness,
general well-being and prosperity. With this word, repeated
thrice, he has woven together other words having much the
same sound, one of which is the parallel word "quiet," or
"ease": "*sha'alû' sh'lô'm Yerushalém! yishlayû' 'ôhabháyik!*"
As Staerk beautifully puts it: "Jerusalem is the bell-note which
accompanies this religious song with its gentle swingings
(v.6 ff.), where the poet intentionally plays with this name,
out of which the Israelite heard the word 'peace'."

Needless to say, the thing that most characterises our Psalmist is this love of Jerusalem of which we have been speaking.
He stands out in the Psalter as perhaps the man who had
Jerusalem most in his heart. It meant so many things to him!
Its stately compactness, its solid unity of stone buildings surrounded by massive ramparts, its memories of past greatness;
but most of all its House of Yahweh and the Church of Yahweh which centers in it—a great church now scattered throughout the lands—a church of brethren, for do not all know
one God? And back of all, in all, bearing all in His mighty
care, Yahweh, who gives significance to everything. For of
whom else but Yahweh could the Psalmist and his brethren
"ask peace" for Jerusalem?

And his love for the city is singularly free from that thirst
for dominion and vengeance which stains too many utterances
of Israelitish patriotism. He lets fall no word of coming exaltation over the nations, still less does he gloat over their future
discomfiture. He is not even thinking with pride of the material splendor of the temple, as was the disciple who said to
Jesus: "Master, behold what manner of stones and what manner of buildings!" (Mk. 13:1.) What thrills him most is the
unity of Israel for which Jerusalem stands and what he desires
for it and his brethren is peace. In reading his Psalm one is
reminded of the Collect for the Fifth Sunday after Trinity:
"Grant, O Lord, we beseech thee, that the course of this world
may be so peaceably ordered by thy governance, that thy
Church may joyfully serve thee in all godly quietness...."

It may well be that our Lord had his Psalm in mind when beholding the city He wept over it, saying, "If thou hadst known in this day, even thou, the things that belong unto thy peace!" (Lk. 19:42).

# II

## THE AUTHOR OF A PSALM OF
## YAHWEH'S ENTHRONEMENT

IT NOW FALLS to us to consider one of those Psalmists who
created a kind of Psalm which has only recently been
recognized by scholars. This Type is called by Gunkel "Psalms
of Yahweh's Enthronement." It is the merit of Mowinckel[1] to
have pointed out that there existed in later Israel an annual
feast celebrating Yahweh's mounting the throne of the world.
It was held at the Hebrew New Year, which fell in the autumn
and was the occasion of great rejoicing. One feature of its celebration was the singing of Psalms written specially for it.

This feast is a genuine discovery of modern research for it
is nowhere mentioned in the Old Testament itself and its existence and nature had therefore to be inferred and established
from a number of diverse data. All that we say about it therefore rests on indirect evidence and must be accepted with that
reservation. Nevertheless Gunkel feels confident that such a
feast did exist and that we can identify certain Psalms as composed to be rendered during its course. He does not indeed go
so far as Mowinckel (whom Hans Schmidt follows in part)
and find in many Psalms echoes of this feast. Mowinckel, he
thinks, pushes his views regarding it to an extreme, seeing in it
the "most important transaction of Israel's religion," drawing
to itself as a powerful magnet a great portion of Hebrew
Psalm writing. But he is quite clear in his mind that six Psalms

[1] *Psalmenstudien* II: Das Thronbesteigungfest Jahwäs etc.

78

were composed for it: 47, 93, 96, (at least in part), 97, 98, 99.[1]

These Psalms then had as their "seat in life" the celebration of Yahweh's Enthronement festival and in order to understand them we must try to picture to ourselves what such a festival was like. Unfortunately, as we have said, we must rely wholly on allusions but this does not prevent us from regarding Gunkel's sketch as fairly reliable.

The feast took its origin in the experience of Israel during the Exile[2] when the people were forced to witness an annual celebration of a similar festival at the Babylonian shrines. With characteristic vigor and independence they invented a feast of Yahweh to offset it. The time of its popularity was therefore the Post-Exilic Age. Among its features were a procession in which Yahweh was represented as "going up" (Ps. 47:5) towards the temple, and "entering into" the holy precincts (Pss. 96:13, 98:9)—an entering which we still proclaim in our American version of the *Venite:* "For he cometh!" Along with this went the adoration by the assembled worshippers, who in their festal garments ("the beauty of holiness") entered Yahweh's outer courts, fell down before Him and presented their offerings. All this was accompanied by their "joyful noise," the singing and blowing of trumpets. These features of divine worship were surprisingly like those which characterized the accession of a king to the throne in secular life. Yahweh is pictured as a King sitting on His throne adorned with costly robes, His subjects assembled before Him from far and near. But we cannot know how far the actual copying went; whether for example some sort of a symbol of God was carried in the procession and placed on a throne, and if so what it was.

It was out of such a feast then that the Psalms of Yahweh's Enthronement sprang. Their fundamental note is glad rapture over the God whose nearness is felt in the solemn transactions of the day. Their basic thought is that Yahweh is becoming King *today* and is entering in. But the "today" is really

---

[1] Of the Psalms treated in this book Mowinckel regards the following as written for the feast of Yahweh's enthronization: 8, 15, 29, 46, 84, 95, 97. *Psalmenstudien* II, p. 3f.

[2] It may however have been a Pre-Exilic observance.

eschatological: "He cometh!" Their content falls into three divisions:

1. Many summons to rejoice, in which they are like the Hymns and therefore exhibit at times a mixing of the two Types.

2. Brief references to Yahweh's deeds, which are thought of as just now taking place.

3. All sorts of descriptions, which depict conditions after Yahweh becomes King. Utterances of both these latter kinds are not unlike those that are customary in the Hymns.

Gunkel adds a fourth element, which he feels is a new thought—the idea that a new world-kingdom is coming. It is easy to explain why the Israel of that later age, oppressed and despised as it was, should portray with enthusiasm a day when the kingdoms of the world would be humbled and Yahweh reign over all nations, making Zion the center of the world. For these utterances, Gunkel believes, are prompted by the spirit of the Prophets and look forward to the time of the end.

Having thus got before us an idea of this Type of Psalm let us now proceed to select one from the comparatively few examples surviving and to consider its Author. In spite of their common theme each of these Psalms has an individuality of its own, yet no one stands out above the others in so marked a way that choice is easy. Perhaps the most striking personality exhibited is that of him who composed Psalm 97.

*The* LORD *is King, the earth may be glad thereof*

He has been brooding over the meaning of the great feast which Israel is about to celebrate and as he meditates his thought takes on glowing colors, his heart leaps with emotion. In such a mood is his poem born. He is the child of a late age and much that could be said of Yahweh has already been well said by the greater poets of an earlier day. His mind is full of their sublime word-painting, he looks as it were through their eyes; and yet he too has his gift. "The author of this Psalm," says Kirkpatrick, "was not an original poet, but he was a masterly Hymn-writer. There is scarcely a phrase in the Psalm which is not borrowed; but he combines the language of earlier Psalmists and Prophets into a 'costly mosaic' with a skill which is worthy of the occasion."

> 1. Yahwéh is kíng!   Let the eárth exúlt,
>    Let the mány íslands rejoíce!

When a new king was proclaimed a wave of gladness swept over a land, for people hoped things would now be better. Songs, rejoicing, feasting were the order of the day. And this in spite of the disappointment that was almost sure to follow. But now it is no earthly king who is proclaimed, it is Yahweh. His domain is no one country but the whole world. He is to take the place of the present emperor—of Persia, probably—who is holding under his iron despotism a multitude of peoples. The Psalmist thinks especially of those to the west and northwest, out over the Mediterranean Sea—the new regions of the Gentiles brought to the attention of the Hebrews by the Persian conquest of the Greek states (Gunkel). Now they groan under injustice but the new King will change all that!

And yet what a terrible King He is! Terrible in his very justice.

> 2. Cloúd and dárkness aroúnd him,
>    Ríghteousness and jústice the foundátion of his thróne.

3. Fíre befóre him goés,
   And sets abláze his ádversaries round aboút.
4. His líghtnings líght up the wórld,
   The eárth seés and wríthes,
5. The moúntains like wáx mélt     (before the face of Yahweh)
   Before the fáce of the Lórd of the whole eárth.
6. The heávens proclaím his jústice
   And all peóples seé his glóry.

Thus the Psalmist has learned to think of Yahweh's final coming; it will be in storm and volcanic eruption, the most awful manifestations of nature. For Yahweh since the days of Sinai has ever been a God of fire. The solid earth twists before Him, the mountains melt, His encircling enemies shrivel in His flame—the flame of righteousness. There can be no doubt now who is King; all nations see His blinding light. So the infant Church pictured the manifestation of Christ:

> Behold, He cometh with the clouds;
> And every eye shall see him—and they that pierced him (Rev. 1:7).

One effect will be immediate: men will know that the idols in whom they have put their trust are nothing. Our Psalmist lives in a world that adores many gods. Its cities are crowned by proud temples, multitudes everywhere prostrate themselves before images. Processions, hymns, dances, sacrifices—all of majestic pomp and costly splendor—hold the crowds in sway. Who among the heathen gives a thought to Yahweh, the God of a pitiful little people in a corner of Palestine?

But now they will *see!*

7. Let all the sérvers of ídols be put to sháme
   That brág of nóthings.
   Bow dówn before hím, all góds.[1]

Yes, the arrogant divinities of the great peoples are shown up, they give in, they fall in the dust to Yahweh. The Psalmist speaks of them in one breath as "nothings" and in the next as joining the congregation of worshippers. Probably he looks on them as real, but of no account—now they have found their proper place! What can their devotees do but follow suit?

But while the masses of idolaters see their gods bankrupt, how different it is with those who have trusted to Yahweh!

[1] Herkenne thinks that these words are uttered by a divine voice breaking in upon that of the Psalmist.

8. Zíon héars and rejoíces,
   And the daúghters of Júdah exúlt
   Becaúse of thy júdgments, Yahwéh.
9. For thoú, Yahwéh, art Most Hígh over all the eárth,
   Exceédingly art thou lifted úp above all góds.

Notice how his fervor breaks away from the third person to
the second. Yahweh is so near him he must say *Thou*. But with
his joy goes the solemn thought of what such a God demands.
So he turns to his fellow worshippers with a word of warning,
meant for himself as well as for them.

10. Lóvers of Yahwéh háte évil!
    He keéps the soúls of his gódly ones,
    From the hánd of the wícked he delívers them.

If indeed they be godly, Yahweh's burning fire is only brightness for them. It is like the brightness of the dawn.

11. Líght has arísen * for the ríghteous,
    And for the úpright of heárt gládness.

And so he comes spontaneously to the final outburst of his
Conclusion, calling to his fellows in the manner of the Hymn
writers. All this happiness is for them since they are, he believes, living truly religious and good lives:

12. Be glád, ye ríghteous, in Yahwéh,
    And give thánks for the remémbrance of his hóliness!

What has become of the vast rejoicings of the many islands
with which the Psalmist began? Has he forgotten them? All
that he has to say of the Gentile world after his opening
proclamation of Yahweh's accession is that the worshippers of
heathen deities are discredited, abashed, "put to shame." And
he implies that so far as they are unjust they will not be able
to endure the consuming fire of Yahweh's presence. It seems
that at the end he has got down to Israel, and not all Israel
at that, but only the "righteous" in it.

But we can hardly feel that the joy of the islands has disappeared. For the Psalmist does not really reverse his catholic
attitude. Surely the righteousness and justice on which the
throne of the new King is built will profit not Zion only.
Yahweh's consuming fire of justice is not to destroy mankind,
but only His enemies. As for the rest, and especially these who

now suffer from oppressing wickedness, it will save them. No, they need not give over their joy; the terrors of the oncoming King will not hurt them. True, they will be ashamed of their idols, but through that shame they will learn to come to the true King and find a happiness they have never known before. We cannot indeed find all this in our Psalmist's actual words; but we feel that we should do him less than justice if we did not read it into them.

What he is really interested in (as Kittel says) is not the victory of Israel over the heathen but Yahweh's victory over the gods. He wants to see the triumph of the true knowledge of God and with it of justice, righteousness, character. Therein lies the joy of Zion. To be sure, there will be a deliverance; and the people of the true God will share in His glory. If Yahweh becomes the world-God, His people will be the people of world dominion (Gunkel). But he does not dwell on this material side.

Such are the thoughts that move our Psalmist when he meditates on Yahweh's accession to the throne. Of the quality of the poem in which he embodies them Staerk says rightly: "The Psalm is a simple and beautiful expression of Israel's *religious* hope for the future. There lies upon it a breath of inwardness, of that holy joy over the coming of the Kingdom of God which rises from a deeper understanding of the divine purpose of salvation. It knows something higher than the outward compulsion of the enemies of Israel through God's judgment of the world. It hopes for the victory of the living God in the hearts of men, for inner conquest. That is the right liberation of Israel out of the hand of sinners—that these, compelled by its God, renounce the false gods and enter into the Kingdom of God."

# III

## AUTHORS OF LAMENTS

W E COME now to the study of composers of Psalms which stand in almost complete contrast to the Hymns which we considered at some length. These Psalms are called by Gunkel *Klagelieder,* which we translate by the English word "Lament." Possibly "Complaint" would be more accurate, but that has an unfortunate sound to our ears. "Outcry" might be better. The translation "Dirge," which has high backing in English scholarship, seems quite misleading; for it is associated with mourning for the dead, and that is distinctly alien to the Lament of the Psalms.

These Laments, if we may call them so, fall naturally into two classes: Laments of the People and Laments of the Individual. We shall follow Gunkel in beginning with the Laments of the People. But much that he says about these is applicable also to the second group.

Not many Laments of the People have been preserved in our Psalter, and therefore we shall select but one Author from that Type. On the other hand, the Laments of the Individual are more numerous than any other Type of Psalm and form indeed, to use Gunkel's expression, the proper core (*Grundstock*) of the Psalter.

The Laments of the People had as their "seat in life" the great public fasts of Israel and to understand them we must keep before us the customs and thoughts of such fasts. Fasts had a prominent place in the religion of Israel, as we see from manifold allusions to them in the Old Testament. They

were occasioned by all sorts of troubles which might befall
the nation and therefore did not recur regularly (as a rule)
but came as a response to some particular need. Usually they
were celebrated in the temple though we hear now and then
of fasts that were observed in the streets and market-places
and on house-tops. To the temple flocked all the people without exception, for proclamation went forth demanding it; and
they were purified for the solemnity by ceremonies of some
sort. If we may judge from the example of Naboth (I Ki.
21:9) a prominent man was chosen to lead the devotions.
Everyone abstained from food and drink, from marital intercourse and ordinary business. The customs mentioned in various parts of the Old Testament and Apocrypha and in the
Letter to Bagoas [1] include the following: The worshippers rent
their garments, beat upon their thighs, cut themselves, girded
themselves with sackcloth, shaved off their hair, sprinkled dust
or ashes upon their bodies, fell upon the ground, rolled in
ashes or dust, threw themselves upon their knees or faces
and stretched out their hands to heaven. The priests also did
these same things, covering the altar with sackcloth, weeping
as they stood between the court and the altar, prostrating
themselves in their robes before the altar, and passing the
night in sackcloth in the temple. Now and again we hear
of offerings being brought, and the pouring out of water before
Yahweh is also mentioned.

The central point of the fast was the common weeping
before Yahweh which took the form of loud crying and howl-
ing, of calling upon heaven or of whimpering in low tones.
Trumpets were used to augment the sound of the human voice.
Other groups of the people besides the priests lamented in
common as choirs. At times we hear the actual words of
the prayer used by the people or uttered in their behalf by
the leader.

The ideas that lay back of such a fast can be plainly seen

[1] See G. A. Barton, *Archaeology and the Bible*, Seventh edition, Philadelphia, 1937, p. 487.

and are often enough expressed. In its great need Israel is
thinking of its God who has sent this plague as punishment
for its sins, repents of its transgressions and seeks divine
pity. The fast and other self-chastenings have as their purpose to strengthen the prayer, for the hope is that Yahweh
may *see* the fast and *hear* the weeping. At other times the
idea of sin recedes and the fast has the sole purpose of rein-
forcing the prayer. The divine answer is given now and then
in the form of an oracle; an ancient device of which the
Prophets availed themselves to bring home to the people needed
lessons.

The Laments of the People, which took their rise from such
fasts, exhibit well-marked characteristics. They call upon God
in the vocative. Sometimes the simple name of Yahweh is
enriched by hymnlike descriptions of His qualities or by such
words as "Lord," "my God," "God of our salvation," "Yahweh
of hosts" etc. They use the second person "thou" as is natural
in prayer; for ancient prayer was not a "conversation with
God" but an address to Him. Indeed it had as its fundamental
presupposition that a man can tell God something and can
influence Him. The prayer of the Laments gives rise as it
proceeds to the conviction on the part of the suppliants that
God will hear them and so it passes over into the mood of
*trust*. Here Yahweh can be spoken of in the third person
as well as the second and the two often parallel each other.
The wish too takes the place of prayer. The same is true
in other trains of thought besides confidence, as for instance
when the godless opponents of the congregation are portrayed
and their words of contempt are repeated to God. The Lament
is sung by the congregation (or groups within it), although
at times the leader, speaking in their name, brings in an "I"
instead of the "we" or Zion itself is introduced as the suppliant, thus heightening the effect. Such congregational character, Gunkel points out, is peculiar to the Israelitish Psalms
as contrasted with the Babylonian, where the conception of a
worshipping church is absent.

As to the content of the Laments, the chief elements are:

1. Complaints, sometimes not uttered expressly, but implied in:

2. Supplications, beseeching God to remedy the complaint.

3. All sorts of thoughts, aimed to excite confidence in the suppliant or to move Yahweh.

The Laments that have come down to us complain at times of such calamities as drought or insect plagues but on the whole are concerned for what may be called the *political* situation of the people, their oppression by foreign overlords or their maltreatment by the rich within Israel. The suffering of the godly nation naturally gave rise to the religious question, how God could permit it and still be righteous. Hence we get echoing through the Laments the "Why?" and the "How long?" so familiar to Bible readers.

The considerations employed to move Yahweh to action are, as has been said, of various kinds, some of them exceedingly anthropomorphic. The Psalmist appeals to His grace, to His kind dealings with Israel in the past, to His covenant and promises, which He ought to keep, to His identification with His people which involves Him in their suffering and shame, to His pity for their helplessness—unless *He* helps.

In the Laments of the People that we find outside the Psalter a chief way of moving Yahweh to favor is to confess Israel's sins. Strange to say, this is not true of most of the Psalms of Lament. They are apt to speak of Israel as a righteous people in contrast to its enemies, upon whom they call down divine vengeance. Psalm 44 goes so far as to assert Israel's innocence with passion. The same tone is characteristic of a number of the Individual Laments of the Psalter, although many examples of penitence occur in this Type. In fact, so pronounced is this particular variety of Lament that a special name has been given it: Psalms of Innocence.

Such Psalms do not make pleasant reading and we are apt to be hard upon their Authors; but Gunkel invites us to a kindlier judgment. "Should we see in their feeling of innocence only a sign of Jewish self-righteousness from the age of the Law, or ought we from it to infer a firmness of character in the people of that day, a firmness which is not willing to make the judgment on itself dependent on its fearful fate, and therefore avoids the confession of guilt that from of old had been customary in this context?"

It will be seen from this description of the Laments of the People that they form, as we have said, a strong contrast to the Hymns. "There despairing laments and stormy entreaty, here rapturous shouts of joy and exultation" (Gunkel). Yet the very passionateness and desire for strong contrasts which characterised the Authors of Laments led them at times to use descriptions of God when calling upon Him and these were finally enlarged until the entire opening of the Lament assumed Hymn form. This mixture of praise and supplication was common among the Babylonian Hymn-writers, but with them it was designed to flatter the godhead in order that they might attain their petitions. The Israelite suppliant stood on a higher level. "Before one dared to come to Yahweh with prayer one must praise Him, and such singing of praise places the divine power impressively before the eyes of God and the suppliant at the same time and contains therefore in itself a strong thought of comfort: the mighty and gracious God will hear this prayer also" (Gunkel). In the same way the Church often begins its collects with a beautiful characterisation of God, as the ground of its confidence in addressing Him.

Having now reviewed the chief features of the Laments of the People, let us select one from among their Authors for our study. After that we shall pass at once to the much more important division of this Type, the Laments of the Individual.

# III

## *1. A LAMENT OF THE PEOPLE*

THE AUTHOR OF PSALM 44

### *Arise, and help us*

As may be supposed from what has been said concerning Laments of the People, this Psalm came into being in an hour of great suffering and humiliation for Israel. The Author is not explicit as to the situation confronting the nation but his general complaints bring it home to us with fair clearness. Israel's hosts have been defeated in battle, and the victorious enemy is using his advantage with outrageous cruelty.[1] Property is being seized, people are being killed or sold into slavery among the Gentiles. All the neighbors of Israel are exulting in its downfall and heaping derision upon the proud nation thus brought low. They are particularly delighted that Yahweh, whom they have come to hate, is being dishonored in the calamity of His people. And the Author, speaking for his compatriots, can discover no reason for Yahweh's thus abandoning Israel; for they have not forsaken Him and gone after other gods. In fact, it seems that their very faithfulness to Him has brought slaughter upon them.

All these features appear at first sight to fit in with the Maccabean age. Then for the first time in centuries (so far as we know) Israel had an army, and religious persecution was also making its first appearance. This led Theodore of Mopsuestia, the leader of the Antiochan school of Biblical

---

[1] König thinks that the Psalmist is writing during the Exile and is looking back on past calamities.

interpretation, to apply this Psalm and a number of others
to the Maccabean period. Eleven hundred years later Calvin
sponsored the same opinion. And now not a few modern
scholars reecho the ancient view: Duhm, Kittel, Staerk, Bertholet among them. On the other hand Gunkel feels that a
Maccabean date is by no means certain and both Barnes and
Schmidt place the Psalm in the Persian period, the latter
assigning it to the time immediately after the Return.[1]

For the purpose of this study it makes little difference when
the Psalm was written. Whatever the occasion, the public
misery calls for a great corporate mourning before God and
our Psalmist is moved to utter on their behalf the Lament
of the People.

He begins with an acknowledgment to God of His past help
to Israel in the time of the invasion of Canaan, as it has lived
on in oral tradition handed down from father to son by command of the Law.

> 2. Gód, with eárs have we heárd,     our fáthers have
>      recoúnted to ús
>    The wórk that thou dídst in their dáys,     in the days
>      of óld—3 thoú (with) thy hánd.
>    Nátions thou didst disposséss and planted thém in,     thou
>      didst breák peóples and spread thém abroad,
> 4. For nót with their swórd did they posséss the lánd,
>      and their árm did nót give víctory tó them,
>    But thy right hánd and thy árm     and the líght of thy
>      coúntenance,     fór thou wast fávorable to them.

So far this is not a Lament; it is like a Hymn, except that
it addresses God directly. Our Psalmist is using the hymnic
Introduction with intent. What will move God more quickly
and give more courage to His people than to recall the amazing miracle of the Conquest? For we can see that our Psalmist
has been taught to look back on that accomplishment as indeed
a miracle in which man's part has dwindled to almost nothing.
So it was portrayed in the later tradition of the Priestly
Writers, for instance.

From the heartening survey of God's former help he passes

[1] Herkenne puts it in the time of Hezekiah, and believes that the speaker
is both the military commander and the prince of his people.

naturally over into an affirmation of trust. Here singular and
plural pronouns mingle in perplexing fashion; it is now "I,"
now "we." But whether he is putting the "I" into the mouth
of the leader, as Gunkel and Schmidt think, or is so unifying
the congregation in his mind that he makes them speak as a
single individual, which is Kittel's view, we must bear in mind
that he is holding fast to the corporate nature of his utterance:

> 5. Thoú art my kíng and my Gód,*    who commándest *
>    víctories (for) Jácob,
> 6. By theé we góre our énemies,    in thy náme we trámple
>    those who rise agaínst us.
> 7. For nót in my bów do I trúst,    and my swórd does nót
>    give me víctory;
> 8. But thoú dost give us víctory over our énemies,    and
>    those that háte us thou dost put to sháme.
> 9. In Gód we glóry all the dáy,    and thy náme foréver
>    will we thánk.

This does not make pleasant reading but let us defer any
criticism of our Psalmist's ethical outlook. For the present let
us notice that like so many other Israelites who use Yahweh
as a War-God he has at least the grace to be humble. He
utters no word of pride in his nation's military prowess but
freely attributes any victories it may have won to divine help.
This mood of trust harmonises tunefully with the acknowledgment of God's help in his Introduction. He probably feels that
by speaking so—and he means it—he inclines God to favor
and increases the confidence of the congregation. Such affir-
mations are common in the Psalter and serve a manifest mental
purpose.

But now the misery of the present—so in contrast to the
happiness of the past—breaks upon him, and he turns to
God in passionate complaint:

> 10. Bút thou hast rejécted and shámed us,    and góest not
>     fórth with our hósts.
> 11. Thou túrnest us báck from the énemy,    and they that
>     háte us plúnder at wíll.
> 12. Thou gívest us like sheép to be eáten,    and among the
>     nátions thou hast scáttered us.
> 13. Thou séllest thy peóple for nóthing,    and hast nót made
>     ánything by their príces.

14. Thou mákest us a taúnt to our neíghbors,    a scórn and derísion to those aroúnd us.
15. Thou mákest us a bý-word among the nátions,    a sháking of the heád among the peóples.
16. All the dáy my sháme is befóre me,    and the disgráce of my fáce has cóvered me,
17. Because of the voíce of the taúnter and revíler,    because of the fáce of the énemy and the revéngeful.

It is a terrible picture, whatever it may mean literally. Here we get a cry of the ancient woe that has again and again brought Israel to the dust. How naturally our Psalmist might have seen in this affliction a punishment for the sins of the people. But quite the contrary!

18. All thís has come upón us—and we have nót forgotten theé,    and we have nót been fálse to thy cóvenant.
19. Our heárt has nót túrned báckward,    and our stéps have not bént fróm thy páth;
20. Though thou hast crúshed us in the pláce of jáckals,    and cóvered us óver with deep dárkness.
21. If we have forgótten the náme of our Gód,    and strétched out our hánds to a stránge god,
22. Shall nót Gód séarch this oút?    for hé knóws the sécrets of the heárt.
23. Nay, for thy sáke we are kílled all the dáy,    we are accoúnted a flóck to be bútchered.

Thus far his complaint. Then suddenly he storms out with his supplications—we might almost say his *demands* upon God. They are not clothed in the usual language of prayer but explode in violent anthropomorphisms in which the "why?" of indignant perplexity is mingled:

24. Wake úp!    Whý dost thou sleép, Lórd?    Get úp! Cást not off for éver!
25. Whý dost thou híde thy fáce?    dost forgét our afflíction and oppréssion?
26. For bówed to the dúst is our soúl,    our bélly stícks to the groúnd!
27. Stand úp!, be a hélp to ús!    and redeém us for the sáke of thy lovingkíndness!

Thus the reader leaves him, lying on the ground amidst the agonised congregation, crying aloud with them to the God who alone can save. Ask now what estimate is to be put upon the man and his religion.

To begin with, there are some manifest deficiencies which
we must acknowledge. To him Yahweh is still the War-God
who moves in the pages of the Book of Joshua, whose place
is at the head of Israel's host; and what our Psalmist desires
is that He turn its defeat into victory. Towards the successful
Gentile army our Psalmist displays a quite natural rancor: he
wants to gore, to trample under foot. There is not a hint of
universalism in his words, still less any philosophy of vicarious
suffering which might clothe Israel's torments with meaning.
Yet he must have read Second Isaiah's portrayal of the Suffering Servant who was to give his life for mankind (Is.
52:13 ff.).

Again, his peremptory demands upon God, while they can
be understood, have not approved themselves to the long judgment of religious taste. His contemporaries evidently liked
them enough to take over his whole Psalm into public use.
But succeeding generations quietly let them drop. Men felt
that such was not the seemly manner of addressing God. Our
Lord, who believed in prayer and pertinacious prayer at that,
has left no recorded syllable of petition charged with the
roughness and impatience of our Psalmist. So in the prayer of
the Christian Church. What collect can be found in its liturgies
that breathes such a spirit although the words "Arise and
deliver us" still reecho in the Litany? Nor is it only his
*manner* that is at fault. Back of his explosions lies a conception of prayer quite different from that which prompted
our Lord's supplication in Gethsemane: "Not what I will, but
what thou wilt" (Mk. 14:36). It is the conception that by
prayer God can be shaken into doing something even against
His will—or at least against His inclination.

Another lack in our Psalmist is that he acknowledges no
sin in his nation. He dòes not mean of course that Israel is
sinless, but he does feel that on the whole it has kept the
faith. Certainly it has done no wrong sufficient to account for
its present woes. Now to a real extent he must have been
justified in such a confidence and in asserting it he goes no
farther (as Kirkpatrick points out) than the author of the

Book of Job, who has his hero maintain his innocence to the end. Gunkel pleads for a kindly judgment on this seeming self-righteousness. And it may be freely granted that the Psalmist in avoiding the traditional confession of sin is exhibiting a rugged sincerity which gives freshness and reality to his words.

On the other hand it must be acknowledged that in avoiding it he falls below fellow-Psalmists who reviewed the past history of the nation, such as the writers of Psalms 78 and 106 and the Authors of Laments of the People to be found outside the Psalter. His protestations of innocence seem superficial indeed when read along with the great confession of Daniel 9: "To the Lord our God belong mercies and forgiveness, though we have rebelled against him; neither have we obeyed the voice of Yahweh our God, to walk in his laws, which he set before us by his servants the prophets" (Dan. 9:9 f.).

And yet, after surveying the defects in our Psalmist's ethical and religious attitude, one must in fairness admit that he displays certain qualities which in some measure offset them.

For one thing, he is not self-centered. To a marked degree he exhibits that sense of solidarity with the nation which gives the religion of the Old Testament its peculiarly social character. Not a word does he say of his own misery, except as it is merged in that of his people; and his very assertion of innocence is lifted by its corporate nature above personal self-satisfaction.

Again, he is loyal to Yahweh even in the face of death. If indeed he is speaking from out the midst of the struggles of Maccabean days we meet in him one of the faithful who held fast in that supreme crisis. In any case he is a zealot, perhaps a fanatic, to whom the ease of comfortable acquiescence in Gentile ways is impossible. Whatever his faults, he is not worldly.

Another of his possessions is faith. It is his very faith that makes him so discourteous to God. For Israel's only help is in Yahweh and he intends to get that help. There is a terrible earnestness about him that we his modern critics might well envy. Though (as we have seen) his prayer lacks the element of surrender to God's will it is not so far from the persistence which our Lord commends. Here is a man who seeks and means to find!

His humility, too, commends him. And, finally, his militant courage. Little as one may like the warlike aspect that it assumes one must acknowledge its fiery, resolute character. It is another of his qualities that is found none too often in religion.

In this man therefore we see the vigor and pertinacity which have carried his race victoriously through the persecutions of the centuries. His Psalm, to use Duhm's words, is "a vivid testimony to the obstinate courage and fanaticism of those Jewish Puritans" to whom he belonged.

## 2. *LAMENTS OF INDIVIDUALS*

In taking up the writers of Laments of Individuals we approach, to use Gunkel's expression already quoted, the very core of the Psalter. And here we shall find that Gunkel's theory of the connection of the Psalms with public worship is put to a severe strain. For these Laments of the Individual have so freed themselves from all association with the ritual of the temple that it is very hard to discover what that association originally was. He sums up the probable history of this Type as follows (pp. 260 ff.):

That it proceeds from worship and the purposes of worship is indicated by several allusions which survive in various Psalms. There is mention at times of accompanying sacrifices (Ps. 5[1]—spiritualised in Ps. 141:2). Oracles are introduced which were probably obtained by the priests from observing the signs furnished by the sacrifice. In Psalm 51 we hear of washing and purging with hyssop. The suppliant also speaks of rending his garments, tearing out his hair, throwing himself upon the ground, chastising himself till evening, kneeling in God's house and extending his hands to heaven, fasting a long time, wearing sackcloth, being soiled with dirt and ashes (p. 179). No examples of the earliest Laments have come down to us but we may picture them as set forms speaking in general and colorless terms. They called upon God, uttered complaints, made petitions, possibly expressed the confidence of being heard by God, and vowed a thank-offering. All these

---

[1] Ps. 5:3 presupposes that the Psalmist is standing by his sacrifice.

are elements of the more developed Laments, as will be seen.

A surprising thing about the Israelitish Lament is that it parallels the Babylonian Lament so closely. This might of course point to its having been borrowed from the more ancient culture. But Gunkel is of the opinion that the similarities between the two arose independently from out the same situations and needs, although he is quite ready to believe that the Israelitish Lament was later enriched by features taken from the Babylonian.

In course of time the Lament of the Individual gradually freed itself inwardly from the acts of worship connected with it. The suppliant needed the act of worship no longer but entered directly into relation with his God. That is why the allusions to the rites of worship are after all so scanty. It would, however, be over-hasty to conclude that Laments which contain no reference to acts of worship could not have been used as prayers at sacrifices.

Parallel with this inner detachment went an external separation. A number of Laments bear on their face evidence of having been composed at a distance from the temple (27 I, 42, 61, 120). Nor should we think that this separation first took place in Post-Exilic times, for at least one of these Laments (Psalm 61) speaks of the reigning king and goes back therefore to the time of the monarchy. Thus even in Pre-Exilic days there had arisen what the Germans call "spiritual" Psalms, that is Psalms expressing the poet's own feelings and thoughts quite independently of the temple worship. The Prophets accentuated this drift by their vehement opposition to sacrifices as carried out in their age. So it continued into later times. But along with it went also the composition of Laments intended to be used in worship. And even the purely personal Laments still followed the old forms. That is the reason why they speak so vaguely of the circumstances surrounding the poet, for in worship-forms such vagueness and generality were necessary. Finally the Lament developed distinct species, such as the Psalm of Innocence, the Psalm of Penitence, the Psalm of Cursing or Vengeance and the Psalm of Trust. At the same time the Lament took over forms from the other Types of Psalms so that there arose Mixed Psalms which it is impossible to assign to any of the original Types.

So much for the history of the Type. When we proceed to ask under what circumstances the Individual Laments of the Psalter were composed we are met with the difficulty that their Authors use for the most part only vague general terms in describing these. But some features do appear. The Psalmist is surrounded by a circle of people who sympathise with him and listen to his words. He is not in ordinary trouble but stands close to death because of some terrible crisis. That is why in the Laments we find men facing the thought of dying with all its implications. One easily recognisable cause for the Lament is sickness of desperate nature which the Psalmist feels is brought on by Yahweh's anger for sin or—a thought even more fearful—is due to Yahweh's having abandoned him. At times he seems to be under trial or in prison. But by far the most frequent reference is to enemies who are attacking him. These, Gunkel thinks, may often not be enemies in the usual sense but merely the healthy people who shrink back from contact with a man in mortal illness because they feel he is being visited by God. Yet there are other foes as well, such as the rich and the powerful who are pictured as oppressing the poor sufferer and exulting in his fall.[1] These and many other overwhelming experiences cause the poet to pour out his agony in verses which often enough might have been composed in the painful hours of the night. For now and again there is allusion to his lying on his bed and praying.

Of what material does the Lament consist? Gunkel answers this question with a long and illuminating examination of its various elements which can only be summarised here. Later

---

[1] Mowinckel maintains that in many Laments and Thanksgivings the enemies mentioned are sorcerers and demons. (*Psalmenstudien* I, No. 4.) While there is undoubtedly something to be said for this interpretation in certain passages, it can hardly apply to the Laments and Thanksgivings as a whole.

in the study of the several Authors there will be occasion to describe these in greater detail.

The composer of an Individual's Lament normally begins by *calling upon Yahweh* by name, to direct His attention to the fact that all the poet is about to say is addressed to Him. Often this calling on God does not stand by itself but is incorporated in an *introductory cry for help*. Occasionally the cry for help is preceded by a short *description of the prayer*,[1] as in Psalm 142:1 f: "I cry with my voice unto Yahweh: with my voice unto Yahweh do I make supplication. I pour out my complaint before him: I show before him my trouble." Or the description may stand alone with the calling upon God at the beginning of the Psalm, as in Psalm 7:2: "Yahweh, my God, in thee do I take refuge." The calling on God however is not confined to the beginning but may recur at the most important points of the Psalm.

The calling on God and the cry for help may be followed by the *complaint*, though this may come directly after the address to God if the cry for help is lacking, as it is in Psalm 22: "My God, my God, why hast thou forsaken me?"

Following the complaint comes the *petition*;[2] but when the Psalmist desires to be freed from his woe more passionately than to tell of it he may begin with the prayer instead of the complaint: "Yahweh, correct me not in thine anger..." (Ps. 6:2). A very frequent order is for the petition to come immediately after the cry for help, and in this case the complaint will follow the prayer. Both petition and complaint can be repeated several times in the Psalm.

In connection with petition and complaint stand various *considerations* which are urged upon Yahweh to induce Him to intervene. He is reminded of His grace, truth and righteousness, He is told how His enemies speak against Him, how

---

[1] Just what Gunkel means by this phrase is not quite clear to the writer. Most of the examples he cited (Pss. 31:2f.; 28:1; 71:1f.; 88:2f.; 120:1f.; 130:1f.) seem on the whole to be actual prayers rather than descriptions of prayers.

[2] Frequently varied by a *wish*.

the Psalmist trusts Him and waits upon Him, how the Psalmist is in misery and cannot help himself.

The Lament may close with a complaint or, as is more frequently the case, with a petition. But some Laments conclude with special forms. One of these is what Gunkel calls the *conviction that the prayer is heard,* and is found in those places where the mood of anguish and despair suddenly changes to the jubilant certainty that the Psalmist's troubles are over. We shall discuss this in our study of Psalm 22 where it appears in startling guise. The other special form is the *vow.* The vow in the Psalms differs from that in the Babylonian Laments in its spirit. There it is uttered in order to obtain what the poet desires from God; here it is no longer a means of persuading God but rather the expression of a rising feeling of thanksgiving.

After this very brief introduction to an exceedingly rich and complex mass of material, we may proceed to the study of selected Authors of Individual Laments, trusting that the points so barely enumerated may take on more meaning when illustrated in the concrete.

# III

## 2. a. LAMENTS IN GENERAL

### THE AUTHOR OF PSALM 22

*My God, my God...why hast thou forsaken me?*

The first writer of an Individual Lament whom we shall study is the man whose words came to Jesus in His dying agony. But quite apart from such a claim upon the love of the Christian world this Psalmist has given us one of the supreme poems of the Psalter.

What suffering impels him to utter his complaint? He has so much to say of his woe that one would think we could know its nature easily; but we must remember how the composers of Laments still retain the general way of speaking concerning their circumstances that they inherit from the earlier Laments connected with worship. Our Psalmist is no exception. He speaks of the scorn and hostility of men and he also describes in vivid terms an illness which is afflicting him. From the fact that he devotes more attention to the former some scholars have concluded that his trouble arises entirely from the attacks of enemies, his illness, if indeed he has any, being a result of his mental distress. But it is more probable that *both* afflictions are pressing him down simultaneously.[1]

Such a fearful experience is new to him. For years—indeed all his life—he has been going along in health and peace. This he has attributed to Yahweh's loving care; for he has

---

[1] Mowinckel believes that the Psalmist pictures himself as assaulted by demons who have brought on his illness. (*Psalmenstudien* I, p. 73f.) It is hard to take such a view seriously.

been a sincere servant of Yahweh, and it has been his confidence that Yahweh would continue to care for him all his days. In the naive faith of an ancient Hebrew he has spoken his confidence openly. God, he has said, is pleased with me because of my obedience and I can roll all my anxiety upon Him; for I am not like the irreligious, who need expect nothing but trouble. He might have used the words of the First Psalm: "I am like a tree planted by the streams of water."

And then the pleasant fabric of his life collapsed. Like Job in the story he saw health shattered and found the world no longer a friendly place but full of mockers. Astonished, he turned to God. God would surely right the wrong, give back his health and silence his tormentors. But no! God, who has never failed him before, now remains inactive. In vain does our Psalmist shout aloud; God cannot be roused. In vain does he continue his calling day and night, groaning and roaring to quicken God's sympathy. God is still silent.

But not so his tormentors. Evidently this man has been well-known in the community for his devotion to Yahweh; he has stood out among the faithful as a leader; he has not, as has been said, refrained from what must have seemed very like boasting in Yahweh. Naturally the worldly element of the neighborhood has disliked this: they have resented his confident assertions that their course would end in misery, while he was sure of happiness. Now he is down. What has become of all his bragging? They crowd about him to remind him of his high words, to gloat over his fall. Nor do they stop at this: they press upon him with hostility, they threaten him, even do him injury.

But what of his friends? Do they not come to his defense? Apparently not. At any rate he says nothing of them in his hour of darkness. It is not to them that he looks but to the God who has failed him.

That is his chiefest woe before which illness and enemies pale into insignificance. For he can attribute his sufferings to nothing else. They are not a punishment or a chastening visited upon him by an angry God. This thought does not occur to him because he is evidently without any sense of having committed sin. He does not indeed protest his innocence, as do some Psalmists, and he utters no word tainted with self-righteousness. His is the childlike confidence of the sincere earnest man whose conscience bears no load of guilt. In this he is like Job; but Job looked on his affliction as coming from an angry God; and our Psalmist does not so interpret his own. His reading of the matter is much more devastating. God has not so much brought his troubles on him—he speaks only once as if he thought so—God has simply left him to them. It is unbearable! And so to the God who will not hear he goes with passionate outcry:

2. My Gód! My Gód! whý hast thou forsáken me?    Fár from
       my crý,* the wórds of my roáring!
3. My Gód!
    I crý by dáy and thou ánswerest nót,    and by níght, but
       there is no rést fór me.

This is his Introduction. We notice that he passes at once from the calling upon God to the complaint, without any intervening petition. Here appears the "Why"? of remonstrance. He is crying out brokenly, violent emotion tearing asunder his ejaculation.

Yes, he is forsaken. And yet God is *there*—

4. But *thoú* art hóly, sítting    upon the praíses of I'srael.

The sick man's thought flies to the temple with its worshipping congregation whose praises roll upward like incense smoke, making a throne for Deity. Holy—very God—He sits.

And this God has proved faithful in the heroic past:

5. In theé our fáthers trústed,    they trústed and thou didst
       delíver them;
6. Unto theé they críed and were réscued,    in theé they
       trústed and were not disappóinted.

All true! He is using hymnic language to depict the overwhelming contrast. *Thou* in glory, saving past generations; and *I* here, unrescued! Notice how the pronouns, very emphatic in the Hebrew, introduce new divisions in the Psalm.

7. But *I* am a wórm, and not a mán,    a taúnt for mén and
       despísed by the peóple.

8. All that seé me rídicule me;     they thrúst out their líps,
   they sháke their heáds:
9. "Róll it on Yahwéh!" "Let him delíver him!"     "Let him
   réscue him, for he delíghts in him!"

That is what men are saying, throwing back upon the Psalmist
his own words in time past. God must do something to silence
them! For they are not right!

10. But *thou* dréwest me out from the wómb,     thou madest
    me trúst upon my móther's breásts;
11. Upon theé was I cást from the wómb,     from the wómb [1]
    of my móther *thou* art my Gód!

Is it too much to suppose that he is here giving a glimpse
of the home into which he had been born, with its quiet assurance of Yahweh's care? As a little child his mother had
taught him that he belonged to Yahweh! Surely that gives
him a claim upon Him in his need. So he breaks out for the
first time in petition:

12. Be not far awáy from mé; for troúble is neár,     for there
    is nó one to hélp.
13. Mány búlls have surroúnded me,     stróng (bulls) of Básan
    have encírcled me.
14. They ópen their moúths agaínst me,     a líon téaring and
    roáring!

His foes are passing beyond ridicule; they are dangerous
beasts, about to destroy him. And now his complaint turns
to his sickness:

15. Like wáter have I been poured oút,     áll my bónes have
    pulled apárt;
    My heárt has becóme like wáx,     it is mélted in the mídst
    of my ínward parts.
16. Dried úp like a pótsherd is my stréngth,     and my tóngue
    cleáves to my jáws,
    And to the dúst of deáth thou hast broúght me.

It is one of the most convincing descriptions of the prostration caused by serious illness that we have in literature!
Yet it tells us nothing of the nature of his sickness, gives
no recognisable symptoms. We might notice in passing that
the end of verse 16 is the only hint we get in the poem of the
Psalmist's trouble being due to God; and the text here is not
certain.

[1] The Hebrew has different words for "womb" in this verse.

But now he is back to his enemies again:

17. For dógs have enclósed me,　a bánd of evil-dóers have
　　surroúnded me;
　　They have piérced * my hánds and my feét.
18. I may coúnt áll my bónes;　*théy* are loóking, they gloát
　　over me;
19. They are divíding my clóthes amóng them,　and upon
　　my gárments they are cásting lóts.

His meaning is not clear. Is he comparing them to a gang
of bandits who have beaten him and now portion out his
possessions? Are they executioners who cannot wait to get
their perquisites? Or are they inhuman heirs seizing his poor
belongings before he is actually dead? No one can tell; but
the picture burns itself upon the imagination for all its vagueness. Someone is treating him as if he were already gone.

Once again he passes to petition, using the same pathetic
word ("far away") as before, a word that runs through his
poem like a refrain. And he begins with the pronoun, marking
the transition:

20. But *thoú*, Yahwéh, be not far awáy!　my hélp, hásten to
　　my aíd!
21. Sáve my soúl from the swórd,　my ónly one from the
　　pówer (hand) of the dóg!
22. Delíver me from the moúth of the líon,　my poór * life
　　from the hórns of the wild búlls!

It is his last frantic cry for help. Far away! Unless Yahweh
comes near, all is over!

Then suddenly everything is changed. The man who has
been appealing to God in the agony of despair begins a mighty
Hymn of exultant praise. He who was alone with none to help
is surrounded by his brethren.

23. I will téll of thy náme unto my bréthren,　in the mídst
　　of the congregátion will I praíse thee.
24. Feárers of Yahwéh, praíse him!　all ye seéd of Jácob,
　　glórify him!
　　And be in áwe befóre him, all ye seéd of Ísrael! [1]

It is because of what Yahweh has done for him that he
summons them to praise!

[1] Löhr regards v.24-25, 27-31 as a liturgical addition. (*Psalmenstudien*,
p. 6.) It is more fitting however to look on these verses as the very
climax of the Psalm.

25. For he did nót despíse,    he did nót abóminate,    the
    afflíction of the afflícted;
    And he did nót híde his fáce fróm him,    but when he
    críed unto hím, he heárd him.

What, we ask, is the meaning of the transformation? Are
the troubles of our Psalmist really over? Has something happened in an instant to make his night day? Impossible, some
scholars answer: here another poem is beginning, composed
under different circumstances. The Psalmist, Schmidt thinks,
has got well. His Lament is a thing of the past, and now in
the midst of the joyful company of his friends he is bringing
to the temple the thank-offering of which he is about to speak.
Duhm goes farther and declares that there is here a second
poem of much inferior quality which has nothing at all to
do with the noble Lament. It is merely a liturgical composition, full of stock phrases, quite lacking in merit. But
the prevailing opinion of recent writers (Staerk, Kittel,
Gunkel, Barnes, Herkenne) is that it is no new poem but the
very crown of the Lament. For what has taken place is an
inward revolution in the soul of the Psalmist. In the midst
of his crying upon God, yes, because of it, confidence has
come flooding into his heart. He *knows* that God is no longer
far away, God is with him! All will be right. "Thus this
Psalm," says Staerk, "witnesses to the deep psychological
truth that the suffering told of in real prayer is by the very
telling inwardly overcome."

This is the "certainty of being heard" which Gunkel lists
as one of the features of the Lament. In more primitive times
it was perhaps created by an oracle of comfort spoken by
the priest to the sufferer. But here there is no oracle save the
faith of the Psalmist's own heart. For that on which he now
rides high is a tide of *faith*.

26. From theé is my praíse in the greát congregátion,    my
    vóws will I páy before thém that feár him.

Yes, he will spread the sacrificial feast in the sanctuary,
bringing the thank-offering which he promised to God in the
midst of his trouble. To it he will invite the hungry, the poor
people who really care for God, blessing them as his guests:

> 27. The lówly shall eát and shall have all they wánt,    they
>     shall praíse Yahwéh who seék him.
>     "Let your heárt líve for éver!"

But the humble Israelites whom he can gather about his
table are not enough to raise the chorus of praise. In his
rapture he looks far beyond them, out to the Gentiles over
all the earth. They too shall sing!

> 28. Remémber and túrn unto Yahwéh    shall áll the énds of
>     the eárth;
>     And bów before his * fáce    shall all the fámilies of the
>     nátions.

And this homage is only His right, for they are really His:

> 29. Fór Yahwéh's is the kíngdom    and he is rúling among the
>     nátions.
> 30. They have eáten and wórshipped—all the fát ones of the
>     eárth!

He sees them with his mind's eye, the happy well-fed multitudes of the world, prostrating themselves before the God
who has taken care of them—giving praise at last where it is
due. But even so the congregation of Yahweh-worshippers is
too small. With a sheer leap of faith he beholds it extended
into the realm of the dead where so many Israelites felt that
Yahweh could no longer be praised.

> Before hím shall kneél    all that go dówn to the dúst,
> And whoso képt not his soúl alive.

And yet the chorus is not enough. To the living and the
dead he adds the generations unborn:

> 31. Descéndants shall sérve him;    it shall be tóld of the
>     Lórd to the cóming generátion.
> 32. And they shall decláre his ríghteousness    to a peóple
>     that shall be bórn, that he hath dóne it!

So he closes, with a great crash of Halleluias resounding
through the world, through Sheol, through the future. It is
like the Conclusion of a Hymn, except that he does not put it
into the form of a summons. The vastness of his chorus reminds us of Psalm 103 where the heavenly multitudes are
called upon to swell the Hymn; only with our Psalmist all the
voices are human.

But what does he mean by his words about the dead? Has

he attained to a belief that in their unseen realm beneath the earth God is really present to be worshipped, that they too can raise their joyful Hymns to Him? Probably not. His enthusiasm may be carrying him into poetic expressions which probably exceed the actual content of his faith. And yet Schmidt is right when he says that even such a poetic flight would not be possible "if the poet had not stood inwardly at least before the door of that faith." This Psalmist may therefore be compared to the Author of Psalm 139, who was assured that not even in Sheol could one escape the presence of God.

Another thing that stands out in this depiction of the great "Halleluia Chorus" is the Psalmist's universalism. Like so many other wide spirits of the Old Testament he looks for a conversion of the nations to belief in Yahweh. And we should notice that it is a real conversion—no compulsion by crushing blows, no cringing submission, as too many Israelites like to picture it, but a voluntary joyful acknowledgment of Yahweh's power and goodness. They will "remember and turn."

And the theme that shall fill their praises is His power and goodness. "They shall declare...that He hath done it." This is what enraptures the Psalmist himself. Indeed his whole stupendous vision of praising multitudes rushes forth from out his own experience, or at least his *expected* experience of divine salvation. "For he did not despise, he did not abominate the affliction of the afflicted!"

He himself therefore has something to tell of Yahweh and it is so wonderful that he would have all know it: then they will turn! What does that mean but that our Psalmist has in him the making of a missionary? Like Second Isaiah he is thinking of a "light to lighten the Gentiles," though it has not yet dawned upon him that the light must be spread by men.

Another trait which all scholars point out is akin to this universalism: he wishes no evil upon his enemies. It is indeed strange that in all his outcries against their cruelty he never once asks for their punishment. Even Jeremiah falls below him in this (Jer. 12:3, 15:15). If he does not rise to the

height of the dying Stephen and pray for their forgiveness he
at least remains silent. One might almost think that he is so
absorbed in his struggle with God that he is not interested in
vengeance. But that would be to put it negatively. His nature
is one of abundant love, a love that goes out to the poor and
hungry, to the Gentiles, to the dead, to the unborn. For surely
his passionate desire to bring them into the great chorus arises
from something more than his loyalty to Yahweh, it contains
a warm feeling for them also. They too are his "brethren."

He is significant for religion in yet another way. For nowhere
in the Bible do we get a more triumphant example of the
power of prayer to lift the soul from out despair and prostration into joy, confidence and strength. If the prevailing contemporary opinion is right his passage from darkness to light
is due to no outward change in his circumstances; he is still a
seriously ill man beset by enemies. But he has broken through
into the sunshine of faith leaving these sufferings beneath him.
To use a phrase of Fosdick's, he has made prayer a battlefield
and has come off victor. One is reminded of the words of
the First Epistle of John: "This is the victory that hath overcome the world, even our faith" (I John 5:4).

It is no reflection upon our Psalmist however when we point
out that his faith rests still upon an unsure basis. Suppose that
God had not intervened. Suppose that his uprush of faith had
been followed by no change in his condition. Suppose he had
realised that he was dying—no thank-offering in the temple
for him, no feast, no throng of guests—only the darkness!
Would his faith have continued? For it is essentially a belief
that God *will* intervene. Doubtless in this instance he was not
disappointed; otherwise his Psalm would probably never have
been given out among his friends. But often no intervention
takes place. And that possibility he does not envisage. He is
still within the bounds of the old retribution dogma. He has
not, like Jeremiah, Job and the Author of Psalm 73, found his
solution quite apart from outward happiness.

But this limitation cannot detract from the beauty, tenderness, sublimity of his Psalm. It will always remain the classic

expression of the devastating sense of being without God in the midst of life's deepest agonies, and the sunshine of its close will continue to light with hope the faithful who in such desolation still hold fast to God.

Nor can we forget that it was this man whose words were in Jesus' mind as the torment of the cross brought Him to the hour of death.[1]

[1] Herkenne regards this Psalm as a direct prophecy of the Messiah, like the picture of the Suffering Servant in Isaiah 53. He thinks however that it falls below the Isaianic passage in that it portrays the salvation of the world as coming through the Messiah's *deliverance* from suffering, not through the suffering itself. König rejects the idea that the Psalm was written directly of the Messiah but maintains that it is a *typus verbalis* containing many unconscious foreshadowings of Christ. Such is the view of the present writer.

LORD, *let me know mine end*

The Author of Psalm 39 is one of those Psalmists who tell their personal experience. He has gone through a time of deep and painful brooding in self-imposed silence and has at last found utterance in prayer. Omitting the calling upon God which marks the beginning of the usual Lament he plunges at once into narrative:

> 2. I saíd, I will keép my wáys,     that I sín not with my
>     tóngue:
> I will keép for my moúth a brídle     as lóng as the wícked
>     (man) is wíth me.

We can see from these words something of what had been in his thoughts. It was the kind of brooding that might easily be interpreted as disloyal to Yahweh, especially by an irreligious man. And it happened that just such a one was in his company—the "wicked" he calls him. It is of course possible that he is speaking collectively of people who pay no attention to God but the more likely view is that he has a particular person in mind—perhaps an acquaintance or a relative. Now we know from other passages that such worldly people liked nothing better than to see the faith of religious men breaking down under the stress of pain, disappointment and trouble. But this Psalmist was determined not to give the "wicked" that satisfaction. Whatever he had against God, it was all "in the family"; outsiders should hear nothing of it.

But he found after a while that utterance must break forth.

> 3. I was dúmb with sílence,     I kept sílence from goód (words);
> And my paín was stirred úp,     4. hót grew my heárt withín me;
> In my broóding a fíre was kíndled—     I spáke with my
>     tóngue!

And so at last he pours forth what is in his mind. But not to men! It is for Yahweh's ear alone.

5. Make me knów, Yahwéh, my énd,     and the meásure of my
    dáys, what it ís;
    Let me knów how mórtal I ám.[1]
6. Behóld, hándbreadths hast thou máde my dáys,     and my
    contínuance is as nóthing before theé!

That is what has been troubling him—the briefness of his
life.[2] His realization of it may arise from a fact to which he
presently alludes: God's hand has struck him, probably with
illness. The dreadful feeling has come over him that he is not
going to get well; and this combined with the melancholy
naturally induced by sickness has brought home to him the
exceeding shortness of his days. He asks Yahweh indeed to
make it known to him but this is only to spread the matter
before God: he himself has and gives the answer. "Behold,
as handbreadths!"

Yet his personal transitoriness is only an incident in a
vaster tragedy. With eyes sharpened by his own misery he
looks out over the world and sees the same doom written everywhere.

Súrely, as * vánity,     is évery mán standing fírm!
7. Súrely, as * a shádow man goes aboút.
    Súrely, for vánity they are in a rúsh.     He accúmulates
    and does not knów whó shall gáther it in.

It is not so much mortality as futility that weighs him down.
Nothing to it all! We are reminded of Qoheleth. He too found
the world and human life absolutely empty, he too brooded
over the death that takes all alike.[3] But our Psalmist is unlike Qoheleth in one cardinal respect—he has religion. Qoheleth really had none to speak of and so it was only to be
expected that he took refuge from this sense of futility (so
far as it was possible) in pursuing what goods life (or God)

[1] Herkenne emends the text so as to make this an exclamation of impatience at the delay of death: "I would know why I am still living!" But
surely the Psalmist wants to live, not to die.

[2] Oesterley would seem to have little ground for believing that what
troubles the Psalmist is the prosperity of the wicked and the adversity of
the godly. *Fresh Approach to the Psalms*, p. 241. König shares Oesterley's
view.

[3] Most recent commentators think that what troubles our Psalmist is
the prosperity of the wicked (Gunkel, Kittel, Schmidt, Kirkpatrick,
Staerk). But nothing in his words seems to bear out such an interpretation. Here the present writer agrees with Duhm.

offers, while they may be had.[1] Quite different is the escape
here.

> 8. And nów, what do I loók for, Lórd?     My waíting is for theé.

The author of Ecclesiastes never could have said that for he
had long ago given up the idea of a God who intervenes to
help. To this Psalmist however God is the supreme factor in
the situation—indeed the only factor from which one can
expect anything. But what can God do for him? Can He reverse the doom of mortality? Hardly! Whatever a later age
might come to believe of a life with God beyond death, our
Psalmist gives no place in his thought to such a possibility.
But God can do *something!*

> 9. From áll my transgréssions delíver me,     máke me not a
>    taúnt for the foól!

Yes, God can forgive his sins; for he acknowledges that he
has transgressed. That to his mind is the reason for the divine
visitation under which he is suffering. Apparently his wrong-
doings have not been such as to cause agonies of conscience;
he speaks of them only in passing, as a known element in the
situation with which it is necessary to deal. He needs pardon;
let God grant it. And by so doing God will take from the
irreligious person any ground for ridiculing the Psalmist's faith.
For pardon involves remission of his present punishment. He
has indeed endured it in silence—a fact that of itself ought
to move God, for his silence has been due to reverence. God
was at work [2] in his pain, and he must not resent it.

> 10. I was dúmb, I ópened not my moúth;     for *thoú* dídst it.
> 11. Remóve from upón me thy stróke!     by the blów of thy
>     hánd I pérish.

Then once more he goes back from his own case to the universal fate of man:

> 12. With rebúkes for iníquity     thou dost chásten a mán,
>     And thou dissólvest, like a móth, his beaúty.     Súrely, a
>     breáth is évery mán!

And now he returns to his passionate petition:

[1] Eccles. 2:24 etc.
[2] Barnes' translation.

13. Heár my práyer, Yahwéh!    And give éar to my crý!
    At my teárs be not sílent!
    For but a guést am I' with theé,    a temporary séttler, as
    áll my fáthers were.
14. Look awáy from mé, and let me bríghten up,    befóre I
    go hénce and be no móre!

That is all he asks—all he or any man *can* ask: a respite
from premature death, a little sunshine before the final darkness. For such as he understands it is man's lot: to stay with
God on earth for a brief season, to settle down in temporary
possession, but always at the last to pass on.

To pass on! The Psalmist is one with his contemporaries in
that. Death ends man's intercourse with God. No more sacrifices, no more prayers, no more hymns: only silence. For man
himself "is no more."

We see here by contrast how amazing is the originality of
those other Psalmists who thought of God as present in Sheol
and of the dead as praising Him (Pss. 139 and 22). Our
Psalmist is incapable of such a flight.[1]

And yet what a heroic quality marks his faith, that in spite
of oncoming separation he lays hold of God mightily while
there is time! We cannot but wonder at these men of the Old
Testament, all of whom (with very few possible exceptions)
faced the fact that they were only stopping with God for a

---

[1] Oesterley however agrees with Duhm that the Psalmist does look
beyond death. "We feel that there is every justification for Duhm's view
when he says: 'It appears to me that no other explanation is possible than
that of assuming that the poet in silent thought hoped for the continuance
of life after death, though without being able to base this hope on any
demonstrable proof, or on any teaching that had been put forth. God had
vouchsafed no such promise, no such revelation. Might not the poet,
nevertheless, hope? and for what might he hope? Whatever the hope might
be, it must center in God. The psalmist does not count on metaphysical
immortality for men, as such; but he looks for God's mercy on the godly.
Therefore, since he is unable, or unwilling, to rely on any general doctrine
of immortality, which might solve the riddle of the forlornness of human
existence, whereby to still his perplexity, he pleads sadly with hesitation:
What may I hope for? Everything depends on Thee. It is a silent prayer,
the prayer of one sighing in this fleeting life for that which is abiding—
the complement of: Yahweh, make me to know mine end, and the measure
of my days, what it is.' " (*Fresh Approach to the Psalms*, p. 267f.) Beautiful as this interpretation is, it necessitates (as Oesterley candidly admits)
the rejection of verses 13 and 14 and the consequent altering of the whole
tone of the Psalm. König, who cites the same opinion of Duhm, rejects it.

season, that they had no part in His eternity, yet loved, served, enjoyed Him, made Him the center of everything, with an intensity which puts to shame the feeble devotion of the modern Christian who has everlasting life at his disposal!

But to return to our Psalmist's conclusion. In the manner of suppliants throughout these Laments he is giving the reason why God should hear him; and a pathetic reason it is. Do not take away from the little that is my portion! And he uses a strange expression in his prayer: "Look away from me." Most of the Psalmists plead that God may look upon them; but he, like Job, asks to be let alone. It sounds as if that were all he wishes—for God to cease afflicting him. Yet if we read between the lines we see that he does not really want God to look away. For he loves God; and if it were possible (as Job for a moment dreamed—Job 14:13 ff.), with what rapture would he embrace the thought that God might wake him from the sleep of Sheol to companionship with Himself!

It is a true Lament that he has given us, yet one not governed by the prevailing forms. He breaks at the beginning into narrative—something quite distinctive. His petition is indeed the common one—to be delivered from his trouble. But his real pain goes too deep for deliverance, and leads naturally to meditation on human mortality rather than to complaint proper. There is thus an incommensurability between what is troubling him and what he asks for and an element of reflection which separates this Psalm sharply from the other Laments of the Psalter.

Nor does he win the "certainty of being heard" even for his modest petition. His Lament closes without any burst of confidence in God's answer.

# The Author of Psalms 42-43

## *Like as the hart desireth the water-brooks*

Up in Northern Palestine,[1] near the source of the Jordan where it rushes from the foot of Mount Hermon, roaring down in cataracts as it starts on its long way to the Dead Sea, there once lived a deeply devoted Israelite whose homesickness for the Jerusalem temple has given us a poem of exceeding beauty. Psalms 42 and 43, by common agreement of scholars, constitute a single composition. This is evident from the fact that taken together they form three strophes, each of which is concluded by the same refrain. A unity of thought and language binds them into one, and that they were so combined originally is indicated by the absence of any title for Psalm 43. We shall therefore treat them as a single Lament.

The man who composed it is suffering from some affliction which makes him think God has forgotten him and gives the irreligious occasion to ridicule his trust in divine care. Like the other Psalmists he affords no clear information as to just what this affliction is. It is plain that he is homesick but not at all plain that this is his only trouble. Enemies of course are mentioned, yet their mere enmity does not seem sufficient to account for his woe. In fact it is just because of his woe that they taunt him. In view of this, the usual idea that he is prostrated by homesickness and therefore becomes a taunt to his enemies seems hardly sufficient. Gunkel finds the basis for another view in the Psalmist's words about the waves and breakers of God going over him: these, Gunkel thinks, mean that he is close to death for the deeps he refers to are those of the underworld. The Psalmist then would be mortally ill and his illness would make his homesickness poignant. Schmidt agrees with Gunkel that the Psalmist is in mortal danger, but

[1] The Psalmist in v.7f. speaks as if he were in the neighborhood of the Jordan and the Hermons, and this combined with his mention of breakers and waves has given rise to the common opinion that the Psalm was composed near the sources of the Jordan.

not from sickness. He is under indictment, probably in prison; for he asks God to plead his cause and do him justice (judge him) against a loveless people (43:1). One might add that Schmidt removes from the text all reference to the northern localities, so that for him the Psalmist is separated from the temple not by distance but by imprisonment.

What really is his trouble we shall never know. It seems best to look on it as something more than homesickness, something that brings him low in such fashion that others can see his suffering. Possibly it is the maltreatment of his adversaries, who may be carrying their "oppression" far beyond taunts. In any case it is no light affliction, but one that is overwhelming him, perhaps even to death. He goes about in the dirty neglected dress of a mourner, his soul is prostrate and tumultuous within him. But he *can* "go about," he is not bed-ridden, and he is not in utter despair for he can admonish his soul to "wait for" a return of happiness.

But whatever his affliction its various elements all converge on one point: he wants to get back to the temple because there God is to be found. And to describe his longing he employs one of the loveliest similes of all literature: [1]

2. Like the hínd which lóngs for the broóks of wáter,
   So my soúl lóngs towards theé, O Gód.
3. My soúl thírsts for Gód,    for the líving Gód;
   Whén shall I go ín and seé *    the fáce of Gód?

Evidently this man's religion is no mere attitude or orientation to Reality, no quiet background against which the other interests of life move, absorbing the attention; it is a consuming passion burning in the very center of consciousness. What he wants is a mystical companionship with an unseen Person and he wants it with a wild insistence which will not be denied. God! But how can God be got at, seen? He knows the answer: in the temple. There in the ascending smoke of sacrifice, in the sacred precincts, the holy symbols, the chanting of Levitical choirs, the solemn dance, the halleluias of the worshipping

---

[1] There is no indication that the hind is being hunted although that idea has found expression in the well-known hymn.

multitudes—*there* one meets God—and nowhere else! His homesickness for the temple gives him no rest.

> 4. My teárs have beén to me breád    dáy and níght,
>    While they sáy to mé all the dáy,    "Whére is thy Gód?"

Here as elsewhere in the Laments the two go together: the weeping of the Psalmist and the derision of the by-standers. He does not say who these are, does not even speak of them as enemies, though he presently uses that word. So far they are just the laughing public to whom religious trust is a joke.

But he will divert his thoughts from them to another public which he knew in happier scenes:

> 5. Thése things will I remémber and will pour oút    my soúl
>    upón me;
>    Hów I wént in the thróng,    I léd them to the hóuse of Gód;
>    With the voíce of shoút and thanksgíving,    a múltitude
>    keeping feást.

Then was when he really lived! Through his brief words we discern something of the vast transaction in which he took a leader's part.[1] And the memory brings with it hope:

> 6. Whý art thou bowed dówn, my soúl,    and why múr-
>    murest thou withín me?
>    Wáit upon Gód, for I shall yét thánk him,    the hélp
>    of my * coúntenance and * 7 my Gód!

This is the refrain that recurs after each strophe, sounding the dominant note of the poem: an expectation of better things which seems to rise higher with each repetition until it breaks forth in a triumphant paean at the end. Thus to this lonely depressed man the thought of God brings new strength: "My God!"

But it is God alone who gives hope; he himself cannot lift his mind out of its depression. And so he declares his purpose of thinking upon God from his far-away place of sojourn:

> Upón me is my soúl bowed dówn;    thérefore I will
> remémber thee
> From the lánd of Jórdan and the Hérmons,    from the
> híll Mízar.

---

[1] He seems to have had some leading function in the feast he describes, but it is not necessary to suppose, as does Duhm, that he had been high-priest. Some think he was a prominent Levite.

8. Ócean unto ócean is cálling    at the sound of thy wáter-
   pipes;
   Áll thy breákers and thy wáves    have gone óver mé.

Scholars generally connect his thought of the overwhelming
primaeval oceans with the sight of the thundering cataracts of
the Jordan source. That is what they suggest to him—God's
floods of death. Gunkel sets aside such an interpretation as
"sentimental." It is indeed rare, as Bertholet remarks, for an
ancient Israelite to find in nature the echo of his own moods.
Yet the common view is probably near the truth. To the agonised gaze of the Psalmist the "charm of color and line in the
wonderful landscape...the wild majesty of the young Jordan
that leaps roaring down its narrow bed of rock" (Staerk) can
convey no pleasure but only the thought of the infernal deeps
swallowing him up. Yet over against them he can set God!

9. In the dáy-time Yahwéh will commánd his lovingkíndness,
   and in the níght his sóng shall be wíth me,
   A práyer to the Gód of my lífe.

It is a difficult verse to understand, although the general
sense is clear. Gunkel would emend it to read:

By dáy I shall look oút for Yahwéh    and for his lovingkíndness in the níght,
I will síng with me a práyer    to the Gód of my lífe.

Or it may be taken as a prayer, "May Yahweh command His
lovingkindness." In any case our Psalmist is speaking hope-
fully. The lovingkindness of Yahweh will not fail him. He
seems to look upon it almost as an angelic being, like God's
light and truth of which he will presently speak; God will command it and will turn his prayer into a song—day and night.

This thought emboldens him to utter his complaint before
God:

10. I will sáy to Gód, my róck,    Whý hast thou forgótten me?
    Whý do I gó about in moúrning    while the énemy tor-
    ménts me?
11. Like * a crushing in my bónes    my foés taúnt me,
    As they sáy unto mé all the dáy,    Whére is thy Gód?

And if he speaks thus to God he will get relief. There is no
need to be in despair. So he swings into the refrain again:

12. Whý art thou bowed dówn, my soúl,    and whý múrmurest
thou withín me?
Waít for Gód, for I shall yét thánk him,    the hélp of my
coúntenance and my Gód!

Up to this point he has indeed addressed God twice (in
passing, as it were) but for the rest he has held off from
actual calling upon Him in the manner of the Lament. But now
he begins to pray in earnest:

1. Júdge me, O Gód, and pleád my cáse,    against a nátion
withoút lovingkíndness;
From the mán of deceít and wíckedness réscue me!

This is the verse that makes us wonder whether the Psalmist's woe may not be caused primarily by a group of enemies,
among whom perhaps stands out one man of special ill-will
(Schmidt). But he may only be using a strong expression for
the scorn of an evil-disposed public from which God can save
him by restoring him to well-being and enabling him once more
to visit the temple. In any case it is God who is his hope.

2. For thoú art the Gód of my stréngth;    whý hast thou cast
me óff?
Whý do I go aboút in moúrning    while the énemy torménts
me?
3. Sénd out thy líght and thy trúth,    let *thém* leád me,
Let them bríng me in to the híll of thy hóliness    and
tó thy dwéllings;
4. And let me go ín to the áltar of Gód,    to Gód, the gládness of my jóy,
And thánk thee upon the hárp, O Gód, my Gód!

That is his heart's desire, how passionately expressed! And
as he utters it to God, making strong his appeal by urging his
dependence on God and his misery under the taunts of his
foes, the confidence comes to him that his petition will be
granted. Light and truth, like guiding angels, will bring him
home to God's house, God's altar. How he will sing! And so the
refrain rings out victoriously:

5. Whý art thou bowed dówn, my soúl?    And whý múrmurest
thou withín me?
Waít upon Gód for I shall yét thánk him,    the hélp of my
coúntenance and my Gód.

The poem that this Psalmist has given us is indeed an Individual Lament but it follows the usual forms of such a com-

position very loosely. At the beginning there is no calling upon God, no introductory cry for help, no description of the Psalmist's prayer. He enters at once into his complaint, addressing God only in passing, as it were, and he continues it through his first two strophes, weaving into it what we may call meditations. But the complaint is tinged with hope, and his remonstrance with his soul for its depression—a feature unusual in the Laments—strikes a note of expectancy that dominates the whole poem. Not till he enters his third strophe does he really present his petition, giving in the customary way the reasons why God should hear him. The second petition passes over into wishes: "let them bring me...let me go in...etc."— as is frequent in the Lament. Finally, he does actually arrive at the "certainty of being heard," though he expresses it differently from the Author of Psalm 22.

All commentators unite in praising the marvellous beauty of our Psalmist's creation. He is a consummate artist, exhibiting even the power of symmetrical structure so uncommon in Hebrew poetry, for he divides his poem into three equal strophes, each concluding with the refrain. But of course the supreme charm of the poem lies in its content. Schmidt finds in it two unique things which raise it above the level of most of its kindred Psalms. "The first is the completed beauty of the poem, the poet's gift of seeing. At the very beginning he portrays the deadly anguish and despair into which he has fallen by an unforgettable figure: When in the dry season of the year the deep-cut wadis of the Palestinian table-land are dried up, when one spring after another fails, then might the hind—it is certainly intentional that he chooses the weaker female animal—with trembling legs and languishing tongue stand between the burnt-out stones, where so short a time ago she could bend down to the purling brook, and helplessly seek after a drop of water. 'So longs my soul, O God, for thee.'

"And now the poet sees himself, and we see him in his words: how in the past, 'stepping in the dance,' 'in the noisy throng of pilgrims,' 'amidst the tumultuous joy and thanksgiving' he ascended in the midst of the congregation to the temple...

And now the primaeval floods roar about his soul answering each other, the 'conduits' which lead down from the upper surface of earth resound in reply—a mighty, monotonous, horrible music! There are few poems in the Old Testament that can so paint!

"The peculiar charm of the prayer, however," Schmidt proceeds, "lies—here is the second thing—in its wonderful religious profundity. This prayer is in truth a conversation with God. Beginning in the abyss of despair ... and with the start of every strophe hurled back into it anew, it lifts itself up each time in its refrain to full confidence, to the wonderful repose in which the suppliant views his despondency almost with amazement. Even yet he has tears in his eyes; even yet there storms through his words the despairing question, 'Why? why?'. And now suddenly the quiet wonder that has arisen within him: how could I have been so despairing? I am now certain: 'I will yet give him thanks ...' Here one sees again, as one sees elsewhere indeed only in the written words of the Prophet Jeremiah, the power of a prayer uttered so that the most inward being of a man shares in it—how it brings the heart of man out of stormy unrest, out of anguish and deathly gloom to stillness and to an indescribable joy."

This long citation from Schmidt passes beyond the consideration of the Author's poetic genius to that of his religion. No one would gainsay the truth of what Schmidt says regarding its intensity. But one aspect of it has caused Kittel to look on it with qualified admiration. For there can be no doubt that this Psalmist's religious life and aspiration center in the worship of the temple. It is there—and apparently there only—that he meets with God. And that, Kittel thinks, is a serious limitation. "The religion of our poet," he says, "is still wholly preoccupied (*befangen*) in the outward worship. The highest things he knows are the uplifting feasts in the temple. That, along with passages like Psalms 26, 27A, is a beautiful testimony to the power which worship had over the souls in Israel and to the way in which God himself comes here into sensible nearness, yes is made for them a living and beautifying possession.

But there is also no doubt that passages like Psalms 40 and 50, which stand under prophetic influence, have an incomparably higher apprehension of the relation to God. The more impressed we are by the attachment to the holy place, the more we recognise how much the religious life of the suppliant is still dependent on the locality itself. It is to him more than a mere symbol of the presence of God; it is to him the proper vehicle of that presence."

Gunkel however does not allow the Psalmist's dependence on the temple-worship to detract from the value of his religion. "Such an immediate connection of the feeling of God's nearness with the deliverance out of dire external necessity and with the inspiring experience of a pilgrimage, is a characteristic of the religion of that ancient time, which cannot possess the inward and spiritual without the outward and sensible; and this very trait may appear alien to the present generation. Nevertheless, one recognises from the heart's tones which the Psalmist utters that what he longs for in the bottom of his soul is the same thing that true religion in all times thirsts for —the sure experience of the living God; and we comprehend the Psalmist, who from out the dark valley of his sufferings looks up to those heights of life."

But it remained for Staerk to place upon our Psalmist's religion its true valuation. The roots of our Psalmist's feeling for the temple, he declares, "rest in the deep need of man for sensible guaranties of faith in God and his salvation." He means of course man's need for *sacraments*. And those who find in the supreme Christian sacrament of the Holy Communion the most enriching and quickening approach to the Divine have no difficulty in understanding what our Psalmist means, even though they may with shame acknowledge that he far surpasses them in his longing for the "living God." This Psalm indeed is charged to thrilling fulness with that love of the sanctuary which is natural to the Christian heart. And it is specially attuned to the atmosphere of the Holy Communion, as the Church has recognised in using it through centuries as the perfect Introit Psalm.

O send out thy light and thy truth, that they may lead me,
And bring me unto thy holy hill, and to thy dwelling;
And that I may go unto the altar of God, even unto the
  God of my joy and gladness;
And upon the harp will I give thanks unto thee, O God,
  my God.

# III

## 2. b. PSALMS OF PENITENCE

### THE AUTHOR OF PSALM 51

*Wash me throughly from my wickedness*

The man who composed Psalm 51 is one of the great men of the Bible. His Psalm attains heights of religious thought and experience that bring it almost if not quite up to the level of the best of the New Testament. We shall speak again of his preeminence. What he has given us is the classic Psalm of penitence to which later ages return continually when they try to express the sense of sin. For this man who has gone so high is a sinner. Not in the sense that all men are sinners but in some special, devastating way.

Scholars indeed are not in agreement as to his situation. From his mention of broken bones some infer that he is prostrated by sickness (Schmidt, Gunkel, Staerk, Barnes, Duhm, Leslie), while others (Kittel, Kirkpatrick) take this to be mainly an expression of his mental agony. Schmidt thinks that in addition to sickness he is threatened by prosecution which may result in his death and that he is referring to this when he asks God to deliver him from blood. Opinions differ also as to the nature of his sin. Gunkel takes him literally when he declares that he has offended against God only, while Kittel and others believe him guilty of some flagrant wrong towards his fellow-men. Again, they divide on the question whether his sin has come home to his conscience of itself or only after the divine penalty of illness brought him to think of it.

But however they may differ on these minor matters they are
all at one in pointing out that what concerns our Psalmist
when he utters the impassioned words of his Psalm is his overwhelming sin. He has done *something* that lays him in the dust
before God, that takes away from him all the joy he has had
in God in the past, that fills his mind with unbearable pain.
And he feels God's punishing hand upon him, giving terrible
reality to his own remorse; his bones are broken. God is against
him, and all through his own fault! That is the fearful thing
about it.

And now what can he do? He cannot go to God with complaint when he knows the complaint is all against himself. He
cannot cry for help to a God whose help he has rejected by his
own deed.

And yet there is something on which he can place his hope:
it is the very character of God whom he has offended. For
the deepest quality of God is just that which he needs now—
His love. So he turns to Him.

> 3. Have mercy upón me, O Gód, according to thy lovingkíndness,
>    according to the múltitude of thy compássions blot oút my
>    transgréssions;
> 4. Thóroughly wásh me from my iníquity    and from my síns
>    make me cleán.

This is his Introduction—the calling upon God—and it
comes out from the midst of petition; for he must utter his
prayer at once. And in that prayer all he has to say of himself is that he is a sinner! He throws himself completely on
the mercy of the God from whom he deserves no mercy. Yet
this admission of his guilt is another reason why God should
hear him.

> 5. For my transgréssions *Í* knów,    and my sín is befóre me
>    contínually.

There is no need for God to bring it home to him nor for
God to contend with him over it. He will not maintain his
innocence; nay, it is his own conscience that is his ceaseless
accuser. Freely he makes acknowledgment to God.

> 6. Against theé ónly have I sínned,    and the évil in thíne
>    eyes have I dóne—
>    Thát [1] thou mayest be jústified when thou spéakest,    be
>    cleár when thou júdgest.

Against thee only! That is the feeling of a man who stands face to face with God. *All* sin is against Him. Our Psalmist is hardly denying that he has wronged his fellows, as Gunkel thinks; nor is he appealing, as Schmidt imagines, to be acquitted of an indictment brought against him for such injury. He means merely that here in the presence of God whom he has alienated the single aspect of his sin which counts is its Godward side.

But his personal wickedness is only part of the burden which he carries, which he must confess.

> 7. Behóld, in iníquity was I brought fórth,    and in sín did
>    my móther concéive me.

He is not really speaking of his mother or the circumstances under which he was born; he is referring to something universal, a common taint of human nature. Every child that comes into the world inherits a fatal load of evil from the generations that went before him; for man is wicked and any son of man shares in the sin of the race. This fact, which makes it hard for him to do right, might indeed be urged in extenuation of his transgression. Gunkel thinks that the Psalmist is so using it here; that it is one of the reasons urged so commonly in Laments, showing why God should be merciful. But the majority of recent commentators reject such an interpretation. The Psalmist is not trying to soften God's wrath by an excuse; he is rather telling God the whole desolate truth about himself—he is a sinful man, born of sinful woman. There is nothing good in him! And he must acknowledge the very depths of his wickedness for God demands utter honesty in one's dealing with Him.

---

[1] We must supply some such phrase as "I confess this that..." (Bertholet, Duhm, Gunkel, Kittel, Leslie). I cannot go along with the view of those who look on the justification of God as the effect, if not the purpose of the sin itself (Kirkpatrick, McNeile, Staerk).

8. Behold, trúth thou desírest in the ínward parts [1]    and in
the hídden part thou dost máke me know wísdom.

This is a saying difficult to understand and the commentators
disagree as to its interpretation. Kirkpatrick seems to think
that the Psalmist is holding up the *standard* which God exacts
of him—perfect sincerity. Kittel and Leslie believe that he is
stressing the necessity of complete openness in confession to
God. One is tempted to follow Kirkpatrick's lead and imagine
that the Psalmist is here contrasting his own utter sinfulness
with God's demands—and, let us add, God's expectations for
him. Even he, the sinner born of sinners, is held up by God
to perfect truth; his conscience deep within him is instructed
in the way of the divine wisdom! If such be his meaning it is
a thought of hope that he utters.

And now he returns to the petition which he had offered so
pasionately, yet so briefly, in the beginning.

9. Un-sín me with hýssop and I shall be cleán,    and wásh
me, and I shall be whíter than snów.

This is the language of the ritual but the Psalmist has no rites
in mind; all the terms in his Psalm taken from the ancient
outward ceremonies of cleansing are figures of what he desires
in the realm of the spirit. He wants to be *clean* and only God
can make him white. Oh what a happiness such a cleansing
would be!

10. Make me heár of jóy and gládness,    let the bónes which
thou hast crúshed rejoíce!

Is he asking for recovery from illness? Such is the view of
several scholars who find, as we have said, a reference to sickness in the broken bones. But it seems more in keeping with
what we know of this man to look on his agony as that of the
heart. Forgiveness, not physical health, is what he longs for
and the joy of which he speaks is the rapture of a soul reconciled to God. So he goes on with the prayer:

11. Híde thy fáce from my síns,    and áll mine iníquities blot
oút.

[1] The meaning of the Hebrew word is uncertain. Some scholars, following the Syriac, omit it.

Yes, let them disappear forever! And yet that will not be enough; for what he really needs is the power not to sin again.

12. A cleán heárt creáte for me, O Gód,   and a steádfast
      spírit make néw withín me;
13. Cást me nót away from thy fáce,   and the spírit of thy
      hóliness táke not fróm me;
14. Restóre to me the jóy of thy hélp,   and with a spírit
      that is wílling suppórt me.

Each one of these petitions invites our scrutiny, for taken together they mark our Psalmist as one of the pioneer thinkers of the Old Testament. What he wants, as has been said, is a clean heart that will be enabled to continue clean; and this, he feels, is so far beyond his own capacities that it can come only by the creative act of God. It must be brought forth from nothing, as was the world from primaeval chaos, by the divine word—a miracle no less astonishing than creation itself. Such a heart will not vacillate between good and evil but remain steadfast in God's will—a thing new and fresh, the gift of God. He prays to abide in the presence of God who is of purer eyes than to behold evil and he can meet the demands of that high place only by the constant work within him of God's Spirit—the Spirit that effects holiness in men. Such is the "salvation" he asks for—moral victory keeping him close to God with the joy that it alone can bring; and to remain in this state of salvation will not require tense struggle for he himself will *want* to do right—he will be supported, as he says, by a willing spirit.

These are conceptions of the religious life that may be familiar enough to us, but coming from the lips of a man of the Old Covenant they startle us with their originality. Gunkel comments at length on this fact. The prayer for a clean new heart, he declares, "is entirely unique in the Psalms. Elsewhere the Psalmists usually ask only for deliverance from their need or at most that God will teach the poet concerning His will and make his heart obedient to it. The only things comparable to such a prayer in the Old Testament are certain predictions of the Prophets, who, in despair of the fruit of their own work with their people, confidently expect that Yahweh

Himself will take this work into His own almighty hands. Then God—so they hope—will sprinkle pure water upon Israel and free it from all its uncleanness; He will give them a new heart and a new spirit in their breast; He will give His Spirit in their breast and cause them to walk in his commandments. His longing for a pure heart and a new spirit however is naturally not produced by what he has read but by what he has experienced in his own life."

Again, Gunkel finds the prayer for God's holy Spirit remarkable, along with the accompanying petitions for continuance in God's presence and a spirit that wills to obey God. "These prayers also stand almost alone in the Old Testament. The only passage to compare with them is Psalm 143:10: 'Teach me to do thy will; may thy good Spirit lead me on a level track.' It was to ancient Israel no usual thought that the Spirit of God in men is a power for the good. On the contrary, the workings of the Spirit were from the most ancient times seen where men were arrested by certain mysterious phenomena such as unusual courage, wisdom and even drunkenness, unchastity or insanity, without any regard at first as to whether these phenomena occurred in the ethical sphere or not. But here the Psalmist speaks of a 'spirit of willingness,' which pours into the heart a wonderful obedience, and of Yahweh's 'holy Spirit' ...i.e. the Spirit which effects in men a good and holy life."

All this brings the Psalmist very close to the faith and experience of the New Testament. He is speaking almost as a Paul or a John might speak. And notice, he is not theorising but basing what he says upon his own actual religious life. For the gifts that he longs for are not something totally new to him; to a real extent he has enjoyed them in the happy past. And so he prays God to *restore* to him the joy of salvation. Surely Gunkel is mistaken when he draws a sharp contrast between this saint of the Old Testament and the saints of the New on this very point of experience: "the Psalmist longs for it, the Apostles of Christ exult in its possession." On the contrary, our Psalmist has so exulted in the past, and therefore hopes to exult again.

He has voiced his *complaint,* or rather his confession which takes the place of the complaint (vv.5-8), and his *petition* (vv.9-14). Now he passes to his *vow* and a unique vow it is.

> 15. I will teách transgréssors thy wáys,     and sínners to theé shall túrn.
> 16. Delíver me from bloód, O Gód,* my tóngue shall cry aloúd of thy ríghteousness.
> 17. O Lórd, ópen my líps,     and my moúth shall decláre thy praíse.

Like so many other Psalmists he promises to tell God's goodness; but not to the same people as they. For they picture their listeners as the faithful, the "great congregation;" but this Psalmist wants quite a different audience. He will seek out the sinners, the people who have gone astray like himself; and he will have such wonderful things to recount of God's kindness to him in his sin that they will be compelled to repent and come back to God. As the Author of Psalm 22 became through his own expected deliverance a potential missionary to the nations, so this Psalmist will be an evangelist, a saver of lost men. And the gospel he will preach will be the same that rings through the New Testament—the gospel of God's love!

If only God *will* deliver him, open his lips, give him something to tell! But what does he mean by speaking of a deliverance from blood? That has puzzled the commentators and still remains a mystery. Our Prayer Book and Bible translate the word "blood-guiltiness," and McNeile, Barnes, König and Herkenne hold fast to this interpretation. Schmidt and Kittel think it refers to a danger at the hands of men, who threaten his life by an indictment (Schmidt) or by ill-will which will visit upon him the punishment they believe he has deserved from God (Kittel).[1] Kirkpatrick has another idea and paraphrases "from the power and punishment of my sin." Duhm thinks he means death through sickness; while Gunkel and Staerk emend the text to read "death" (silence) instead of blood. Amidst such disagreement one can hardly expect to

---

[1] Peters and Baethgen interpret it to mean mortal peril of some sort.

come to a satisfactory opinion of his own, and it is better to leave the expression uncomprehended. Yet his idea is fairly clear; he must be delivered before he can speak.

Such is his vow. And he feels that what he promises will be more acceptable to God than costly animal sacrifice.

18. Fór thou dost not delíght in sácrifice,     and should I gíve
     a whole burnt-óffering thou wouldst not be pleásed;
19. The sácrifices of Gód are a bróken spírit,     a heart bróken
     and [1] crúshed, O Gód, thou wilt not despíse.

The man who can say that has entered deep into the mind of the Prophets; for like them he throws aside the requirements of the ritual Law and deals with God on the broad basis of ethics. Here again our familiarity with such an attitude may easily obscure for us its amazing boldness in a saint of the Old Covenant. Our Psalmist would understand what St. Paul meant when he said that for freedom did Christ make us free; for he *is* free—he treats God as a son treats his father.

And his reading of the heart of God in this matter gives him assurance. Perhaps it is too much to say that he closes with the "certainty of having obtained his prayer," as Gunkel claims. But he has at least reached a mood of quiet confidence; and the thing that makes him so sure is his very prostration in the dust before God, his "heart broken and crushed." God *cannot* reject that!

Here his Psalm closes. The two following verses, by the almost universal agreement of recent commentators, do not come from him [2] for they express a devotion to sacrifices which can scarcely be harmonized with the great prophetic utterance we have just been considering. It is generally thought that they were added by a well-meaning man who was shocked at the Psalmist's seeming disrespect towards ritual offerings and wished to turn the reader's mind back into the proper reverence for these. They make the Psalmist speak as if Jerusalem were in ruins, suggesting that its fallen condition is what ren-

---

[1] Some scholars, following the Syriac, omit "broken and."
[2] Baethgen is an exception in holding that they are an integral part of the Psalm.

ders sacrifices unfitting in his day. But let Yahweh build the walls of Zion again and *then* its offerings will once more meet with divine acceptance.

The Psalmist, however, knows nothing of these verses! We take leave of him still praying in humility and penitence and presenting before God his own broken heart as the one thing God desires.

*Out of the deep have I called unto thee*

We shall conclude our survey of the writers of Individual Laments by the study of the man who has given us the sixth of the seven Penitential Psalms of the Church. He has forever endeared himself to the suffering and the distressed by his opening words: "out of the deep"; and his Psalm will always be known as the *De Profundis*.

It is in these words that he depicts his situation. Scholars seem to agree that by "deep" he means the deep waters of the underworld, the floods through which the soul passes on its way to the realm of the dead. He feels himself already sunk in them, far below the earth on which others are enjoying life and happy intercourse with God. It is hardly necessary to suppose that he is actually face to face with death; he is using this figure to express some abyss of misery from which he cries to God. What then is his trouble? Only one thing can be certainly gathered from his Psalm—that he is laden with sin. Gunkel thinks that we may also infer some outward suffering because the Psalmists generally felt sin only as it was brought home to them by pain. "The devout suppliant is in sore trouble, perhaps in critical illness, and he sees in his sufferings the punishment of God for his sin." This may be so but the Psalm does not reveal it. We are more likely to do the Psalmist justice if we pay attention only to what he *says*. His silence as to his outward circumstances is, as Schmidt points out, the uniqueness and the greatness of this Psalm. "This suppliant has only one sorrow—his sin—and only one concern—forgiveness."

He begins with what Gunkel terms the description of his entreaty, combined with his calling upon God.

1. Out of the deéps I cáll to thee, Yahwéh;   2 Lórd, heár my voíce!
   Let thine éars bé atténtive   to the voíce of my supplicátions.

Out of the deep! God is so far above him that perhaps his voice will not reach all the way to Him; and God is furthermore estranged from him by his own deed. Yet this is just the reason why God *will* hear him. His supplication however he does not utter. Instead, he hints at it shyly, bringing forward two further reasons why God should show him mercy (Gunkel). From the first of these we see that what he desires is forgiveness. He pleads the common weakness of human nature:

> 3. If thou shouldst keép iníquities, Yahwéh,   Lórd, whó would stánd?

He says this not to excuse himself but rather to merge himself with the universal guilt of humanity. He appeals to the mercy of God—for what else is left man? So the writer of Psalm 51 asked for pity solely on the ground of God's great goodness. Our Psalmist does this in confidence.

> 4. For with theé is párdon,   thát thou mayest be feáred.

God's nature is not to condemn but to forgive. Over against the universal wickedness of humanity is set the universal pardon of God. And as a second consideration moving God to be kind he reminds Him of the object He has in mind when He remits guilt—that men may fear Him. The Psalmist can hardly mean the fear of terror but rather what Kirkpatrick calls the "devout reverence which is the animating spirit of Old Testament religion." And yet even this has in it an element of fear, a sense of sternness in the divine character. What God desires in blotting out men's sins, our Psalmist would say, is not that they may feel themselves on free and easy terms with Him. Quite the contrary! Schmidt puts it well: "That there is forgiveness with God—and with God alone—does not make the heart light. No, for it is not till one rightly considers this that the true feeling of fear comes: the fear which is other than all fear besides, greater and deeper. For now one knows that there is no way of man's own, no means administered by man, whereby one can come out from the anguish of sin. We are in the depth of our guilt fully dependent on God, who can pardon if He will, and can hold in sin whomsoever it seems

good to Him." Perhaps we cannot quite enter into this last
thought, which is more likely to appeal to Germans than to
Americans. But we can understand how the Psalmist attributes
to God the purpose of creating in man a sense of seriousness
and awe by His kindness. And yet this cannot do full justice
to his thought for he sees in God's aim an *ethical* aspect also.
Man is to obey Him. "This precious confidence of all the sin-
laden, that God is forgiveness, is for them no pillow of rest but
becomes for true religion the spur to full surrender to His
holy will." So writes Staerk; and Kittel adds that what God
really has in mind when He forgives the sinner is the sinner's
own progress.

If these modern commentators comprehend the Psalmist's
thought correctly we perceive that he is uttering a subtle and
profound truth. In his own case, so he implies, forgiveness
would result in more wholehearted conformity to God's demands. And in any case the verse is one of the most arresting
in the Bible, for it flies straight in the face of the common
idea that fear is called forth by severity rather than by love.
It manifests generous confidence in man when it asserts that
he would not take advantage of divine clemency. Altogether
it is a saying of poignant beauty which first challenges, then
compels assent.

Since now he is sure of divine forgiveness being granted, soon
or late, what is his part?

> 5. I loók to Yahwéh—my soúl loóks—    and for his wórd
>    do I waít;
> 6. My soúl to the Lórd—    more than they that wátch for
>    the mórning.*

The Hebrew is broken and almost incoherent, yet there is no
necessity of adopting any of the emendations proposed for who
can fail to see what he means? The next move, so to speak,
is God's and he can do nothing until God acts—nothing but
look. Gunkel believes that he is here offering yet another mo-
tive to induce God to intervene since the portrayal of this
attitude of expectancy is frequently met in the Laments. These
men felt that God loved to have them so wait upon Him. What

the Psalmist is depicting is that eager forward straining of the soul's attention which in the New Testament is called *hope* and is enshrined by the Church in its triad of theological virtues.

Exactly what is he hoping for? The word of God, he says. Now this can hardly be the promises uttered by God in the past (Kittel, Kirkpatrick, Barnes) for he means something not yet existent, something for which he waits. He seems to have in mind rather an absolving word which God shall pronounce in due time, blotting out his sins (Gunkel, Schmidt, Herkenne, Staerk: "a word of comfort"). Just how God will give it he does not indicate but he feels sure he will know it when it comes. Probably he is thinking not of an oracle delivered by a priest, such as we find in some Psalms, but of the inner assurance which coming suddenly to a man turns his night into day.

And how passionately he looks for it! The beautiful comparison by which he would show the intensity of his longing is one of the jewels of the Psalter. More, he declares, than men who high on a tower have kept vigil during the interminable night and now peer into the east for the first gray of dawn.

Thus far the Psalmist has been concerned with his personal need although already he has seen it in its universal setting (v.3). That need has been answered by the tranquil sense of assured forgiveness, which may indeed be delayed but will not disappoint him. Yet he does not stop with this; his thoughts are upon the beloved community to which he belongs. For Israel shares his guilt; it also is laden with iniquity. Like Isaiah he knows that, a man unclean of lips, he dwells in the midst of a people unclean of lips (Is. 6:5); and his heart yearns over his brethren's pain. Why should they continue to suffer when there is a free escape?

> 7. Waít, Ísrael, upon Yahwéh;
>    Fór with Yahwéh is lovingkíndness     and with hím is
>       plénteous redémption.
> 8. And *hé* shall redeém Ísrael     from áll its iníquities.

So, like the Author of Psalm 51, this forgiven man becomes an evangelist. But it is not to those whom men regard as sinners that he turns; for the good tidings he bears have to do with no sharply distinguished group; they are for all. Indeed it may well be that they who have most to gain from his call are the best members of the community—the true Israel, to use Staerk's phrase—for perhaps only the best can understand what he means when he speaks of universal guilt.

What he tells them is that God loves; it is His nature. For that is the significance of the expression "with Yahweh is lovingkindness," just as in verse 4 he said "with thee is pardon." And he uses another term which is destined to play a majestic part in the thought of the Christian Church; "with him is plenteous redemption." The word "redeem" means to ransom, to deliver by paying a price, and this idea of *cost* is not absent even when it is God who redeems. But cost what it may, God will never shrink from paying; there is always enough to meet the price, to deliver from *all* sins. Back of the term lies of course the conviction that man cannot ransom himself—it can only be done by God. For the religion of both the Old Testament and the New is a religion of redemption. The Son of Man gives His life a ransom for many (Mk. 10:45). However difficult this thought may be for modern people, there is no doubt that it is there.

In interpreting this man and his Psalm we have adopted the usual view of recent commentators, that he is burdened with his personal sin, that in some way he has himself destroyed the peace between him and God. But it is possible that the deeps from which he calls are those of national humiliation and guilt while he personally has not offended. There is about his Psalm an undeniably corporate quality which led earlier commentators often to characterise it as the prayer not of an individual but of the congregation. This view has been discarded but it may have contained an element of truth. Perhaps, as Kirkpatrick thinks, our Psalmist is a "representative godly Israelite" of blameless life who comes before God, like the author of Daniel 9, to plead the cause of his people. But even if his own way be pure he takes no comfort in that; he knows that fundamentally he also shares in the universal guilt: who shall stand?

It is this universal note that draws men to him. They who are in *any* deeps, laden with *any* sin, in need of *any* redemption, find in his Psalm the words with which they can voice their longing. Willingly they take their place by his side in the guilt-burdened ranks of a common humanity; they let him speak for them, solaced by the very delicacy with which he forbears to utter any prayer save the prayer that he may be heard; they join in his eager looking for the dawn of divine grace; their dry hearts are watered by the dew of his hope; their agony comes to rest in his gospel of God's lovingkindness and sufficient ransom.

# III

## 2. c. *PSALMS OF TRUST*

The reader may have noticed that the last two men whom we have studied have composed a kind of Lament which differs from those considered previously in that they speak mainly of sin and repentance. And indeed these Psalms do belong to what Gunkel terms a sub-species of the Lament, the *Psalms of Penitence*. Their Authors display the painful consciousness of having sinned against Yahweh and of having therefore merited the punishment threatened by Him. For this reason the complaint over outward troubles, so common in the Laments, is lacking in these Psalms; indeed complaint of any kind does not appear. In their petition they ask for nothing but cleansing, pardon, remission of penalty, renewal of a life pleasing to God. The reason they urge for the granting of these petitions is also unique, for they appeal to God's grace and truth and His kind readiness to forgive sins.

The Psalms of Penitence however are not the only sub-species of Lament that Gunkel notes. There are also the *Psalms Protesting Innocence*,[1] the *Psalms of Cursing and Vengeance*[2] and the *Psalms of Trust*.[3] Each of these is marked by the prominence of some single element of the Lament which dwarfs all others, giving them a distinct character. The first two of these sub-species are not favorites with the modern reader and

---

[1] Pss. 5, 7, 17, 26.

[2] e.g. Psalm 109.

[3] Pss. 4, 11, 16, 23, 27I, 62, 131. It is a weakness in Gunkel's Type scheme that he is compelled to assign to other Types Psalms like Ps. 91 which also express trust in God.

the personalities of their Authors repel us more than they attract or inspire. We may be excused therefore if we pass them over and take up the third sub-species, the Authors of Psalms of Trust. Here we meet with some of the most appealing of all the Psalmists.

"The Psalm of Trust" says Gunkel "is the most effective transformation which the Type of the Lament has undergone. Its germ-cell is the *expression of trust,* in the very form indeed where this mounts to the level on which the one praying no longer needs to lean upon Yahweh. It is therefore not surprising that the Psalm of Trust speaks predominantly of Yahweh in the third person. It is very instructive to notice how the emotion of trust, as it attains independence, increasingly represses the other motifs of the Types."

Psalm 27, which we are now to consider, has carried this process of repression very far, and yet even here the plan of the Lament glimmers through. This will appear as we review the words of its Author.

# The Author of Psalm 27

### *The* Lord *is my light and my salvation*

It is a common opinion among recent commentators that Psalm 27 is not a unit but falls into two independent Psalms, of which the first, Psalm 27:1-6 is a Psalm of Trust, while Psalm 27:7-14 is more of a Lament proper. This division is upheld by Bertholet, Duhm, Gunkel, Kirkpatrick, Kittel, Leslie, McNeile, Herkenne and Staerk. It is grounded on several considerations. Duhm thinks that the Author of the first part is a leader because he speaks of war and hosts being against him, while in the second part the speaker is obviously an ordinary man. Others make more of the difference in *tone* between the two parts, the first expressing trust, the second anguish and fear, though (as Kittel admits) trust also comes to utterance in it. Gunkel lays great stress on the *form* of each part, which is complete in itself, and indicates (he thinks) complete independence of each unit.

There is much truth in what these scholars urge but none of their arguments need be final. Barnes inclines to regard the Psalm as a unit and Schmidt urges the same view. Our own study will be based upon the whole Psalm as the work of a single Author. If the reader disagrees on this point he may use as much as he likes of the material we present, discarding the rest or assigning it to a second personality.

The background of this Psalm is *enemies*. The Psalmist says nothing of sickness or other calamity but much of men who attack him. In the first part he rises above his terror of them, in the second part he succumbs to it again for a moment of agonised calling upon Yahweh but ends with a strong cry of faith. These enemies seem to be bringing accusations against him and Schmidt is led by that fact to suppose that the Psalmist is under indictment and about to be tried in the temple on a capital charge. He therefore puts the Psalm into a Type which he believes he has discovered; it is a *Prayer of One under*

*Indictment,* uttered during the night preceding the trial while
the Psalmist is confined in the sacred precincts, or just before
the trial. Gunkel sets aside this Type as unproven and in fact
the arguments used by Schmidt to establish it are not convincing. But without accepting the Type we may well believe
that in this case the Psalmist is indeed under accusation which
endangers his life. Gunkel adds another factor in his trouble—
that he is far from Jerusalem, a member of the Diaspora, shut
off by distance from coming to the temple that he loves. But
there seems to be no proof of this. We should think of him
rather as living in Palestine, perhaps in Jerusalem.

Let us now turn to his Psalm. He begins with the divine
name, as is so common in the Laments, but Yahweh is not
called upon. The Psalmist has attained a measure of peace
and feels no need to cry to God for help. So he enters upon an
expression of trust, in which Yahweh is used in the third person as subject of the sentence. And yet for all his peace we
can see the trouble above which he has risen for the moment;
the material of a complaint shows plainly through his happy
words of confidence.

> 1. Yahwéh is my líght,[1] and my salvátion;    whóm shall I
>      feár?
>    Yahwéh is the strónghold of my lífe;    whóm shall I
>      dreád?

Yahweh! He, the Power greater than all powers, is my light;
to Him I look for all that makes me glad—"health, rescue,
joy, comfort" (Gunkel); to Him I flee for protection; who is
able to stand between us?

> 2. When evil-dóers cóme upón me    to eát my flésh,
>    Ádversaries and fóes of mine—'tis théy    who must
>      stúmble and fáll.

It is faith that is speaking, not experience. The perfect tenses
which he uses are probably not recounting a past event; they
utter the finality of a great conviction. It *must* be so! (Gunkel).

---

[1] These words in their Latin form, *"Dominus illuminatio mea,"* are the
motto of the University of Oxford.

3. If an encámpment should encámp agaínst me     my
   heárt will not feár;
   If wár should aríse agaínst me     even thén will I trúst.

This is faith! Like the Prophets, he sees God, and before that sight all things earthly shrink into insignificance. And now he utters his heart's desire; yet it is not a petition, as in the Laments, but a simple statement of fact.

4. Óne thing have I ásked of Yahwéh,     ít I seék:
   That I may dwéll in the hoúse of Yahwéh     all the dáys
   of my lífe,
   To gáze upon the pleásantness of Yahwéh     and to con-
   síder his témple.

Here the heart of the Psalmist speaks. He wants nothing material, but only the vision of God, the companionship with Yahweh. And he finds this in the sanctuary and its worship. Here he can see the friendliness, the cheerful kindness, the loveliness of Yahweh. In the Egyptian religion men felt that they beheld the beauty of the god by looking upon his image; but this Israelite can find no statue of Yahweh in the temple nor does he need one; sufficient to him are the holy symbols of the divine presence, the holy places, the acts of worship (Gunkel). The temple with all it contains is to him a sacrament, an outward and visible sign of an inward and spiritual reality. The God he meets there is a God of delight. Within those walls he feels no irksome restraint, no repelling severity. All is intense joy. "When he speaks of 'considering God's temple' we can picture him as he walks through the sanctuary and takes in everything with love and gladness" (Gunkel). "To understand this one must have in mind what the public worship and especially the great feasts in the temple with all their pomp and their tumultuous rejoicing and exulting meant to the oriental, taking captive his innermost soul. Here the Godhead was near to him—its very self, absolutely, immediately" (Kittel).

But the temple is more to him than the place of meeting God; it is an asylum (Gunkel).

5. Fór he hídes me in his tábernacle [1]     in the dáy of évil;

---

[1] The Hebrew word means "hut" or "booth."

> He conceáls me in the sécret place of his tént,    upon
> a róck he lifts me hígh.
> 6. And nów my héad is lifted úp    over my énemies aroúnd
> me.

God not only shelters him, He gives him victory. The sense of
security passes over into the certainty of triumph. In overflowing gratitude he now utters his *vow*.

> I will sácrifice within his tént    sácrifices of shoúting;
> I will síng and make mélody to Yahwéh.

Here, as in the rest of the Psalm, this man's religion blends
the inward with the outward. What he promises to God is material as well as spiritual—animal sacrifices and his song of
thanksgiving. For he seems to mean real sacrifices. Why should
he not? They are to him the channel of intercourse with God,
the ladder reaching up to heaven, no less than the offering of
the lips.

Thus the first part of his Psalm closes with victorious faith
and gratitude. But suddenly, if we accept what follows as a
continuation of his Psalm, an unhappy change descends upon
him. His troubles now sweep over him as a flood and he sends
upward his call to Yahweh:

> 7. Heár, Yahwéh!    with my voíce I crý;    and have
> mércy upon me, and ánswer me.
> 8. Thíne (sáys my héart) is the "Seék ye my fáce";    thy
> fáce, Yahwéh, am I seéking.

He is pleading the divine promises of olden time, perhaps
the words of Jeremiah: "Ye shall seek me and find me" (Jer.
29:13). But it is not, as Kirkpatrick says, necessary to suppose that he has any definite passage in mind for "the invitation is the sum of all revelation." Like the Author of Psalm 51
he sets his hope in the divine love alone, urging nothing else
in his behalf except that he is indeed seeking God. And God
*must* respond to that seeking!

> 9. Híde not thy fáce from mé;
> Túrn not thy sérvant away in ánger; [1]    thou árt my hélp.
> Cást me nót off    and leáve me nót,    O Gód of my
> help.

[1] This sentence hardly gives Kittel ground for saying that the Psalmist
has *deserved* to be turned away.

Then his faith reasserts itself. God will never fail him!

> 10. Though my fáther and móther forsáke me,      yet Yahwéh
> gáthers me up.

We do not know whether he is speaking literally or not. Perhaps his parents have indeed abandoned him, for Job's complaint of the alienation of wife and kinsfolk in extreme trouble (Job 19:13 ff.) shows only too plainly how the fearful belief that a sufferer was under divine wrath could terrify into flight even those closest to him. But he may mean only that God's love is greater, more to be depended on, than the love of father and mother. If so, we have here one of the tenderest portrayals of God's care in all the Bible. Yahweh "gathers him up" as one takes up a foundling child adopting it for his own (Gunkel) or as the rear guard of an army picks up the fainting stragglers [(Is. 58:8) Barnes].

He has uttered one petition—not to be forsaken. Now he asks for another boon:

> 11. Teách me, Yahwéh, thy wáy;
> And leád me in an éven páth      becaúse of those that lie
> in waít for me.

He wants God to show him where he is to go. He himself is in distraction; how can he pass safely through the ambushes of his foes? But Yahweh has a level path for him and can guide him in it. Yet it is a question whether a deeper meaning is not implied in his words. For the path of Yahweh is not only level, it is right; and when he asks to be shown it he makes an ethical surrender to the will of God. Such at least is the impression Staerk receives from his words. "In this trouble he prays for the one thing that to him is needful, the power of an ethically pure life, for a walking in the way of the divine will which indeed he knows but in his human weakness is in danger of leaving."

It is to his immediate perils however that his mind returns.

> 12. Gíve me not over to the desíre of my ádversaries
> For fálse wítnesses have rísen up against me,      and men
> that breáthe out víolence.

> 13. If I had nót beliéved that I would seé    the goódness
>     of Yahwéh
>     In the lánd of the líving.... !

Yes, his situation is indeed desperate. His enemies mean death.
But his faith saves him from collapse—for that is the significance of the broken sentence in verse 13.[1] He is not going
to die![2]

And now this faith surges upward to a triumphant close as he
cries to his own soul:

> 14. Loók unto Yahwéh, be stróng!    and let thy héart be
>     bóld, and loók unto Yahwéh!

So he attains to his "confidence of being heard." The end of
his Psalm returns to the sure trust of its beginning and the
agonised calling upon God of its middle portion is forgotten.
What he has given us is a great Psalm of faith.

And with the faith is mingled a tender, passionate love of
God, in whose house he would fain be forever. Whether he
means this literally or not, we cannot doubt that it utters the
deep joy of his heart in the God whom he meets in the temple.

A final thing that characterises him is his lack of vindictiveness. However much he has to say of his enemies he utters
no imprecation against them. In this he is like the Author of
the 22nd Psalm.

---

[1] Some scholars, omitting the "if," translate "I believe that I will
see...." Here they follow the LXX and the Syriac.

[2] The "land of the living" means the present world of living people.

# The Author of Psalm 16

*Thou shalt show me the path of life*

Psalm 16 stands nearer the Lament than any of the Psalms of Trust. It begins with the Lament's "calling upon God" and its "description of the prayer," and the second person is used in address to God in several verses at the beginning and the end.[1] But in spite of this dependence on the Lament our Psalmist has given us an unmistakable Psalm of Trust, for the mood of glad confidence in God prevails throughout his song. It is this joyous faith combined with the loftiness of the Author's religious tone that has made his utterance so beloved. As McNeile truly says, "the poem is one of the purest gems of the Psalter."

Unlike the writers of Laments, our Psalmist seems to be free from external pressure of any sort. True, he has been in trouble and the echoes of it still resound in his verses; but his present situation is so happy that such echoes are very distant. "The danger, if special danger there was which prompted the prayer of verse 1, lies entirely in the background" (Kirkpatrick). Not all recent commentators indeed share this view. Barnes seems to feel that his past trouble is very vivid still in the Psalmist's mind. Kittel goes even farther and maintains that he is "apparently in great trouble of soul and body" as he writes. But most would agree with Kirkpatrick. "Here," says Schmidt, "all is quiet, brightening joy, deep certainty."

But we must make a distinction. The Psalmist is for all his gladness hardly in a position of worldly ease. Duhm inferred that he was and asserted that "Psalm 16 is the composition of a fortunate man who has Yahweh alone to thank for his good fortune." But Gunkel is surely nearer the truth when he says that this man is "not blessed with earthly treasures." His wealth lies in another sphere, as we shall see, and his gladness

[1] Gunkel-Begrich, *Einleitung*, p. 255.

springs up from within him. All we are pointing out here is that
he is under no load of anguish.

He begins indeed as if he were in some need:

> 1. Presérve me, O Gód, for I have taken réfuge in theé!

This "calling upon God," however, seems from what follows
to be different from the cry of distress that we hear in the
Laments. It is more a petition for constant aid through a life-
time; and the "description of the prayer" portrays an equally
lasting attitude on the Psalmist's part. For in the succeeding
verse he confesses that his soul is permanently centered in God:

> 2. I have saíd * to Yahwéh, My Lórd art thoú,
>    I have no goód but in theé.

There lies the Psalmist's real treasure:—God! And yet God
is for him not a Being to be possessed in isolation; a chief part
of his joy in Yahweh is the companionship of the faithful into
which his own faith brings him:

> 3. As for the hóly that are in the lánd,
>    Théy are * the éxcellent;    all my delíght is in thém.

He knows the pleasure of the "communion of saints."[1] How
such an utterance—and there are others like it in the Old
Testament—enables us to see the fellowship existing in the
ancient Jewish Church among earnestly religious people! The
Psalms are full of it and we must think of these Psalmists as
bathed in its bright warmth for the most part, though at times
they may call out from the cold shadow of loneliness.

But outside that society, set over against it in bitter contrast,
move the people to whom Yahweh is nothing. These look elsewhere for their help, imagining that they find it in the pagan
deities whose worship is evidently wide-spread even among
Israelites. As the Psalmist gazes out from the happy society
of saints his mind contemplates such recreants with horror and
aversion. This he expresses in words which have come to us so
misshapen as to be meaningless.

[1] Gunkel, Schmidt, J. M. P. Smith and Barnes (substantially) read this
difficult passage differently and maintain that the Psalmist is speaking
not of saints but of heathen gods. But the ancient versions all understand
him to mean saints.

4. Their sórrows shall be múltiplied who give gífts for
   anóther god.

That is what we read in the American Revised Version, and
it may be put down for want of something better; but one
can get neither this nor any other clear rendering from the
Hebrew, which is hopelessly corrupt. But the drift of the
Psalmist's words is fairly plain in spite of the condition of
the text. He is speaking of the worship of heathen deities and
renounces it with all the vigor at his command:

> I will not pour oút their drínk-offerings of blóod,
> And I will not take úp their námes upon my líps.

Evidently his fellow Jews, in their recourse to foreign gods,
do not stop short of degrading and cruel rites. Perhaps he has
in mind the sacrifice of children, which seems to have been
revived in Post-Exilic times by desperate people who thought
thus to obtain divine favor by the giving of their most precious
possession. "They slay the children in the valleys, under the
clefts of the rocks," declares a later Prophet (Is. 57:5). Once
this had been done by mistaken men in honor of Yahweh but
the fierce protests of the Prophets had apparently burned into
the minds of all that the God of Israel would have none of
such offerings.[1] Now those who performed these monstrous rites
"took up the names" of other gods "upon their lips." But there
is only one Name that our Psalmist will utter:

> 5. Yahwéh is the portion of my posséssion and of my cúp;
>    Thoú maintaínest my lót!

Thus the Psalmist returns to his favorite thought. Yahweh is
enough for him! "The idea that the grace and companionship
of God, which he apprehends as nothing less than a possessing
of his God, is for him a compensation for everything else, is
clothed by the poet in images taken from the division of the
land and from the feast. As every citizen holds his portion in
the land, as at a feast there is assigned to every guest his cup,
and with it his share of drink and food, so to him God Himself
has been assigned for his whole life as portion and property.
And this inheritance does not pass. Earthly goods can be dis-

[1] cf. Jer. 7:31, Ezek. 20:26, Mic. 6:7.

sipated or seized by force: this lot...Yahweh holds fast with his own hand" (Kittel).

He goes on to tell the delight that he has in God:

> 6. The línes have fállen for me in pleásant places
> Yes, my \* inhéritance is beaútiful to mé.

Here again he is using the metaphor of land division; he has come off well in the clan allotment of the common glebe (Schmidt). In his words echo the farmer's love of the soil, his sense of the loveliness of some fair field, free of stones, with its trees[1] and perhaps its spring of water welling up. Only it is not of any field that he is speaking but of the living God.

The thing above all others which makes him happy in his possession of God is the fact that God directs him in his way:

> 7. I will bléss Yahwéh who gives me coúnsel;
> Yes, in the níghts my reíns admónish me.

He does not want a God who lets him have his own desire; he craves rather the stern discipline which shapes him to higher ends. Evidently he has in mind the warnings of conscience, in which he sees the instruction of God himself. Thus the Psalmist with extraordinarily fine and profound perception brings out the uniqueness of the experience of God in Israel's religion: it is the religion of the holy "Thou shalt," of the moral command (Schmidt). "In the nights," he says; for "his conscience speaks to him especially in the night, when the soul becomes quiet and thinks on itself and what it owes God" (Kittel: cf. Pss. 4:4, 42:8, etc.).

From the thought of discipline he passes over to that of the life-attitude which brings him complete repose of mind and un-failing joy:

> 8. I have sét Yahwéh befóre me álways,
> If hé \* is on my right hánd I shall not be sháken.
> 9. Therefore my heárt rejoíces and my glóry[2] exúlts,
> Yes, my flésh dwélls in cónfidence.

He has been mounting up to his climax and he reaches it as he declares what is the ground of his trust:

---

[1] cf. Gen. 23:17.
[2] Probably "my liver."

10. For thou dost nót abándon my soúl to Shéol,
    Thou dost not gíve thy gódly one to seé the pít.
11. Thou makest me to knów the páth of lífe,
    Fúlness of jóys is in thy présence,
    Pleásures in thy right hánd for éver.

If we had nothing else from our Psalmist but these two verses, we should owe him a great debt; for they gather up in a little cluster of sayings his chief contribution to religion.

First, his trust. God, he declares, will not permit him to die. At first sight his words seem to affirm a belief in survival of the grave; and so they were interpreted by St. Peter in his Pentecostal sermon, being applied to the Messiah. St. Peter's point, it will be recalled, was this: David (whom of course St. Peter took to be the Author) thus predicted that God would not allow "my soul" to remain in Hades; yet David manifestly could not have meant his own soul, for he had continued in Hades since his death; he must therefore have in mind the Messiah, and be foretelling Christ's resurrection (Acts 2:25 ff.). The Messianic part of this interpretation is accepted by no Protestant scholar of the present era, so far as I know.[1] There is, on the other hand, some disposition to look on the Psalmist's words as referring to life beyond death. The late A. B. Davidson held that the Psalmist is asserting his own freedom from death because of his possession of God. "He does not contemplate dying and being restored to life. Rather, those gigantic personalities, Sheol and Shahath, that open their mouth for him, shall have no power over him."[2] Of contemporary writers both Welch[3] and Barnes retain the same general view of the Psalmist's meaning. "God will not suffer all this (his life with God) to come to an end in the cul-de-sac of death, for what is of real must be of enduring worth." So Welch interprets and adds: "It (Ps. 16) is the culmination of the attitude on human destiny which appears throughout the Psalter" (p. 117). Barnes argues at length that the Psalmist means survival, basing his

---

[1] Herkenne attributes the Psalm to David, who in v.1-8 is speaking of himself and in v.9-11 of the Messiah. Oesterley denies its Messianic application. *Fresh Approach*, etc., p. 189.
[2] *Old Testament Theology*, New York, 1904, p. 447.
[3] *The Psalter*, p. 114 ff.

view chiefly on the whole tone of the Psalm and on the expressions in v.11 which go beyond mere earthly goods. König takes the same view.

Attractive as this interpretation is it does not commend itself to the majority of recent writers. They would agree with Gunkel when he says: "Verse 10 is only a magnificent triumphant utterance of the certainty that the Psalmist will remain preserved from sudden, premature death." This view, Gunkel holds, is established by the parallel passages in the Thank-Psalms, where the poets speak of having been lifted or brought up from death,[1] plainly referring to recovery from mortal peril. The majority of scholars range themselves on this side.[2] Kirkpatrick a generation ago interpreted the verse in the same way, citing Cheyne's words: "His (the Psalmist's) antithesis is not this world and the next, but life with God and life without God."

It seems safer therefore to claim for our Psalmist no clear vision of immortality. His complete confidence in God's protecting care contemplates only preservation through his threescore years and ten. But the fact that it does not go all the way should not obscure the peace which it bestows. And that brings us to his second contribution, his delight in God.

No one can read his Psalm without being struck by the frequency with which there occur in it words expressing happiness and enjoyment: "my good," "my delight," "pleasant," "beautiful," "rejoices," "exults," "confidence," "fulness of joys," "pleasures for ever." It is as if the whole Psalm were flooded with dancing sunlight. There can be no question but that this man has somehow found the secret of gladness; he is not merely talking about it, he *has* it. And he tells where he gets it—in his "possession" of God. Here is the "path of life," concerning which the Wise Men have so much to say; for the true life, as Cheyne reminds us, is life with God.

God, he declares, is his *only* good; and there is no reason

---

[1] e.g. Pss. 9:14, 30:4.
[2] Bertholet, Duhm, Kittel, Leslie, Oesterley (*Fresh Approach*, etc., p. 265), McNeile, Staerk and Eichrodt (*Theologie des Alten Testaments*, Leipzig, 1935, II, p. 114). Cook (*Old Testament*, p. 135) is non-committal.

why we should not believe him. We have seen that he is probably not rich or successful or honored by the world, as Duhm imagines. Surely something more is impelling him to sing than "his feeling of prosperity." And again we have seen that he has chosen the good part which shall not be taken from him. Duhm is mistaken here also in wondering whether he would stand such a testing as that of Job. Indeed Duhm has quite too low a concept of this man's inner life when he says: "To the Christian idea of the world and life his naïve joy in external well-being and his confident faith in its continuance would hardly be satisfying." On the contrary, the modern Christian might well be thankful if his own heart were thus "fixed where true joys are to be found."

For the fact is that this saint of the Old Testament has attained a height in the life with God that most of us today must acknowledge to be above us. He belongs, with the Author of Psalm 73, to those purest souls who fly to God as the moth to the flame. God to him is not a background, not something added to life, not merely one among many interests; He is all. His mystic communion with God is toughened and made vigorous by the stern ethical sense which chastens and disciplines his mind; nor is its joy thereby dimmed, for in this very "counselling" of God he finds his supreme reason for thanksgiving. It bears its fruit in that cleansing of his heart which restrains him from malediction upon those who wilfully turn from the happiness Yahweh can give. In all his Psalm there is not one false ethical note—nothing, that (to use Horace's phrase) one "would take away." Its single lack is of the widened horizon which belief in survival gives. And perhaps Kittel is right in thinking that he is not so far even from that faith. The thought of such companionship with the eternal God might well lead on to the thought of its outlasting death. "The veil over the bound of human life is for our poet not yet lifted; but it needs only the push, so to speak, of a finger to lift it." So his last word "for ever" trembles on the verge of the "life everlasting."

*The* LORD *is my shepherd*

Psalm 23 is the supreme classic of the Psalter. For a classic is that which is used and does not wear out, but grows fresher and more satisfying always. Many of the Psalms are classics in this sense, but Psalm 23 is more used today and doubtless in the past has been more used than any other, and continues to satisfy the needs of the religious heart more widely than perhaps any other. It is learned by heart by so many that in almost any gathering of religious people in North America enough persons will be found to make possible its being said in concert from memory, as the Lord's Prayer can be said. Doubtless this is due to its use in the public schools. It seems to fit in with almost any situation in life, to be welcomed in hospitals and homes, in joy and sorrow, among young and old. One needs only to begin repeating it and a hush falls upon any group; they listen as to the accents of the soul's mother tongue. Childhood knows and responds to it; and at the other end of life the dying repose in it as they go down into the shadow of death.

The man who composed it could not foresee this. He did but express in six short verses his own trust in God. How could he know that after two thousand years they would be a household word to millions? Yet to him it was given to say something which the heart of man needed to have said, to say it briefly, completely, with a beauty that is final. It can never be said again as he said it; the mould is broken in which his poem was cast.

As we approach our study of such a man we are conscious of the needlessness of our undertaking. Has he not been speaking to generations for himself? Why should any presume to interpret him who has interpreted to humanity its own deep childlikeness towards God? And yet there is always something to be gained by looking once more upon the intimate and the

familiar, by striving to know afresh one whom we know as we
know few others.

He has given us a Psalm of Trust. In it he tells what Yahweh
is to him, how in the varied experiences of life he has found
Him satisfying. As is natural in a Psalm of Trust the tone is
one of quiet confidence, or happy brooding. The Psalmist is
evidently not a young man; few young men could speak as
he speaks. He has lived long enough to know the vicissitudes
of man's lot, "the sundry and manifold changes of the world,"
and he has learned what God does for him in them all. For the
moment he is apparently free from stress. A serene sunlight
falls upon his Psalm, it opens and closes with words of peace.
Yet he tells of darkness and enemies; the time has been when
he came to grips with these and the time will be again. He
knows it and yet the thought does not terrify him; for the
sunlight now about him is greater than they, it will outlast
them and overcome them.

We have seen that the Psalm of Trust has so attained this
mood of peace that it need not address God in the second
person, calling on Him to save; it can think upon Him in the
third person. That is what our Psalmist does, beginning his
meditation with the great divine Name which is its theme.

1. Yahwéh is my shépherd,    I láck nót,
2. In pástures of gráss he makes me lie dówn,
   Beside wáters of rést he leáds me; 3 he restóres my soúl,
   He guídes me in páths of ríght    for his náme's sáke.

Here is the first of the two metaphors which our Psalmist
employs to portray God's relationship to him: the shepherd.
Every one in Palestine knew the shepherd; he was one of the
commonest of sights, as he is today in the same country. The
modern traveller as he goes about the Judean landscape often
meets him, a bearded man in flowing head-dress and graceful
striped robe, walking at the head of his sheep, sometimes
carrying a lamb in his arms. He has two responsibilities; to find
food for his flock and to protect them from beasts and robbers.
Without him the sheep are helpless; they starve or fall an
easy prey. With him they are secure and they know it.

Our Psalmist is by no means the first to see in this well-known figure a symbol of God who cares for His trusting people. Prophets and other Psalmists use it freely in speaking of Yahweh's relationship to Israel as a nation and in this sense of a responsible ruler over a community it is commonly applied in the Old Testament to kings and other public officials. The new thing in this Psalm is that an individual appropriates it to himself. Yahweh is *my* shepherd. The Psalmist does not of course separate himself from the flock, he recognises that he is part of a group which share in the benefits of God's provision; but his thought is none the less upon the personal relationship between the Shepherd and the single sheep.[1] And indeed he is justified in making much of this for the human shepherd knows his sheep as individuals, he cares for each one, calls each by its name. When it is lost he leaves all the others to seek it out, and if he finds it he rejoices over it more than over all the rest. So at least the New Testament, itself a Jewish book, tells us; and there is no reason to doubt the accuracy of the picture.

Of the shepherd's two responsibilities the opening verses deal with the first. In his endeavor to see that the sheep lacks not he guides it by right paths to one of the rare spots in arid Judah where water welling through the soil keeps the grass green. Here beside a pool or trickling brook the sheep eats its fill, slakes its thirst and lies down at noon-tide to rest on the pleasant sward. Its strength is revived, its "soul restored."

Such is the idyllic picture whose delightful imagery has done much to endear the Psalm to Bible readers. Translated into plain speech it means that the Psalmist has always been richly provided for by God's care; that he has had enough of sus-

---

[1] It is strange that Baethgen and Theodore of Mopsuestia whom he follows could have overlooked the intensely personal nature of this Psalm and have thought that the Psalmist was speaking in the name of Israel. Mowinckel is not guilty of this absurdity, but (true to his thesis that most of the Psalms were written for occasions of worship) does not regard Psalm 23 as a "purely private outpouring of the heart, individual in the modern sense, occasioned by nothing special, an expression of a continuous mood of a single, individually-stamped saint," but as a Thanksgiving Psalm composed for the thanksgiving sacrifice feast. At the same time he feels that the poet's own experiences echo in it. (*Psalmenstudien* I, p. 126.)

tenance and beauty and joy; that he is confident that God is ever leading him in "right paths," paths going surely to their goal of life and health and gladness, not paths which wander aimlessly. And God does this "for His Name's sake," because He Himself is what He is; just as the shepherd guides his sheep truly because he is a shepherd.

From food, drink and rest the Psalmist now turns to the other good which it is the shepherd's duty to provide—protection; and here the third person gives place to the warmer "Thou."

> 4. Yeá, though I wálk    in the válley of dárkness [1]    I will
>     feár no évil;
>     For thoú art wíth me,    thy ród and thy stáff    théy
>     cómfort me.

When the sun gets low and the shepherd starts homeward with his flock it is presently necessary to descend into some deep ravine where the shadow of night has already fallen. In it may be lurking a wild beast ready to leap upon the passing sheep or a still more deadly robber famished for meat. The shepherd strides ahead, his formidable club ready for any assault; and the sheep follow, seeing him there with weapon in hand; follow trembling but secure—comforted, our Psalmist quaintly says. So in the hour when enemies rush on him the Psalmist walks unafraid for is not God with him, able to overcome them all?

And now the metaphor shifts. God is the host who receives the traveller into His tent, affording him asylum from his pursuing foes and entertaining him with His best while they look on impotent and abashed.

> 5. Thou prepárest befóre me a táble    in frónt of my
>     énemies;
>     Thou hast anoínted with oíl my heád,    my cúp runs
>     óver.

Hospitality in the East calls for lavish expenditure; men are to be found who boast that their generosity to guests has

---

[1] The rendering "shadow of death" is based upon an ancient vocalisation of the Hebrew consonants which is now generally discarded.

brought them to poverty. God falls no whit behind the most
generous of them. He proffers the Psalmist all that heart could
wish, the loaded table, the overflowing cup, the festal oil upon
the hair; and He does this to rebuke those who seek the
guest's hurt, the enemies who would discredit him. It is as if
God said: "See, this is my friend; let him alone!"

As it has been and is now, so shall it ever be:

> 6. Only goód and lovingkíndness shall pursué me        all the
> dáys of my lífe.

Many a time he will hear pursuing footsteps behind him
and his heart will throb with quick fear; but when the supposed enemies overtake him he will look back into their faces
and behold none but the dear familiar friends sent after him
by God—Good and Lovingkindness! But in a deeper sense he
will never leave the tent of his Host:

> And I shall dwéll [1] in the hoúse of Yahwéh        to the léngth
> of dáys.

Like the Author of Psalm 27 this Psalmist pictures as his
highest good a lifetime spent within the temple. Not that he
will forsake the outer world, but he will continually visit the
sanctuary and find his real joy there. There will he abide "to
the length of days!" [2]

Having now reviewed this Psalmist's poem let us pause to
consider its place in the religion of Israel. He speaks throughout of what he receives from God and he means that he gets
quite literally the things he mentions—food, drink, rest, protection, vindication. His theme then is God the Supplier of
man's needs, physical as well as spiritual. True, he also loves
God for Himself and takes pleasure in His companionship; for
this appears plainly in the Psalm in spite of the fact that it is
not expressly spoken of. He is likewise aware of the condition
of such companionship with its attendant blessings. One must

---

[1] The Hebrew text has "I shall return" instead of "I shall dwell." The
ancient versions however have "dwell" and the American Revised and the
Jewish Versions adopt this reading. Most modern commentators do the
same, though Barnes and Schmidt keep "I shall return."

[2] Herkenne thinks that the Psalmist does not have in mind the temple
but is speaking figuratively of the continued enjoyment of God's presence.

walk in the paths of righteousness. He is glad that he has such a God, who cannot but exact this "for His name's sake," because He is what He is. For the metaphor of "right paths," when transferred from a sheep to a man, can mean only righteousness; it is ethical through and through, as Kirkpatrick and Davison correctly perceive.

And yet the note of *receiving* does predominate in the Psalm. This note indeed is good and the mood of the Psalmist is a necessary strain in religion. But it has its dangers. Of one such danger several clear thinkers of the Old Testament were fully aware. There is no guarantee that the Psalmist will continue to receive the divine favors which now make him so happy. In a sense, he knows this for he recognises that there are dark valleys dividing the sunny pastures; but one wonders whether he has ever had the experience of Job who saw the Shepherd apparently turn against him, saw all the rich divine gifts he had enjoyed rudely snatched away while the hand that had bestowed them "took him by the neck and dashed him in pieces" (Job 16:12). It seems that in the Psalmist's case the Shepherd's club has always been used to beat off enemies before they could inflict real "evil"; and he expects that to be true in the future also. But the reverse may happen, as it has countless times. And then what will he say?

Once more, even if he himself escapes such a fate how can he close his eyes to the grim fact that too many do not escape it? His happy song then cannot be for all, but only for the fortunate ones who come clear of great adversity. This too was seen by Job, whose own harsh lot took on new horror against the wider background of God's apparent misgovernment in the world (Job 21). Qoheleth perceived it also and it deepened the sombreness of his despair (Eccles. 3:16 ff.).

Finally, his mood tends to a naïve acceptance of well-being as God's gift, to a repose in prosperity which approaches complacence. After all, how does the Psalmist know that God really intends him to lie down in the green pastures? He seems to ignore another strain in Israel's religion which goes deeper than the mood of his Psalm and has wrought greater things—

the strain which may be called heroic. We find it in men like Moses and Jeremiah and indeed all the Prophets. It comes to perfect flower in Him who said: "The Son of Man is not come to be ministered unto but to minister, and to give his life a ransom for many" (Mk. 10:45). It is a mood which turns its back on grassy meadows and waters of rest, on loaded tables and overflowing cups. The head of him who cherishes it is not anointed with oil but grimy with the dust of work. It carries heavy burdens in dry places. Instead of being shepherded it shepherds.

The Psalm then is no complete expression of the religion of Israel or of our own. It is a Psalm of Trust, not of Aspiration or even of Penitence. But a realisation of this fact only brings out its value. For, as has been said, the strain which it utters is a necessary element in religion. Even those who renounce the green pastures of earth need to find others in which they may lie down, and the most selfless servants of mankind are often the very ones to win from this Psalmist's words a meaning which only they can understand. The Son of Man, who had not where to lay His head, who came not to send peace upon earth but a sword, did yet dwell in the very heart of sunlit peace and could bid all who labor to come unto Him and find rest for their souls.

"The LORD is my shepherd." There is no one in our restless sophisticated age who does not need the peace and healing and strength which still pour fresh from our Psalmist's words upon any soul that will receive them as a little child. This is the more true because in our English Bible they have taken on an overtone which comes not from the Psalmist but from the Christian faith in Christ and immortality:

> Yea, though I walk through the valley of the shadow of death, I will fear no evil: for thou art with me; thy rod and thy staff they comfort me....
>
> And I will dwell in the house of the LORD forever.

# IV

# AUTHORS OF THANKSGIVINGS
# OF THE INDIVIDUAL

THE STUDY OF the Laments of the Individual has brought us by the way of the Psalms of Trust to the threshold of another Type of Psalms which we must now consider. These are the Thanksgivings of the Individual. In ancient Israel it was the custom, when a man had been delivered from some mortal trouble, to bring to the temple a thank-offering and at the same time to express gratitude to God for his goodness. Both these gifts—the sacrifice and the words of gratitude—were called in Hebrew by the same name—*tôdā*.

It is perfectly plain therefore what connection the Thanksgiving had with worship. And indeed in the score of Thanksgivings now extant in the Psalter there are allusions to the sacrifice offered,[1] to the presentation of the cup of salvation before the drink-offering,[2] to the sacred meal accompanying the sacrifice[3] and to the joyous procession which began outside the temple[4] in order to pass through the "gates of righteousness,"[5] concluding with the dance of the festal congregation around the altar.[6]

The occasion of the Thanksgiving was personal and it was therefore not connected with any public feast. The man who had received the benefit from God came to the temple as soon

[1] Pss. 66:13ff., 107:22, 116:17, 27:6, 56:12.
[2] Ps. 116:13.
[3] Ps. 22:26.
[4] Ps. 100:2, 4.
[5] Ps. 118:19.
[6] Ps. 118:27.

as convenient after his deliverance to render thanks and pay
his vows. This might take place, so far as we know, on any
day. He was the center of it all and it was his feast. But he
did not come alone. With him appeared as his invited guests
his relatives, friends, acquaintances and those bound to him
by any other tie, prepared to rejoice with him. They surrounded him when he presented his sacrifice, took part in the
joyous procession and ate with him the festal meal. The poor
also might be brought in as guests. To this company would
be added the rest of the people who were at the time gathered
in the temple, who would take their share gladly in the rejoicing. All this shows the mood prevailing in these festivals:
"they were the fairest hours in the life of the religious man."

In most of the Thanksgivings the offerer alone speaks or
rather sings. He addresses himself to the friends and companions who surround him, calling them by such names of
honor as "religious people," "righteous," "holy," "worshippers
of Yahweh," "lowly" and the like. And his song is the central
point of the feast. To give *words* this position of honor is
in accord with the spiritual loftiness of Israel; and that these
words should be clothed in poetic form is explainable from
the poetic gift of the people. In early days the Thanksgivings
were composed by priests or temple singers and put into the
mouth of the individual; but the time came when lay-poets
of genius created their own Thanksgivings. Harp and lutes
accompanied the rendering of the song.[1]

The Thanksgiving usually falls into several parts:

1. The *Introduction,* like that of the Hymns, in which the
Psalmist declares that he intends to praise God for his goodness, or calls on his friends to do so. In this Introduction
one word is never omitted—*Yahweh.* "From the very beginning the Psalmist must declare to which God his Psalm is
addressed ... *Yahweh* is written on the front of his poem, as
it were, in great capital letters."

2. One of the most important parts of the Thanksgiving,
one that is never omitted and therefore constitutes an abso-

[1] Pss. 43:4, 71:22.

lutely certain indication of the Type, is the *Narration* of his trouble by the Psalmist. He feels in duty bound not to keep to himself what Yahweh has done but to tell it to his friends, often giving it the first place in his Psalm and even repeating it or taking up the whole Psalm with it. From the prominent place he gives it we can see that this Narration of God's gracious gifts is the most important thing he has to say. It is therefore the characteristic content of the Thanksgiving.

These Narrations show that the trouble out of which God has delivered the Psalmist is no common one but a matter of life and death; only such is deemed worthy of a Thanksgiving. Yet when we ask what it is, we are baffled by the vagueness of the expressions used, a vagueness inherited from the days when such Psalms were merely formulae used in worship.

The Narration usually contains three portions: the recounting of the *trouble,* of the Psalmist's *calling upon God,* and of his *deliverance.* In many cases the trouble seems to be a serious illness bringing the sufferer near to death. Psalm 107 however exhibits various kinds of misfortune, each told of by a group of rescued pilgrims—travellers losing their way in the wilderness, prisoners languishing in jail, seamen in a storm. Or it might be inability to get home from a strange land,[1] or sore need of help in battle.[2] Again, the Psalmist may have experienced the onset of foes, their false accusations and malicious slanders;[3] or in sickness have felt the contempt of the community.

Often the Psalmist acknowledges that the trouble was due to his own sin and speaks of it with penitence, telling how his suffering brought him to contrition and how on confession he obtained God's forgiveness.

3. Another principal element in the Thanksgiving is the Psalmist's *Acknowledgment* of Yahweh's deliverance from trouble; indeed, the Hebrew word to thank (hôda) means

---

[1] cf. 2 Sam. 15:8, Gen. 28:20, 31:13.
[2] cf. Num. 21:2, Jud. 11:30ff., Is. 19:21.
[3] cf. Pss. 9:3, 30:1, 71:24, 92:11, etc.

"to acknowledge." Yahweh alone, he cries, is true; Yahweh alone helps. Trust him! With such words the Psalmist commonly exhorts his hearers, telling the faith he himself has come to after his experience.

4. The Psalmist may conclude with the *Announcement* of a thank-offering which he is now presenting. In later days, when some Psalmists had come to reject animal sacrifice, the poet may declare that he is bringing to God his Thanksgiving itself instead of announcing a thank-offering.[1]

Along with this individual form of the Thanksgiving stands another. We have seen how the Psalmist is surrounded by friends and relatives to whom he sings his acknowledgment of Yahweh's benefits. In Psalm 22 we find him urging these companions to praise Yahweh for themselves.[2] It must have been quite the rule for them to do so and we may picture these "poor" accompanying the Psalmist into the temple with a Thanksgiving of their own. This commonly took the form of the verse preserved in Jeremiah (33:11) and recurring in a number of the Psalms:[3] "Thank Yahweh, for he is good, for his mercy endureth forever."

It was easy then for such chorus Thanksgivings to be woven into a Thank-Psalm, forming a single unit, in which the Psalmist is answered by the chorus and in turn answers, or the reverse.[4] This is done in Psalm 118, a great Liturgy of Thanksgiving "where the voices of all the participants, the Individual and his friends, together with the blessing of the Priests, resound antiphonally." Or again, groups of thankful persons could be assembled to sing a Mass-Thanksgiving, in which group after group utter their gratitude for various deliverances from trouble.[5]

As time went on the simple form of the Thanksgiving was thought to be too cold and it was enriched by drawing upon other Types. One of these, strange to say, was the Lament.

[1] cf. Pss. 116:13, 17-19, 27:6, 118:19ff.
[2] Ps. 22:26.
[3] Jer. 33:11, Ps. 106:1, 107:1, 118:1-4.
[4] e.g. Ps. 66.
[5] Ps. 107.

It might be thought that between the Thanksgiving and the Lament there could exist no common tie; but the contrary is the fact. For in the Thanksgiving the Psalmist has just emerged from the suffering and danger which give rise to the Lament and thanks God for delivering him from them. Hence the two Types are closely related and fit together, as Gunkel says, like the halves of a shell. So we find the Author of a Thanksgiving, when he narrates his trouble, giving the words he uttered in the midst of his agony; and these take the form of a Lament.[1] The reverse happens when the Author of a Lament, suddenly becoming certain that God has heard his outcries and will deliver him, passes from complaint to gratitude and praise.[2]

Another Type on which the Authors of Thanksgivings drew was the Hymn. This lay near at hand, for the same note of rejoicing in Yahweh is fundamental to both Types. The difference is that in the Thanksgiving the Psalmist exults over a particular benefit which God has just conferred upon him while in the Hymn he sings of God's great deeds and glorious attributes in general. It is hard to keep these two things apart and so we meet in the Thanksgivings hymnic portions and in the Hymns bits of thanksgiving.[3] The Authors of Thanksgivings became indebted also to the Prophets, though more for the prophetic depreciation of sacrifices than for any features of detail.[4] They obtained a contribution likewise from the Wise Men, introducing didactic bits where the Psalmist assumes the role of a teacher giving instruction to his friends on the basis of experience.[5]

To Gunkel's mind the most important development of the Thanksgiving from the point of view of the history of religion took place when it began to free itself from the Thank-offering. Here it followed a line already taken by the Type in Babylonia and Egypt. In some instances one cannot be sure

[1] e.g. Pss. 30:9f, 31:22a, 32:5ab, etc.
[2] e.g. Ps. 22:22ff.
[3] e.g. Pss. 30:12, 103:2-5.
[4] e.g. Pss. 40:6, 50:14, 51:16f.
[5] e.g. Pss. 32:8f, 34:12-15.

whether the apparent ignoring of sacrificial worship implies any abandonment of it; but there are Thanksgivings in which the Psalmists unmistakably reject sacrifices and speak of the Psalm as the only gift God desires, the only gift worthy of Him.[1] Here the soul, loosed from the bands of the cultus, comes before its God. And yet, strange to say, these very Psalmists still continue to sing their Thanksgivings in the temple. "The impression of the holy places with their lovely adornment, their many inspired men, their antique memories, their ineradicable feeling that here man is near his God and may 'see his face,' was still, even for these spirits who no longer prized the crude sacrifice, so great that it remained the accepted thing, when they wished to utter a song of thanksgiving, to choose the temple as the place for doing so."

As development went further even the use of the temple gave place to the singing of Thanksgivings in private houses; but we cannot be sure how general this custom became. A number of such Thanksgivings do not mention the temple yet their silence does not prove that they were rendered in the home of the singer.[2]

Originally the Thanksgivings were composed by temple officials; and to this group we may assign such of the Thank-Psalms as exhibit a markedly stereotyped, monotonous and impersonal character. Later however the laity took over the Type and used the traditional forms to produce poems out of their own experience, some of them works of genius revealing unmistakably the hand of a great poet. It is from these that the Psalms will be selected for our own study.

The Thanksgiving as it existed in Israel did not stand alone; in Babylonia, Egypt, Phoenicia and even Greece we find poems of the same Type, exhibiting a noble spirituality. Among them are two of remarkable beauty, both antedating the Israelite poems; the so-called Psalm of the Babylonian Job, and the Thanksgiving of the Egyptian Neb-re for the recovery of his

---

[1] e.g. Pss. 40:6, 50:14, 51:16f.
[2] e.g. Pss. 7:17, 13:6, 28:6f., etc.

son.[1] These show that the Israelites were the inheritors of a general world-culture, in which Thanksgivings had an already recognized place.

Consider now several Authors of Individual Thanksgivings preserved in the Psalter.

[1] See G. A. Barton, *Archaeology and the Bible*, 7th ed. Phila., 1937, p. 491. Also D. C. Simpson, *The Psalmists*. Oxford, 1926, p. 185f.

# The Author of Psalm 32

*Blessed is he whose unrighteousness is forgiven*

We have seen that a Thanksgiving might be offered to God for different kinds of deliverance, the most common being recovery from serious illness. The man whom we are about to study however stands almost alone among the Psalmists in that he thanks God for the gift of forgiveness. His trouble has been the burden of a guilty conscience and God has removed it.

It is this fact of his liberation that distinguishes him on the other hand from those writers of Laments who tell of their sin, such as the Author of Psalm 51. They are in the midst of the anguish of penitence, but he has come through to the other side. Looking back on his experience he is conscious of unutterable happiness. His heart is bursting with thanksgiving and he begins by pouring it out.

But instead of declaring that he is about to praise Yahweh for His goodness, or calling upon his companions to join him in doing so, as is usual in the Introduction to this Type of Psalm, he breaks forth into an opening beatitude:

1. Bléssed he whose transgréssion is taken awáy, whose sín is cóvered!
2. Bléssed the mán to whom Yahwéh does not réckon iníquity,
   And there is nót in his spírit deceít!

He means himself of course; and yet he means something transcending self, something universal. For as Gunkel points out (*Einleitung*, p. 277) a beatitude differs from the usual utterance of thanks in this, that the Psalmist who employs it looks away for a moment from himself and thinks of the great body of religious people, for whom he wishes his own gladdening experience. Such thought for others characterises our Psalmist throughout his song.

We must remember also that he is giving thanks to God.

Now the beatitude is a very beautiful way of doing this. It puts the Psalmist and his happiness in the wider setting of God's mercies to mankind. And its very indirectness, its seeming to be occupied in the blessedness of him who receives the divine favor, brings out all the more the goodness of God from whom it flows.

He has begun, so to speak, with the end of his story. Now, after his Introduction, he presses on at once to the Narration of his trouble:

3. While I kept sílence my bónes wore awáy     through my roáring all the dáy;
4. For dáy and níght thy hánd     was heávy upón me, My moísture was túrned to the droúght of súmmer.

What a picture of fevered suffering! But it is described in the usual vague way of the Psalmists which prevents us from knowing whether he is speaking of physical illness or only of mental distress. In either case he leaves no doubt as to the cause of his anguish. It was his refusal to confess. Some sin was on his conscience and he persisted in glossing it over. We get no inkling of what it may have been but we can see that it was serious—one that held him back from peace with God. Down in his heart he knew that relations would never be right between him and Yahweh until it should be cleared away. Yet he refused to grapple with it. To use a phrase of today, he was probably "rationalising" his conduct. In consequence, he persisted in shutting his eyes to the meaning of his pain. He roared over it in violent protest and all the while he knew that it was only what he must expect from God.

So things went from bad to worse till his resistance broke:

5. My sín I acknówledged to theé     and my iníquity I did not híde;
   I saíd, I will conféss concérning,     my transgréssion to Yahwéh;
   And thoú didst take awáy the iníquity of my sín.

Simple words but telling of how great a revolution within! We can see the final resolve: "I said." We can hear the outpouring of the guilty heart, perhaps in words like those of Psalm 51. And we can feel the immediate relief, the assurance of the answer. For his words imply that it *was* immediate.

From that moment the Psalmist entered into the blessedness of which he speaks in his opening beatitude. How plain to him now is the true course for any one burdened with guilt!

> 6. For thís shall every gódly man make supplicátion to theé
>    In the tíme of fínding.[1]

The moment one can get at God—can find Him—let him ask God's forgiveness. How foolish to imitate his stubborn silence when acknowledgment and penitence open the door to gladness! And along with the gladness, security.

> Súrely in the overflówing of greát wáters    unto hím they
>    shall not come neár.

As has been said, this Psalmist has a tendency to look beyond himself and put his personal experience into the universal frame of God's dealings with mankind. He is doing that here. But now he comes back to what the divine forgiveness means to him.

> 7. Thoú art a híding-place to mé,    from troúble thou dost
>    guárd me,
>    With sóngs of delíverance thou dost surroúnd me.

Perhaps, as Schmidt thinks, he means the songs and ringing cries of joy which are resounding all about him as he stands in the temple court in the midst of many who have come to utter their Thanksgivings. But more probably his mind is upon his whole future. On every side will be safety and jubilations!

Once more he turns to his fellow-men and assuming the role of a Wise Man—for has he not gained Wisdom?—he addresses them in the person of friends and companions. Thus his Thanksgiving is enriched by a dash of the didactic.

---

[1] Finding what? Grace, says König. Baethgen, Barnes, Kirkpatrick, Kittel and Leslie (apparently) say, God. The passage is thus a reminiscence of Is. 55:6. This is the interpretation that appeals to the present writer. On the other hand Bertholet, Briggs, Gunkel, Herkenne, Schmidt and Staerk emend to read: "in the time of distress."

8. I will instrúct thee and teách thee in the wáy that thou
     shalt gó,
   I will give coúnsel, my éye upón thee.
9. Bé ye not like hórse and múle, without understánding
   Whose tráppings must be brídle and hálter to hold them ín
   Else they will nót come neár theé.

The Hebrew of this passage is obscure and probably corrupt
but it is easy to see what the Psalmist means. He is thinking
of the manner in which he had himself acted towards God,
going his own way with no more sense than an animal till
God's bridle brought him up short. Such stupidity can have
only one result:

10. Mány the paíns for the wícked!    But he who trústs in
    Yahwéh—lovingkíndness surroúnds him!

Then leaving off his strain of Wisdom he brings his song to
its close with a genuine hymnic Conclusion:

11. Rejoíce in Yahwéh and exúlt, ye ríghteous,
    And sing for jóy, áll ye that are úpright of heart!

In forming an estimate of this Psalmist we are confronted
with two diverging views among scholars, a high view and a
low one. To begin with the low view. Gunkel warns that Christians are apt to admire him more than he deserves because
they find in his words an echo of their own experience. Our
Psalmist, he believes, would never have accused himself of
any sin if he had not become ill. In fact, he had not really
sinned in any serious way and he ought like Job to have
refused to accuse himself. He did indeed begin like Job.
When his illness came he would not look on it as a punishment. He kept his head high for a long time. But after a
while his spirit broke. He was no titanic fighter like Job and
he gave in. He succeeded in finding in his past a sin that
would account for his trouble and that he confessed. Then he
began to get well and knew from this that God had forgiven
him. His confession then is an evidence of weakness not of
true penitence.

Duhm is even more severe. The Psalmist, he declares, has
given us the classical expression of the retribution dogma[1] and

[1] That is, the dogma that God infallibly rewards the righteous and
punishes the wicked.

he displays the infallibility and the didactic urge which characterises its exponents. In this he is like the author of the Elihu speeches of the Book of Job. That he has the standpoint of the Law is shown by his speaking of his sympathisers as "godly" and "righteous." "His conceptions of sufferings, of sin, of prosperity are sub-Christian and the Church in choosing this poem as one of the seven Penitential Psalms only testifies to the dogmatic and legalistic nature of its own idea of the world and religion."

Over against these two scholars stands Kittel who on the whole praises the Psalm. "It is a Penitential Psalm of powerful and (in its first part) of moving effect. Its effect is founded upon the fact that—and here it is like Romans 7—it flows from the quite immediate experience of a conscience oppressed and torn by its sin." Kittel agrees indeed with Gunkel that the Psalmist did not realize his sin till he was stricken with illness but this is true of thousands of others whom one cannot therefore accuse of a lack of purity in their religious sensibility. At the same time, Kittel says, the effect of the Psalm is weakened by its naive retribution teaching and its apparent limitation of forgiveness to the pious.

Staerk also may be counted on the same side as Kittel. While admitting that the retribution dogma gives a defective conception of the nature of sin he goes on to say that it was probably not only outward suffering but the inward voice of conscience as well which brought the Psalmist to recognise and confess his sin. Schmidt likewise admires the Psalm. To him the acknowledgment of verses 3-7 is "especially inward and thoughtful (*besinnlich*).... The beautiful liturgy" (for such he deems it) "has its deep and eternal truth in the proclamation of the liberating power of the acknowledgment of past sins. To be sure, the liberation for which the Psalmist gives thanks is not solely and not primarily the feeling of inward loosing from the pressure of the burden of conscience but the joy over his recovery. But still this joy would not be as great as it is unless the Psalmist saw in this outward fact the guarantee of God's absolution." We may cite Barnes, Kirkpatrick, McNeile, Davison and probably Bertholet as yet other exponents of this high view of our Psalmist. Bertholet pronounces his poem a "step on the way to Romans 7." Barnes cites Montefiore who upholds the Psalm as a true instance of the joy of penitence. Kirkpatrick reminds us that it "was a favorite with St. Augustine,[1] who 'often read this Psalm with weeping heart and eyes, and before his death had it written upon the wall which was over against his sick-bed, that he might be exercised and comforted by it in his sickness!'"

It will easily be seen that the present writer is entirely on the side of the admirers of the Psalmist. He can see in his words no evidence that the sin he confesses is artificially constructed; this man is talking about a real and devastating misdeed. The fact that he would not acknowledge it at first does not mean that he was unaware of it but rather that he was deliberately shutting his eyes to it. Nor is it certain that the trouble which made him roar all the day may not have been primarily the torture of this repression. So McNeile thinks: "Mental misery expressed itself in physical misery."

Again, Duhm's condemnation of the Church's choice of this as a Penitential Psalm is indeed shallow. As a matter of fact, it illustrates ideally the four elements of penitence: contrition, confession, amendment, absolution.

First, *contrition*. When our Psalmist at last came to face his sin he was heartily sorry for it. Not because it had brought punishment or chastening upon him; that would be mere *attrition*, or sorrow over the consequences of sin. No, he hated it because it was hateful to God and separated him from God whom he loved. He was determined to cast it out utterly— no half measures—and be right with God honestly and completely.

Then, *confession*. We do not know what he said when he confessed but we are sure that he made a clean breast of the whole matter, keeping nothing back.

Third, *amendment*. From now on he is steadfastly pur-

---

[1] Herkenne, who also mentions this fact, adds that St. Augustine coined the saying: *Intelligentia prima est ut te noris peccatorem.*

posed to lead a new life, to obey God's will in "uprightness."
And there is nothing perfunctory in his resolution; he is enthusiastic over it. In fact, it forms a chief part of his joy.

Finally, *absolution*. He has no doubt that he has obtained
it, and neither have we. Indeed, he stands as the great ex-
emplar of a forgiven man; and in God's forgiveness he finds
the first and most moving reason for his exultation, as he
tells us in his opening beatitude.

If all this be true, then our Psalmist can be acquitted of
the charge that he is now serving God for material reward;
for that is what Duhm means when he says the Psalm is the
classical expression of the retribution dogma. Like every son
of the Old Covenant our Psalmist does expect God's favor
to show itself in outward gifts. But if this is *all* he means
when he speaks of God's being a hiding-place which the waters
shall not overflow, when he tells of lovingkindness and songs
of deliverance surrounding him, of rejoicing and exulting and
singing because of God, then we have misunderstood the whole
tone of his Psalm. For if we find anything there it is the love
for God. So far from his ideas being sub-Christian, they may
well put most Christians to shame.

There are many things that combine to make our Psalmist
one of the most attractive Personalities of the Psalter. The
reality of his experience, his passion for sincerity, his dedication to God's holy ways, his interest in giving what he has
to others, his love of God—these all make a warm appeal to
the Bible reader. But the thing in him that will always draw
men closest is his story of sin, repentance and forgiveness.
If we may borrow a beautiful contrast of Kirkpatrick's, another Psalmist opened the Psalter by declaring the blessedness
of him who has not walked in the counsel of the ungodly; it
was reserved for our Psalmist to utter a beatitude for the sinner
who repents.

## Then said I, Lo, I come

By almost universal consent recent writers on the Psalms regard Psalm 40 as composed of two independent parts, tied loosely toegther by an editor, perhaps for liturgical purposes. The first part is a Psalm of Thanksgiving; the second a Lament. The division falls after verse 11. The Lament is repeated in Psalm 70 and several bits of it have been worked into Psalm 35. We shall confine our study to the Author of verses 1-11, or (in the Hebrew) 2-12.

It has been seen that two important features of the Thanksgiving are the Narration of the Psalmist's trouble and the Acknowledgment of God's deliverance from it. It is with a telescoping of these two that our Psalmist begins. So eager is he to tell what God has done for him that he passes quite over the usual Introduction. There is no need, he feels, for him to declare that he is about to praise Yahweh, for his story will speak for itself.

> 2. I waíted and waíted upon Yahwéh    and he inclíned to
>     mé    and heárd my crý
> 3. And he brought me úp from the pít of túmult    from
>     the míry cláy
>     And he made my feét to stánd upon a róck,    he made
>     fírm my stéps
> 4. And he pút in my moúth a néw sóng,    praíse to our Gód.

Like his fellow Psalmists he describes his trouble only in vague terms. The metaphor of the pit or cistern in which the feet sink down into mud while its black sides rise unscalable towards the vanishing light of the upper world is symbolical (as we have seen) of the realm of the dead. Perhaps the Psalmist felt himself sinking into the horror of death through illness or was beset by deadly enemies. We cannot tell. We know only that his need was desperate. And yet he had one hope; he looked and looked unto God. "Waiting I waited" he says in his quaint Hebrew, which the ancient versions translate as it stands: *expectans expectavi* runs Jerome's translation and perhaps we ought to keep the original expression in our English, so beautiful and poignant is it. As he waited he cried, doubtless in words such as are preserved in many a Lament. But not, so far as we can see, in penitence for he says nothing of any sin which he had to confess. Waiting and crying had their result. God brought him back to the solid earth again and now he feels himself master of his goings. Then instead of the cry came praise—a new song because everything now is new! The men of the Old Testament believed in a God who was constantly working a new work, intervening afresh to save the individual or the nation.

But of course this amazing rescue is not for the Psalmist alone; he knows that God is showing forth in him the marvel of His doings for all the faithful:

> Mány shall seé and feár    and shall trúst in Yahwéh!
> 5. Bléssed the mán who has máde   Yahwéh his trúst,
> And has not túrned unto the proúd    and to traítorous apóstates.

With verse 5 he is beginning a little Hymn of praise (v.5-6). We have seen how the Author of Psalm 32 chose the beatitude as a subtle and beautiful way of praising God; and our Psalmist does the same. About him are Jews who under the stress of trouble abandon the faith of their fathers and seek help either from heathen deities or by compromise with the world. Happy they who remain true to Yahweh! And his own deliverance will embolden them in their faith, or their "fear of Yahweh," which in the later Old Testament is practically a synonym for religion. Perhaps as he says this the Psalmist is standing in the temple courts surrounded by such faithful people, to whom he pours out his glad testimony.

Now in his rapture he abandons the cooler third person for the passionate vocative:

> 6. Greát are the wónders that *thoú*,   Yahwéh, my Gód, hast dóne,
> Ánd thy thoúghts to uśward.   None is there to compáre to theé!
> If I would decláre and speák of them    they are too míghty to téll.

Other hymnists love to celebrate in detail God's work in creation and His manifold mercies to Israel and to themselves; but this Psalmist, like the Author of Psalm 139, gives up the effort in despair (Ps. 139:17 f.). Indeed he does not even allude to God's creative work but confines his effort to the divine dealings with men. Here two things stand out; God's doings and His thoughts or plans. What *He* does—the pronoun "Thou" is emphatic, to distinguish Yahweh's actions from those of the false helpers to which the apostates seek—are miracles, things wholly beyond human expectation, like the Psalmist's own deliverance. And so are His ideas, His plans. One of these which has just come to the Psalmist in overwhelming force has to do with sacrifice. It is usual when a man has received great good from Yahweh to announce that he will present a thank-offering and such an Announcement, as we have seen, is a regular feature of Thank-Psalms. Our Psalmist would love to bring such a gift—as did the Author of Psalm 22—but God has shown him its inadequacy:

> 7. Sácrifice and meál-offering thou hast no delíght in;     eárs
>     hast thou dígged [1] for me.
>     Búrnt-offering and sín-offering thou áskest nót;
> 8. Thén saíd I, Ló, I cóme—
>     In the róll of the boók it is wrítten concerning mé—
> 9. To dó thy pleásure, my Gód, is my delíght,     and thy láw
>     is in the mídst of my inmost párts.

Not with sacrifices prescribed by the ritual law but with something far more precious must he show his thanks. God has opened a way through his dull ears for the amazing truth that what is wanted is *obedience*. This, he realises, is the true meaning of the sacred roll, the Holy Scripture already recognised by the faithful as the guide of life: there it is written "concerning him," the personal application of the divine teaching, that he should do God's pleasure. To that purpose of God he responds with all his being. "Lo, I am come...." It is like the "Here am I; send me" of Isaiah (Is. 6:8). God's "delight" is met by his own.

[1] A vivid figure for opening the ears. It does not seem necessary to emend the Hebrew. There are a number of uncertainties in the text of vv. 7-11.

But there is something that he can offer beside himself; it is the Acknowledgment of what God has done for him. And this, he says, he has freely given:

> 10. I have told the good néws of ríghteousness in the greát congregátion;
>     Behóld, I do not refraín my líps,    Yahwéh, *thou* knów-est.
> 11. Thy ríghteousness have I nót híd    in the mídst of my heárt;
>     Thy faíthfulness and thy hélp I have decláred;
>     I have not conceáled thy lovingkíndness and trúth    from the greát congregátion.

Gladly and abundantly has he fulfilled this duty of public testimony, which is always "good news" to the faithful. So lavishly does he heap up verbs to express his action that some scholars think the text is overloaded with them and should be pruned! God Himself is his witness—God who knows all. In his impulsive appeal for this divine corroboration we see once more the utter trust and affection with which he looks to God.

Having now done his work as evangelist he concludes with a little prayer whose quiet confidence reminds us of the Lament:

> 12. Thoú, Yahwéh wilt not refraín    thy compássion fróm me.
>     Let thy lovingkíndness and trúth contínually guárd me.

It is a lovely Psalm that he has left us, one that has proven a favorite with Bible readers. Several of its characteristics stand out with remarkable beauty. One is, the wonder of love with which he contemplates God's thoughts towards man. There is in his nature a capacity which he shares with several other Psalmists (Pss. 92:5; 104:24; 106:2; 139:6, 17 f.), a power of seeing in God's ways with man a freshness, a new-ness, a quality of the marvellous that carries him away with emotion. St. Paul had it too, as his outburst in Romans 11:33 ff. shows: "O the depth of the riches both of the wisdom and the knowledge of God! ..."

Then again, our Psalmist is one of the few singers of the

Psalter who dedicates himself to God before our very eyes: "I am come... to do thy pleasure." It is this note of self-offering which led the writer of the Epistle to the Hebrews to see in our Psalm a prophecy of Christ's atoning death. Dismissing the blood of bulls and goats as forever inadequate to take away sins, the Savior in the agony in Gethsemane embraced the divine will and offered Himself once for all upon the cross for our forgiveness (Heb. 10:4 ff.).

A third note which distinguishes our Psalmist is the "delight" with which he thus "presents himself, his soul and body" to do God's will. He knows the joy of complete surrender to a holy will which satisfies his own deepest aspirations, to a transcendent Being with whom he feels himself completely united in adoring love. There is in his obedience no element of constraint, no stern compulsion of sheer duty, much less of the "servile fear" against which Moral Theology warns us, but only romance, passion, abounding joy. He is one of those who prove the saying true that he who loses his life shall find it.

Once more, our Psalmist comes before us as a man who finds God's personal admonition in the Bible. In the roll of the book there was something written "concerning him."[1] It is our custom today to speak of the national and corporate intent of much of the Old Testament. Its Law-givers and Prophets directed what they said to the people as a whole and the individual counted for little. Later indeed the individual came into his own and both Psalmists and Wisdom Writers make much of him; but Israel's earlier scriptures largely merge him with the group. Now it must be these earlier scriptures which our Psalmist has in his "roll"—doubtless his own precious possession. But when he reads them he does not feel that he is left out or merged. Rather he hears in them the voice of God speaking to himself and none other. The Law and the Prophets turn about *him*, they are focused upon *him*,

---

[1] König maintains that the Psalmist is speaking not of a divine book but of his own "book of life" (Ps. 139:16) containing his strivings and accomplishments, which he lays before God. There seems to be no sufficient ground for this view.

all their meaning is concentrated into that single compelling call to *him* and no other. And to that he makes answer, Lo, I come. Self-centered, perhaps, but necessary to living religion.

For it is living religion that he gets in the Bible, or rather in the response of his own heart to the Bible. Modern scholars are prone to deplore the development by which Post-Exilic Judaism came to find the Word of God in the Bible instead of seeking it at the mouth of Prophets. No doubt there was some loss in this change; but we ought not to make overmuch of it. For the Jew who took the "roll of the book" into his hands for guidance and inspiration was in no worse situation than we are today. If we can draw from the Bible the sustenance which our souls need, he could do the same. Everything depended on his own religious sensitiveness, his receptivity and his ability to select.

And that leads up to the final thing which distinguishes this Psalmist: his choice of material from the Scriptures on which to feed his thought. There can be no doubt what are his favorite passages in the ancient writings. He loves the ethical precepts of the Law and the great emancipating utterances of the Prophets. From whom did he learn that God desires obedience rather than sacrifice if not from Samuel (I Sam. 15:22) and Amos (Amos 5:21 ff.), from Isaiah (Is. 1:10 ff.), Micah (Mic. 6:6 ff.), Hosea (Hos. 6:6) and Jeremiah (Jer. 7:21 ff.)? He is no scribe arguing over the interpretation of ritual ordinances of the Priests' Code, keenly interested in questions of ceremonial, of clean and unclean foods, of the keeping of sabbaths and festivals. When he thinks of God it is not of His physical "holiness," nor of His concern to have the procedure of the cult duly carried out; it is of God's justice and truth and lovingkindness and compassion. Of these he delights to read; in meditating on these he rises high on the tide of adoring wonder. And when he turns to the will of God for men, he sees there the same qualities demanded in human relationships. So although he employs none of the *forms* used in Prophecy he moves by virtue of the *content* of his Psalm in the stream of prophetic teaching.

*Turn again unto thy rest, O my soul*

The two Authors of Thanksgivings whom we have just studied belong among the fresh and original thinkers of the Psalter. Before we leave this Type let us consider one who can lay no claim to originality but pours out his heart in thankfulness after the usual fashion. The fact that in his Psalm we detect echoes of earlier Psalms shows that he is dependent upon other poets. But his Psalm for all that has a charm of its own.

This use of earlier Psalms together with the Aramaic expressions employed and the advanced position of the Psalm in the Psalter—all points to its having been composed at a late date. In the Septuagint it is divided, verse 10 forming the opening of a new Psalm. But the verses following, so far from seeming disconnected with verses 1-9, form as will be seen a component part of the whole, being the Announcement of the Thank-offering. We shall therefore follow the Hebrew text in treating the Psalm as a unit.

By Yahweh's help our Psalmist has just emerged from some desperate trouble, but like the Psalmists generally he gives us only vague hints as to its nature. In one place he speaks as if all men had been false to him, but we have seen that such expressions may reflect only the way in which people generally shunned an unfortunate upon whom the hand of God had fallen. The most natural supposition is that he had been mortally ill. But now that is all over. Restored to health he appears in the temple to render thanks, not only before the group of friends who doubtless accompany him, but "in the presence of all Yahweh's people."

He begins with the Acknowledgment of divine help:

1. I lóve Yahwéh * for he heárs    the voíce * of my supplicátions;
2. For he inclíned his eár to mé,    and through my dáys
   I will cáll (on him).

Now he proceeds to the Narration of his trouble:

3. The córds of deáth encírcled me    and the pángs of
   Shéol found me;
   Troúble and sórrow I found    4 and on the náme of
   Yahwéh I cálled:
   Práy, Yahwéh,    delíver my soúl!
5. Grácious is Yahwéh and ríghteous,    and our Gód is
   pítiful.
6. A keéper of the símple is Yahwéh;    I was lów, and he
   sáved me.

Here is a hymnic strain which breaks into his story with
its ringing praise. And like the hymnists he summons his own
soul, not indeed to praise God but to enjoy the refreshment
He has provided:

7. Túrn, my soúl, to thy rést    for Yahwéh has dealt boún-
   tifully with thee.

And from his soul he turns to God, leaving the third person
for the intimate "Thou":

8. For thou hast delívered my soúl from deáth,    mine éye
   from teárs,    and my foót from fálling;
9. I am wálking befóre Yahwéh    in the lánd * of the
   líving.

Then he reverts to his desperate plight in words whose
meaning is none too clear:

10. I belíeved—fór I am speáking—    Í was afflícted ex-
    ceédingly;
11. Í saíd in my alárm    All mankínd are cheáts!

It is broken utterance at best and we shall hardly be
profited by lingering over it to see whether we can through
emendation get it into more intelligible form. Let it pass as
disconnected ejaculation. As such it brings a picture before
us: the Psalmist's trust in Yahweh despite his desperate trouble, his feeling that every one had disappointed him. Yet now
that is all past. From his Narration, enriched by hymnic inter-
jections, he passes to the final division of his Psalm, the
Announcement of his Thank-offering:

12. Hów shall I retúrn unto Yahwéh    áll his bountiful
    deálings tówards me?
13. The cúp of salvátion I take úp,    and upon the náme of
    Yahwéh I cáll;
14. My vóws to Yahwéh I páy    in the présence of áll
    his peóple.

It is no figure[1] but an actual drink-offering of which he speaks, an offering vowed to Yahweh in the hour of trouble. And he accompanies it with a brief echoing of his former Acknowledgment and Narration:

15. Weíghty in the éyes of Yahwéh    is the deáth of his
        gódly!
16. Áh, Yahwéh,    for Í am thy sérvant,
        Í am thy sérvant,    the són of thy hándmaid;    thou
        hast burst ópen my bónds!

It is a cry of "belonging." Before the great multitude he stands alone, face to face with God: "I" and "Thou." All the deliverance has come from that same "belonging," because he is God's.

After this interlude of loving intimacy he resumes his Announcement:

17. To thee I sácrifice a sácrifice of thanksgíving,    and
        upon the náme of Yahwéh I cáll;
18. My vóws to Yahwéh I páy    in the présence of áll
        his peóple,
19. In the coúrts of the hoúse of Yahwéh,    in thý midst,
        Jerúsalem!

As we said at the outset, the value of our Psalmist lies in his very lack of great originality. Instead of uttering truths beyond the experience and apprehension of the plain man he gives expression to simple thoughts and emotions. His religion is one of accepted forms. He does not rise above the sacrificial worship of the church but finds his home within it. The votive cup of wine and the animal victim he presents with no thought of their inadequacy. The sacred places are his soul's delight and his Psalm closes with an address, not to Yahweh but to Jerusalem!

His relations with God likewise move upon the usual level. In trouble he vowed to God with a good conscience. He has been saved by Yahweh from mortal need and he accepts his deliverance with joy. It is sufficient for him; his "rest," as he beautifully puts it. He does not speculate as to why trouble comes to him or to others; he accuses himself of no sin; he

---

[1] Herkenne does indeed regard the cup as a figure of the state, or lot, of salvation which the Author asks for himself (cf. Ps. 75:8).

gives no thought to the implications of his deliverance in the sphere of duty. He seems more occupied with God's gifts than with God Himself.

And yet his Psalm overflows with joyous religious emotion, with the warmth of true piety. He loves God, he belongs to Him. And he knows how to show Him gratitude. In his words thrills the fervor of pure thanksgiving. Nor has he ceased to appeal to the modern Christian. Those who today find their hearts' home in the "courts of the Lord's house," who believe that they gain from sacramental worship a joy and strength not elsewhere to be had, understand him when he speaks of a "sacrifice of thanksgiving"; and in the hour of their own deliverance, reading his words in the familiar Prayer Book Version, may well make their resolve to take in gratitude the "cup of salvation" to the true rest of their souls. It was doubtless with this in mind that the compilers of the Prayer Book incorporated Psalm 116 in the Office of Thanksgiving of Women after Child-birth.

# V

# AUTHORS OF WISDOM PSALMS

THERE existed from an early age in Israel a kind of utterance that was characterised by the name of "Wisdom." It had already attained a high development in other countries, especially Egypt, and seems to have been taken over from them into Israel. This Wisdom was of a practical nature and occupied itself with reflections upon human life. Gunkel distinguishes three stages in its development in Israel. The first, in which the prevailing interest was in secular life rather than in religion. Here it spoke of such universal facts as the uncertainty of riches, the value of friends, the handicaps of poverty and the like. Later a distinctly religious tone came in, centering attention particularly on the teaching of divine retribution—that God rewards every man according to his works. This is exemplified abundantly in the Book of Proverbs and in the speeches of Job's friends. In both these stages the earlier utterances took the form of single adages or "Proverbs," each expressing an isolated idea. After a while men of poetic genius began to build up groups of such sayings into a unified whole and "Wisdom Poetry" arose. A final stage of development appeared when disillusioning experience led men to question the dogma of retribution, as do the writers of the Books of Job and Ecclesiastes.

This Israelitish Wisdom in all its stages found expression in the Psalter. Some Psalms are completely given over to it, so that they form a distinct Type, while there appear frequently in Psalms of other Types sayings and bits of poetry which belong to Wisdom writing. Conversely, the other Types have had their influence on the Wisdom Psalms, especially where the poet speaks his own thoughts in lyric strain.

As outstanding examples of the successive stages of Wisdom development in the Psalter Gunkel cites three great Psalms. Reflection upon human life in its general aspect appears in the Writer of Psalm 49, who calls all the world to listen while he sings of the vanity of riches and their powerlessness to prevent death. In Psalm 91 the retribution dogma finds classic expression, where the Author assures Yahweh's faithful follower that it will be well with him however the ungodly may fall about his path. This confident teaching, finally, had become a matter of bitter doubt to the great soul who in Psalm 73 tells how he at last won peace in contemplating the quick end of the wicked man's prosperity and joy in his own abiding fellowship with God. We shall study each of these Psalmists in turn.

The Wisdom strain in the Psalter is characterised by certain expressions and forms, the most important of which are given by Gunkel. The Psalmist speaks of his words. as Wisdom, Teaching, Riddles, Proverbs. He describes the "fear of Yahweh." He addresses his hearers as his sons. Sometimes he uses a solemn Introduction in which he summons all the world to listen and appeals to a revelation he has received. He warns and teaches, exhorting to virtue and trust in God or holding out the penalty of ungodliness. He loves striking comparisons and heaped-up figures; he uses question-and-answer and other devices; he utters beatitudes; he describes Yahweh's doings and justifies them.

Some of the grandest poems of the Psalter are Wisdom Psalms. Here we see personality entering into Psalm composition in the same way that we have noticed in the other Types. The earlier detached sayings were spoken, but Psalm 49:4 indicates that the more developed Wisdom Poems were sung to the accompaniment of the harp. The appearance of a priestly oracle in Psalm 91 shows that it was used in public worship; and Wisdom Psalms are incorporated in early collections which emanate from public worship. There can indeed be no doubt that Wisdom Poetry originally had another home than the temple service, as we see from such Psalms as 49, 127:3-5 and 133. Later on however the priests and singers who had the care of public worship began to employ in it Wisdom Psalms because of their great popularity with the laity. But we cannot discover on what specific occasions of worship they were so used.

As to the dating of the Wisdom Psalms Gunkel speaks at some length. The three stages of development above noted would on the whole succeed each other in time though earlier kinds would continue to be produced after the later had come into being. The Psalms dealing with human life in general go back in some instances far into the period of the monarchy and the latest stage which exhibits a questioning of the retribution dogma could begin as early as Jeremiah's time, for we know that such questioning was then prevalent. But Wisdom continued to flourish on Israelitish soil for centuries and we find poetry of this Type as late as Ecclesiasticus (c. 175 B.C.) and the Psalms of Solomon (c. 50 B.C.). Thus the bounds within which individual Wisdom Psalms may be set are very wide. The date of the several poems must be determined, so far as possible, from such indications as they themselves furnish.

# The Author of Psalm 49 [1]

## *For he shall receive me*

One problem that continually exercised the minds of men in Israel was the prosperity of the wicked. As they looked about them they saw all too plainly that ungodliness often seemed to bring no penalty while righteousness failed to win success and happiness. How could this be reconciled with the belief in a just God? It is to this perplexity that we owe the noblest productions of the Wisdom Writers, the Book of Job and several of the Wisdom Psalms, especially Psalm 73.

The Author of Psalm 49 has also thought much on this general problem but in his mind it has taken a somewhat different form. What concerns him is the phenomenon of wealth in the midst of poverty. His difficulty is not so much that the rich are wicked, although he does speak of them as dishonest and oppressive. His mind is disturbed rather by the fact that there *are* rich people, and that they have the elation, the solidity, the magnificence, the prestige and power that wealth confers. His heart is moved for the poor who are cowed by the rich. He himself is poor and he knows what it is to be browbeaten and mulcted by the power of money.

But as he brooded over this fear he has come to see something which takes it away and gives him the confidence of unbounded security. So happy is he in his discovery that he feels himself obligated to disclose it to others. Thus his Psalm begins with the invitation to hear so characteristic of Wisdom Writers:

> 2. Heár thís, all peóples!    heárken, all inhábitants of the
>     wórld!
> 3. Both sóns of the lów man and sóns of the hígh man,
>     rích and poór togéther!
> 4. My moúth shall speák wísdom,    and the meditátion of
>     my heárt is understánding;

[1] Mowinckel regards Pss. 49 and 73 as Thank-Psalms, not Didactic or Problem Psalms. (*Psalmenstudien* I, p. 127.)

5. I will inclíne my eár to a sáying,     I will ópen upon the
    hárp my ríddle.

What he has to say therefore is not for any one group; it
concerns all nations and especially the two social classes on
whose lot he has been pondering. His message, like that of
the Wise Men generally, is to be broadly human, not limited
to Israelites. And he professes to impart the truth about life
for that is the meaning of Wisdom.

But whence does he obtain it? From a "saying," he tells
us. It is the common term for an utterance of the Wise Men
which we translate "proverb." But this "saying" has not come
from himself; he must "incline his ear" to it. Barnes thinks
that he means simply a proverb of the past—the saying that
he repeats as a sort of refrain: "Man will not abide in honor."
But it seems more probable that Kittel, Kirkpatrick and
Schmidt are right in thinking that he is speaking of something
more authoritative and awful. That to which he inclines his
ear is the voice of God, who reveals to him a "riddle" which
he is to tell mankind.

6. Whý shall I feár in the days of évil,     when the guílt of
    my treácherous (foes) * surroúnds me?
7. They that trúst in their weálth,     and in the greátness
    of their ríches make their boást!

There you get the contrast: the timid poor, the overbearing
rich! Yet the fear is quite unnecessary; for after all there
is one Power which money cannot buy off:

8. Súrely * the hígh man will not at áll ransom himsélf,*
    he will not gíve to *Gód* his príce.
9. (But cóstly is the ránsoming of their soúl,     and it has
    ceásed for éver)
10. That he should líve on for éver,     nót seé the pít.
11. For he seés that wíse men dié,     togéther the foól and
    the brútish pérish,
    And leáve to óthers their weálth.
12. Their gráves * are their hoúses foréver,     their dwéllings
    to generátion and generátion.
    They cálled lánds by their námes!
13. And mán in hónor abídes not,     he is líke the beásts
    that are brought to noúght!

Our Psalmist's words have been transmitted to us con-
fusedly, but it is better to let them stand for the most part

as they appear in the Hebrew text than to try to rewrite them. After all, their general meaning is clear enough. The rich man has a high place in society; he owns great estates which he proudly calls by his name. But he does not *stay*. An inexorable God bids him leave it all for his permanent home, his six feet by two of earth! Then others get his money. As for him, he is gone with the beasts, not one whit better than they.

To our Psalmist's mind then the thought of the rich man's end is full of liberation. Why should one any longer fear him? And now he goes on with this theme, portraying, like the painters of the Middle Ages, a veritable "dance of death"! (Schmidt).

> 14. Thís is the wáy of those who are cónfident    and the
>      énd * of those that applaúd their tálk.[1]
> 15. Like sheép for Shéol they have been appoínted; [2]    deáth
>      shépherds them;
>      And the úpright shall have domínion over thém in the
>      mórning.
>      And their fórm is to waste awáy *    Shéol is their *
>      dwélling.

Again the text is corrupt and the commentaries swarm with emendations; but as we here translate it, using the minimum of corrections, it gives a vivid enough picture. Yes, the rich are very sure of themselves and their bragging makes a great impression on many; yet all—flattered and flatterers—are moving, moving in grim order after a grisly shepherd, on and on, to their dreadful home of decay.

But the darkness is broken into by a gleam of sudden light. There is to be a "morning" when the ranking of the present will be reversed and dominion shall come to the upright. What does our Psalmist mean? Some scholars alter the saying completely but with them we are not concerned, for we follow the ancient versions in retaining the Hebrew text. The "morning" (as in Ps. 46:6) seems to point to the dawn of the great "day of Yahweh" when He will intervene to save His faithful people.

[1] Hebrew: "delight in their mouth."

[2] König, following the Targum, understands this to mean: "they (the rich) have appointed them (the righteous poor) to death, as though they were a flock of sheep."

But what will be the scene of this transaction? Will it, as Kirkpatrick thinks, be the life that now is? Or is our Psalmist looking to some event that will transcend the bounds of death? It appears that the rich over whom the upright are to rule are already dead. If so, the scene lies beyond death.

But our Psalmist does not stop here. The light which has fallen upon his sombre verses blazes out into a moment's noonday glory:

> 16. Súrely *Gód* will ránsom my soúl     from the hánd of
>     Shéol; for he will táke me.[1]

The teacher of others has turned from his pupils to himself— and God. What he utters is no mere possibility, but a great all-vanquishing certainty: "surely!" Just now he said that the rich man cannot buy himself off from death, for the ransom of souls is beyond the reach of money. But there *is* One who can pay the price, and He will! Even the implacable hand of Sheol will yield its prey to *God* when He "takes" the Psalmist to himself!

Such then is God's compensation to the upright poor—life with Him beyond death and "in the morning" dominion over the dead rich. Here the poem of our Psalmist attains its climax (Barnes). For this is the "saying" that has been revealed to his attentive ear, this his "riddle" opened upon the harp. And indeed it is a stupendous utterance for a man of antique Israel. It leaps out from the pages of the Old Testament to take its stand with three or four other sayings in a pioneer confession of faith in an after-life.[2]

And now, having reached his height and caught a vision of his own dazzling future, our Psalmist descends to his former theme again:

> 17. Feár not when a mán grows rích,     when the glóry of
>     his hoúse incréases;
> 18. For when he díes he will táke nóthing óf it,     his glóry
>     will not go dówn áfter him.

---

[1] The Psalmist seems to be echoing the expression used of Enoch in Gen. 5:24: "And Enoch walked with God: and he was not; for God took him."

[2] Job, 19:25ff., Ps. 73:24, Is. 26:19; cf. 25:8, Dan. 12:2ff. and perhaps Ps. 16:9ff.

> 19. Though he blésses his soúl while he líves—(and they
>     applaúd thee while thou doest wéll to thysélf!)
> 20. He * shall énter into the generátion of his fáthers,     for
>     éver he * shall not seé líght!

Then once more his refrain tolls like a knell:

> 21. Mán in hónor does not understánd,     he is líke the
>     beásts that are brought to noúght.

Even the casual reader can see that what our Psalmist has
here given us is a composition quite unlike the Hymns, Laments and Thanksgivings which we have been studying. It is a
meditation in the form of an instruction. It looks for the most
part on life rather than on God. God is never addressed. There
is no prayer, no praise, no thanks, hardly a word about Him.
Only twice is the divine Name uttered.

It is directed, not to fellow-worshippers in the temple but to
pupils in the market place; for he summons them from the
midst of the world's busy life. His theme is one familiar
enough—money, what it does and what it cannot do. But as
Gunkel points out, our Psalmist is unique among the Old Testament thinkers who have pondered on the rich, in that he does
not identify them with the godless or the wicked. He speaks
indeed of the "guilt of treacherous (foes)" and of the fear
which wealth awakens in him. But for the most part he is content to paint the rich as every one sees them—their arrogant
elation (v.7), their illusion of permanence, their imposing estates that bear their names (v.12), their ability to make money
produce more money (v.17), their stupid self-assurance (v.14),
their way of winning the applause of the world (vv.14, 19),
their "glory," their "honor" (vv.13, 17, 21).[1] He utters no
denunciation of their cruelty, their oppression, their blas-
phemous talk against God. He points no sharp contrast between them and the godly poor, he lifts no outcry to heaven
over the seeming injustice of God's distribution of prosperity.
He lets the picture speak for itself.

And as he contemplates it what has our Psalmist to say to
the throng whom he has summoned by his grandiose exordium?

---

[1] Verses numbered according to the Hebrew.

For it cannot be denied that he promises to say something which will make it worth the while of all men—high and low, rich and poor—to listen.

First, speaking as one of the poor he remonstrates with himself for the fear that the wealthy inspire in him. Why should he dread them? For money and all it brings is powerless in the face of inevitable death. Look at the common end of all! For that suffices him. He threatens no special calamity to the rich: let them live out their full time!

No one will deny that he knows how to paint his dreary picture—the ransom offered to God and refused, the shepherd Death stalking ahead of his marshalled flock, the dying hand relaxing its hold on money and glory for another to enjoy. Nor will any fail to see that it does liberate the poor man to hold these realities before him. It would help the rich too if he would let it! The literature of the world contains many such reflections, some of poignant beauty.

But after all there is nothing *new* in what our Psalmist says on this point. However well expressed, it would hardly meet the expectations aroused by his opening invitation. The true revelation which he has to impart comes in the center of light (v.16) which illumines the gloom of his beginning and ending. So sudden and unprepared for is it, so startling in its content, so brief and compressed, so without seeming effect on what follows, that Gunkel and Staerk pronounce it an interpolation by a later hand. Kirkpatrick and McNeile will not go so far as this, but find in it no reference to an after life. The Psalmist, they think, is only saying that he will be delivered from premature death and will be set over the rich in the better day that God is to bring in. But the whole tenor of the Psalm seems to require a greater deliverance than this. What our Psalmist is recalling to us is not that the rich will die before their time, but that they *will die*. And if his affirmation about his own future means anything by contrast, it must refer to a final, not a temporary, rescue from death. Over against the "ransom" offered vainly by the rich he sets the ransom of God who is stronger than Sheol and prevails. It is not surprising therefore that the majority of recent commentators both retain verse 16 and interpret it of survival.[1]

The Psalmist then is declaring that he will survive death by the ransoming power of God. It is of himself that he speaks; yet the fact that he is addressing others, among them the poor, indicates that he is describing no peculiar favor limited to his own case (Barnes), but a general redemptive truth applying to all the "upright" dispossessed of earth (Kittel, Schmidt).

What he looks for therefore is a divine compensation beyond this mortal scene. This has its manifest lack, for it leaves the present life wholly in the hands of the wealthy. The rich we shall always have with us! Our Psalmist does not share the passionate conviction of Isaiah (11:1 ff.), Ezekiel (34) and the Authors of Psalms 72 and 146 that God will intervene here to redress the inequalities of our society, filling the hungry with good things and sending the rich empty away (Lk. 1:53). The "upright" must wait till "the morning" for their domination!

But the "otherworldliness" of our Psalmist's affirmation (which may well be more apparent than real) detracts little from the fact that he breaks through the bounds which hem in so rigidly most of the Old Testament writers and boldly declares that in a great hereafter God will give the poor life and dominion forever.[2]

[1] e.g. Barnes, Bertholet, Duhm, Kittel, König, Leslie, Löhr (*Psalmenstudien*, p. 35), T. H. Robinson (*The Psalmists*, ed. D. C. Simpson, p. 108). Davison is doubtful. Mowinckel seems to regard the verse as referring to a past deliverance of the Psalmist from death (*Psalmenstudien* I, p. 128).

[2] Löhr believes that the whole Psalm with its division of men into rich and poor, its bombastic opening, its awkward development of thought "betrays the authorship of a man from the non-literary ranks, whom his religious ponderings have compelled to take up the pen. But just in this its manifest origin lies the value of the Psalm. In the circles of the simple folk the thought of a hereafter as a postulate of divine compensation for the privations of this life has arisen and come to be at home." *Psalmenstudien*, p. 35.

*Whoso dwelleth under the defence of the Most High*

The Author of Psalm 91 has given us one of the most familiar and best loved poems of the Psalter. He knows how to clothe in beautiful and varied imagery a truth of religion that the heart of mankind longs to make its own—God's loving care of the faithful. Amidst the perils of the world he summons the soul of the believer to quiet trust.

In content therefore it might well be included among the Psalms of Trust. But its form is different. The Author of a Psalm of Trust tells what God means to him personally while our Author speaks as a teacher of others.[1] If he had not concluded with a divine oracle in which God is introduced as speaking for Himself we might think his Psalm a page taken from the more intimate portions of the Book of Proverbs.

But though he has chosen a different literary vehicle for his message he is really speaking from out his own experience just as much as the Authors of Psalms of Trust. For the teacher must first learn before he can instruct others. And one reason for the power of his Psalm is that the reader feels this in all that he says. He is passing on the comfort with which he himself has been comforted of God.

> 1. He who dwélls in the sécret place of the Most Hígh  in
>    the shádow of the Almíghty abídes....

We can see of whom he is thinking—the loyal people of God. And he expresses their loyalty in a peculiarly beautiful way, as the choice of a home, an abiding place. It is the hiding-place of God, which He alone knows, His shade under which they can be refreshed in security and peace. To make his sonorous

---

[1] According to the present Hebrew text indeed our Psalmist does refer to himself in two places: vv. 2 and 9. But in v. 2 the ancient versions give the third person and in v. 9 the sense so plainly demands the third person that we have adopted the slight emendation restoring it which is employed by a number of recent commentators.

verse more majestic, to give it more of the quality of the
"numinous," he uses the ancient names for God that come
down from patriarchal times: Elyon, Shaddai.

In this their faith he would encourage them:

> 2. Sáy * to Yahwéh, my réfuge and strónghold,    my Gód,
>    in him I trúst.

Then in the concrete detail that the Hebrews love he pictures the effectiveness of their security against three common
dangers.

First, the treacherous slander of enemies:

> 3. For *hé* will delíver thee from the snáre of the fówler,
>    from the deádly péstilence;
> 4. With his pínions he will cóver theé,    and únder his
>    wíngs thou shalt find réfuge;
>    A shiéld and búckler is his faíthfulness.

Our Psalmist crowds metaphor upon metaphor.[1] His figure of
the mother-bird gathering her young under her wings must
have sunk deep into the mind of our Lord, for He used it of
His own yearning over Jerusalem (Mt. 23:37, Lk. 13:34).

Next, the contagion of an epidemic:

> 5. Thou shalt not feár the térror by níght,    the árrow that
>    flíes by dáy,
> 6. The péstilence that wálks in dárkness,    the destrúction
>    that dévastates in the noón-day.

All these seem to be images of the same thing. Gunkel and
other commentators remind us of the superstitions then current. At night fearful demons of disease were thought to stalk
about, passing at will through closed doors. In the heat of the
summer noon the sun-god shot his mortal arrows of sun-stroke
and plague. We can understand from reading these verses how
faith in the supreme God delivered men from the terror of
unseen superhuman enemies, much as Christianity liberates
the uneducated convert in a non-Christian land today.[2] "Thou
shalt not fear."

---

[1] Oesterley thinks that the Psalmist meant quite literally that Yahwen,
like the sun god of Egypt, has wings. (*Fresh Approach*, etc., p. 208.)

[2] Oesterley develops at great length this idea that the Psalmist has
demons in mind. He even regards the lion and cobra of v. 13 as incarna-
tions of demons. (*Fresh Approach*, etc., p. 281 ff.)

No, for thou art singled out for special care:

> 7. A thoúsand shall fáll besíde thee,     and tén thousand
>     at thy right hánd—
>     Unto theé it shall not come nígh!
> 8. Ónly with thine éyes shalt thou behóld,     and the réc-
>     ompense of the wícked thou shalt seé.

Our Psalmist is speaking like a typical Wise Man of Proverbs. To his mind there exists no "problem of evil." It is all very simple: these people who fall beside the faithful man *must* be wicked, or they would not fall. How different with the loyal ones whom he addresses!

> 9. For thoú—Yahwéh is thy * réfuge;     the Most Hígh
>     thou hast máde thy dwélling....

And now he passes to the third danger from which Yahweh saves: the perils of a journey, where one's frail tent may be overwhelmed by storm or robbers, where loose stones may send one stumbling headlong, where a deadly cobra may strike unawares, or a prowling lion suddenly appear. But here too "thou shalt not fear": invisible hands sustain thee:

> 10. No évil shall meét theé,     nor shall stróke come neár
>     thy tént;
> 11. For his ángels he shall chárge concerning theé     to keép
>     thee in áll thy wáys;
> 12. Upon their hánds they shall bear thee úp     lest thou
>     stríke upon a stóne thy foót;
> 13. Upon líon and cóbra shalt thou treád,     thou shalt
>     trámple the yoúng lion and the snáke.

Why indeed shouldst thou fear?

But our Psalmist is not content to leave his hearers with merely his own assurance, however inspired. Suddenly his words are broken into by the Voice of God:

> 14. "Because upon mé he has set his lóve, therefore will I
>     delíver him,
>     I will lift him hígh, for he knóws my náme.
> 15. He shall cáll upon me, and I will ánswer him;
>     With him am Í in troúble;
>     I will réscue him and bring him to hónor;
> 16. Of léngth of dáys will I give him his fúll,
>     And I will make him seé my salvátion."

The familiar second person has been dropped; God says not "thou" but "he." It is as if the supernal utterance were pealing high over the heads of the faithful. Yet they hear it and know it is for them. And what a rich cluster of promises it holds out! Safety, the good esteem of men, long life. For God is not unmindful of his own.

As we review his Psalm we are conscious of certain manifest limitations in the religion of our Psalmist; for, as has been said, it is *his* religion which he is recommending to his hearers.

He brings out only one aspect of the manifold life of man with God—trust in divine providence. He says nothing of spiritual gifts such as forgiveness or the power to do right or the joy of God's companionship. And he seems to be concerned mainly with the outward blessings which make life go on securely, pleasantly and for a long time. He does not even mention healing from illness, since apparently he does not expect to become ill. This one-sidedness is not necessarily a blemish for it may be sufficient in a single Psalm to develop one theme fully. We need not infer that the other strains in religion are wholly absent in our Psalmist. Nevertheless there is something lacking in his experience with God, as we shall see.

Again, the promises he holds out cannot be absolute. The story of our Lord's temptation reminds us that they can be abused. What they have in mind are the unavoidable dangers which meet one in the path of duty and normal living. To court peril by casting oneself down from the pinnacle of the temple, for example, would be tempting God. But (a more serious qualification) the promises do not invariably hold good even for these unavoidable dangers. The arrow does not always miss the faithful and find the ungodly. Our Psalmist takes no account of the continuous lack of *discrimination* in God's dispensation of both calamities and benefits. He allows neither for the hurtful forces which strike down good and bad alike nor for the benignant powers of the universe which shed kindness upon the just and the unjust. As we have said, he does not yet realize the "problem of evil," much less attempt its solution; nor on the other hand does he comprehend the measure of God's love which embraces all.

For this reason he applies the doctrine of "special providence" in an almost sinister way, exhibiting a complacence that might easily pass into hard-heartedness: "only with thine eyes shalt thou behold, and the recompense of the wicked thou shalt see" (v.8). The word "recompense" is significant; it means what completes the transaction, rounds it off ideally. Some excuse may be found in the fact that he is here reflecting the usual attitude of the Wise Men, as portrayed in the friends of Job. But he ought to have thought more deeply and truly about God.

The fact is, our Psalmist lives in what William James called a "one-story universe." The fabric of his life plainly remains unbroken. Whatever his dangers or troubles, he is still fundamentally at ease. And as Job reminds us, "in the thought of him that is at ease there is contempt for misfortune" (Job 12:5). There are deeps which he has not plumbed, vistas down which he has never looked. That is why he does not pity.

Yet however real his limitations, there can be no doubt that our Psalmist meets an elemental need of man—the need for security in God. That is the value which his Psalm has ever had for the faithful. It is, as Kittel says, "a high-resounding, inspired praise of the trustful confidence which the religious man enjoys in God's protection.... The poem repeatedly recalls Psalm 46.... Next to it this is the second great Song of Faith in the Psalter, and like it has been in the Church of all ages the true companion of the sore-pressed in a thousand hard situations and in all sorts of dangers." And Kittel declares further that those who use this Psalm quietly disregard its one serious blemish—its exultation over the fate of the wicked in v.8.

This Song of Faith closes with an undeniably aggressive note. Gunkel, to be sure, overlooks this. "It is significant," he says, "that in such poems as this we hear only of divine protection in suffering but almost never of divine power to act. These Psalmists have no desire to offer resistance to the troubles and enemies besetting them but long only to flee and be hid. Such a peculiarly passive attitude is manifestly distinctive of the circles from which these poems have proceeded;

it is the poor, the oppressed, the 'quiet in the land,' who here speak." But Gunkel surely is mistaken. It is true that our Psalmist has no confidence in his own strength; but when the supporting angels of God are about him he feels able to "trample" the young lion and the snake (v.13). And he hears God promise to the faithful more than a safe hiding-place. They will be lifted high, will be brought to honor, will be made to see God's "salvation." This great word with which our Psalmist ends has in it a ring of triumph. We must remember that it is the usual word in Hebrew for "victory." No, the Psalm is not passive; through it blow glorious airs of conquest and exultation. And that is one reason for its hold upon its readers.

It is likewise a Psalm of intimate relationship with God. However our Psalmist may bring forward the outward benefits to be gained by faith, one feels that the heart of his poem beats with a joyous sense of God's personal love for himself. That joins his Psalm to the assurances of God's care uttered by our Lord: "the very hairs of your head are all numbered" (Mt. 10:30; Lk. 12:7). The chief trouble with his teaching of special providence is that it does not go far enough! Instead of being peculiar, it should be universal.

A final reason why men love his Psalm is that he speaks of the angels keeping watch over us. Gunkel indeed inclines to view this as a decline from the "high and pure religion" of the Prophets and most of the Psalmists, which has to do with the supreme God only. But our Psalmist's mention of these "subordinate existences" in no wise detracts from his devotion to God. It merely peoples his unseen world with friendly supporting beings who carry out God's protective will, much as true friends aid us in the world of men.[1] Even those who no longer take the existence of angels seriously would be loath to part with this touch. They like to retain the thought of angels as part of the poetry of faith. They loved angels as children, they love them now.

How much more those who see no reason why there should

[1] cf. Oesterley, *Fresh Approach*, etc., p. 279.

not be superhuman intelligences about us caring for us! To such modern Christians our Psalm is rightly set as a Proper Psalm for Michaelmas, leading up to the old collect which they can still pray:

O Everlasting God, who hast ordained and constituted the services of Angels and men in a wonderful order; Mercifully grant that, as thy holy Angels always do thee service in heaven, so, by thy appointment, they may succour and defend us on earth; through Jesus Christ our Lord.

## THE AUTHOR OF PSALM 73

### *Nevertheless, I am alway by thee*

We come now to the study of the Psalmist who penetrated most deeply into the inner heart of religion. He gained this insight through an experience of doubt which almost led to complete loss of faith in God. For with him the naive certainty of the retribution dogma as we have it in Psalm 91 broke down, just as it broke down for Job. Like Job he had to wrestle with the ghastly sense of God's undeserved mistreatment and like Job he attained to a new assurance of the friendship of God. But his solution of this agonizing problem was in part more satisfying than Job's—so satisfying indeed that the Christian of today can still rest in it.

For this reason the Author of Psalm 73 has won himself a unique place in the minds of many readers of the Old Testament. The present writer can well remember his own introduction to this saint. When yet a graduate student he had occasion to confer with an elderly clergyman whose well-seasoned piety was known throughout a whole city. From a discussion of Greek tragedy the conversation shifted to Hebrew poetry and the older man spoke of the Psalms as supplying something which he could find in no other poetry and indeed in no other book of the Bible. "I think," he said, "that if I were told I must discard every book of the Bible but one I should pass by even the Gospels and choose the Psalms. Take Psalm 73— do you know it? No? Oh, that is the greatest of them all." And then in simple words he drew the picture of the struggle of this soul and its final achievement of peace—drew it so clearly and with such beauty that the picture has remained in his hearer's mind until the present. Indeed, after his later researches, it still approves itself as true; and it will be substantially that picture (in so far as he is able to recapture it) which reappears in this study of the Psalmist. He has since learned that the estimate placed upon the Psalm by this elderly

clergyman is shared by not a few of the most competent Old
Testament scholars of our time.

In spite however of such appreciation by mature minds,
Psalm 73 has never won wide-spread popularity and the usual
Bible reader is unaware of the treasure which lies half-buried
within it. For this there is an obvious reason. The first twenty
verses, which contain the story of the Psalmist's inner con-
flict, are muddied by confusions in the Hebrew text which appear to some extent even in the English translation, and their
lack of clarity combines with a certain uninviting quality in
the matter itself to discourage any but a determined seeker.
It is only when taken together with the last eight verses that
they form a whole of incomparable beauty. Perhaps no Psalm
needs an interpreter more than this one. To the interpretation
then let us proceed.

Our Psalmist, like the writer of Psalm 32, begins at the end
of his story:

> 1. Súrely goód to Ísrael     is Gód, to the púre in heárt!

Yes, he sees that now! But only at long last. He has had to
fight to see it and it is of the fight that he now proceeds to tell.

> 2. But Í—álmost góne were my feét,     well nígh had slípt
>    my stéps.

Another moment and he would have been lost. But why?
Whence this deadly danger? He confesses the shameful truth:

> 3. For I was énvious of the boásters,     the prospérity of
>    the wícked I was seéing.

Yes, it was the old wrong, the defiance God's righteous government which had enraged Jeremiah and Job.

> 4. For there are nó bánds in their deáth,     and fát is their
>    stréngth;
> 5. In the troúble of mén they áre not,     and with mén they
>    are not piérced.

That is what stirs him—their exemption from the common lot
of pain, their special privilege in a suffering world. And instead of bringing out their gratitude it stimulates their arro-
gance.

6. Thérefore their néck-chain is príde,    víolence cóvers them as a gárment;
7. Their éye stands fórth with fátness,    the thoúghts of (their) heárt pass all boúnds.
8. They móck and speák in the evil of oppréssion;    from on hígh they speák.
9. They sét in the heávens their moúth,    and their tóngue wálks upon the eárth.

Not very clear this, for the text has evidently been corrupted; but we cannot miss his meaning. What a picture! Fat middle-aged men with their feet in the trough! To hear them one might think that they, not God, were in control of the world! And this insolent haughtiness, instead of setting men against them, has just the opposite effect.

10. Thérefore túrn his peóple híther    and wáters of a fúll (cup) are draíned for thém.

Again, in spite of the hopeless obscurity of the text, we can probably read his meaning—he is portraying the popularity of evil which has turned many a man into a cynic. How these men flaunt God to his face!

11. And they sáy, "Hów does Gód know?"    and "Is there knówledge in Elyón?"

They are emancipated spirits who conceive of God as too tran-scendent to bother about everyday human conduct! Here the anger of our Psalmist boils over.

12. Behold, thése (are) wícked!    and in perpétual secúrity théy make their weálth tower hígh!

Yes, the wicked! That is, the men who according to all right ought to be overwhelmed by divine wrath. And they—increase in riches! Of what use then the Psalmist's following of right-eousness?

13. Súrely in vaín have I cleánsed my heárt    and wáshed in ínnocency my hánds.
14. And I have beén beáten all the dáy    and my chástise-ment is every mórning!

That is how God has rewarded my goodness—never a day without some fresh calamity! [1] Thus the Psalmist's envy was

[1] I cannot accept Oesterley's view that the Psalmist for the purpose of his argument is here *assuming* a wrong attitude. (*Fresh Approach*, etc., p. 272).

sweeping him on—nearer and nearer to apostasy. For that is what it was coming to. He was trembling on the verge of renouncing the faith of a lifetime and taking up the philosophy of the men he envied. But one consideration held him back:

> 15. If I had saíd, "I will tálk as théy"—    behóld, with the generátion of thy sóns should I have dealt treácherously.

Yes, it was not a matter in which he only was concerned. He belonged to a company, the sons of God, God's true servants— and to them he stood committed. They trusted him. What now if he should go over to the other side!

No, that was impossible. He must find some other solution. But how hard it was to get! And then one day he found it:

> 16. And I kept thínking how to knów thís,    lábor it wás in my éyes,[1]
> 17. Until I went ín unto the sánctuary of Gód—    I understoód their latter énd.
> 18. Súrely, in slíppery places thou séttest thém,    thou mákest them fáll to destrúctions.
> 19. Hów they becóme a desolátion as in an ínstant!    they are énded, fínished by térrors!
> 20. As a dreám from awáking, Lórd,    in aroúsing shalt thou despíse their ímage.

Here once more are obscurities, but we glimpse the scene— the Psalmist thinking and thinking, yet getting no light until in a never-to-be-forgotten moment he entered the temple. Countless times had he entered it before, but that day it was different. In the midst of the "holy places," surrounded by the symbols of a vaster order, the light came to him. Yes, there was the answer!—the *aharî'th,* the last end. This insolent prosperity of the wicked could not last. As in a vision he saw it all—the crash—the end—God arising. How plain it was now!

But he does not stop there. If he had he would have got no farther than the Writer of Psalm 37, who certainly has not penetrated any deeps. Our Psalmist however again turns his attention from the wicked to himself, and in so doing he

---

[1] A number of scholars insert vv.21-22 after v.16, but such a transposition does not seem necessary.

comes upon the great truth which sets him forever upon the mountain-top.

Why, he asks, has he not been able to see God's justice before? And he gives the answer:

> 21. For ferménting was my heárt,    and in my reíns I was
>     piérced.

He had allowed himself to become so enraged that his pain was unbearable. And when a man gets into that condition he is no longer a man.

> 22. But Í was a brúte and did not knów,    a beást wás I—
>     with theé!

Yes, therein lay the enormity of his raging. God had been with him all the while. And he had not realised what that meant!

> 23. But Í am contínually with theé,    thou hast grásped me
>     by my right hánd;
> 24. With thy coúnsel thou dost leád me,    and áfterward
>     to glóry thou dost táke me.

He is speaking of the companionship of God. Never for a single instant does he lose it. He is like a child with his father. Never is his hand let go, never is he left without loving advice, never uncertain of the *afterward,* the final outcome; he will be received with light and joy and honor—for these are comprehended in the Hebrew word "glory." And all the while that he was so envious he had this—which the wicked with all their money and success and popularity can never have! So it had *not* been in vain that he had washed his hands in innocency! A brute was he indeed not to know it! But now he *does* know and knowing realises what it means to him.

> 25. Whóm have I in heáven (but thee)?    and besides
>     theé I have no delíght upon eárth.

And this possession, this delight, are independent of material well-being. His body indeed is succumbing under the blows which continue to fall, his mind (heart) is losing its grip. No matter!

> 26. Faíling are my flésh and my heárt;    the róck of my
>     heárt and my pórtion is Gód for éver.

One is reminded of St. Paul's words: "though our outward man is decaying, yet our inward man is renewed day by day" (2 Cor. 4:16).

And now for a final contrast in this Psalm of contrasts:

> 27. For behóld, they that go far from theé shall pérish;
> thou destróyest every one who plays the hárlot from theé.

How could he envy them—who will not be *with God,* who will not give their love to the true Lover. Well, let them depart if they wish. For him there is but one course:

> 28. But *Í*—to draw neár to Gód is my goód;     I sét in the Lórd Yahwéh my réfuge,
> To téll áll thy wórks.

Thus the Psalmist who but now almost abandoned God, almost decided to "tell" or "talk" of the advantage of insolent wickedness, as the wicked do—has come back with overwhelming conviction to God as his only joy and only refuge and is "telling" of all the things God does. That is why he is writing this Psalm! Like the Author of Psalm 32, his own experience of God is making him an evangelist. For his poem is addressed to his fellow-men, that they may learn what good they have in God, if only they also will "draw near" to Him. Here is "Wisdom." Only it is not cool, as is so often the Wisdom of the teachers; it pours out glowing from a deep inner fire of love. And in this also he is like the author of Psalm 32.

It must be noticed that our Psalmist says nothing of any outward deliverance.[1] So far as we can see, he is just as ill and just as poor as he was when the great temptation assailed him. He has simply awakened to his inward possession. He does indeed say that he will tell of all God's works and possibly outward restoration may constitute a chief element in these. His meaning is not clear. But we can be certain that he will also tell of the works that he has already declared to be

---

[1] Mowinckel, who regards this as a Thank-Psalm, maintains that the Psalmist, on entering the temple to subject himself to the customary rites of purification, has been healed of his sickness, and that the healing has proved to him that God is good to him and hostile to his enemies. (*Psalmenstudien* I, p. 128.) This seems rather fanciful.

the very fabric of his happiness—God's supporting grasp, His
counsel, His welcome with glory. And these seem to be independent of outward circumstances. It is this independence of
the material, joined with our Psalmist's joy in God's fellowship, that makes him perhaps the most spiritual, the most inward of all the saints who have contributed to the creation of
the Psalter. It is hard to see how he falls below St. Paul in his
looking to the things which are not seen (2 Cor. 4:18)—except
perhaps in one point.

Does he look beyond death? When he affirms that God will
"afterward receive him to glory (or, take him in glory)," is
he thinking of a transaction which transcends this present life?
Opinion is divided, and in the nature of the case the answer
cannot be certain either way. The Hebrew text as it stands
seems to indicate the affirmative, but it is not perfectly plain—
not nearly so plain as the English translation! Gunkel and
Schmidt are among those who feel themselves compelled to
emend it so that the verse refers to the present life only.
Gunkel would read: "and in the path thou dost make me strong
in heart." Schmidt contents himself with regrouping the present
consonants so that they give the sense: "thou drawest me by
the hand after thee." Schmidt does not state his reasons for
discarding the existing text but Gunkel has a few words to say
in support of his action. Linguistically, he maintains, the expressions "afterward" and "to glory," while possible, are difficult. The word "take," which implies that like Enoch the
Psalmist will be carried up to heaven, arouses strong doubts.
But the really determining consideration is that the idea of a
future life does not fit in with the thought-world of the Psalmists. "It is a belief which does not appear in the whole Psalter,
but was first naturalized in Israel in a later period, and that
not without the influence of foreign religions. Its place is in
the apocalyptic literature of that period." To find it in our
Psalm constitutes an "anachronism of centuries." One can see
that Gunkel feels intensely on the subject. "It is no page for
our science to be proud of," he adds, "that such interpretations

still remain alive—yes, have actually the reputation of being peculiarly religious and profound!"

His animus is directed against the recent commentators who retain the Hebrew text with its outlook on a future life. Among these he mentions Staerk, Kittel, Duhm and Bertholet. These have on their side the Hebrew words as they stand, which in spite of "difficult" expressions do seem to mean that God will take the Psalmist to (or in) glory after this life is over. Nor is the strain which such an interpretation puts upon the text so great that one is compelled to emend it. The Septuagint, which goes back to a Hebrew text far older than ours, reads "thou didst receive me with glory," though it omits "afterward." This seems to throw some weight on the side of our reading. In answer to Gunkel's objection that the Psalter does not contain such a belief, it may be said that this is a late Psalm, and may well come from a period when faith in a blessed hereafter was stirring in some circles of Judaism. Moreover, it is by no means *certain* that such faith does not appear in other Psalms (e.g. 16, 17, 49), as it probably does (if only in passing) in Job 19. But the strongest indication that our Psalmist held it is the tone of his poem. He seems to be occupied with a good which "flies beyond" earthly experience, which will continue his *even though* his flesh and his heart fail (v.26). The failing of flesh and heart—their coming to an end—means death. But, he says, God is his portion *for ever*. "For ever" here appears to overleap the bound ordinarily set to it in the Old Testament. Kittel may be right in thinking also that he sees the fate of the wicked likewise extending beyond bodily death. As we have said, certainty is impossible in this matter. Each must interpret after his own literary feeling. But however scholars may disagree on the meaning of verse 24, they are in complete accord as to the unique greatness of our Psalmist. Gunkel compares the manner in which he came to see how the fellowship of God could outweigh the loss of bodily health with the revelation Christ gave to St. Paul when he asked for the removal of his "stake in the flesh"; "My grace is sufficient for thee, for my power is made perfect in weakness" (2 Cor. 12:9). "Thus in its loftiest passage the Psalm passes upward into the height of the New Testament." We add this word of Staerk: "Psalm 73 is the confession of a saint of the Old Covenant to which even the Christian can never listen without deep reverence. It is as if there stood over this most personal of all the prayers of the Psalter, in invisible letters, the words of Exodus 3:5: 'Draw off thy shoes, for the place on which thou standest is holy ground.' " [1]

---

[1] For a brief treatment of this Psalmist as representing the religious attitude of mind as contrasted with the philosophic, see W. Temple, *Nature, Man and God*, London, 1935, p. 39ff.

# VI

# AN AUTHOR OF A ROYAL PSALM

THE Psalter contains a number of Psalms which have to do with a king (2, 18, 20, 21, 45, 72, 101, 110, 132, 144:1-11, 89:46-51). Abundant evidence in these Psalms shows that in each case the king is an Israelitish or Jewish monarch actually seated on the throne. The occasions on which they were rendered are seen from allusions in both the Royal Psalms themselves and in the other Old Testament books to be various events and celebrations in the life of the king, from the day of his accession to the day of his burial. They were composed and sung by people belonging to the royal chapel. Such poetic and musical production was highly prized, even King David himself not disdaining to act as minstrel. They were rendered in the presence of the king and his great men in the palace or in the temple amid surroundings of splendor and majesty. We must look upon them therefore as emanating not from the people but from a court-poet.

The various occasions of the Biblical Royal Poems are often clearly indicated by the Poems themselves. They were the festival of the accession to the throne, the king's birthday, his marriage, his dedication of the sanctuary, his joyous return after a victorious campaign, his thanksgiving for victory, his recovery from serious illness, his lament in trouble and finally the elegy sung over his dead body.

For this reason the Royal Psalms do not strictly speaking constitute a single Type like the other Types we have been considering but form a whole series of Types. Some of them

correspond to the Thanksgivings and Laments of the People,
some to Types composed by the Individual; and they borrow
from such Types. Much more common however is borrowing
the other way round. In Psalms composed by private individuals we frequently find expressions which properly could
be used only by a king. An example is Psalm 27:3, where the
Psalmist speaks of a host of men encamping against him; or
Psalm 43:1 in which another Psalmist asks Yahweh to plead
his cause against an ungodly nation. These expressions have
led some commentators to hold that it could not be a private
man who is speaking. But the true explanation is that phrases
of Royal Psalms were taken over by individual poets—a fact
which gives rise to the question whether Royal Psalmody was
not generally older than individual compositions. This borrowing of royal patterns may seem surprising, but it was possible,
as we see from examples in Babylonia and Egypt.

The general content of the Royal Psalms is made up of several elements. There are praises of the prince's glory, depictions
of Yahweh's favor to him—how he is chosen, anointed, exalted
by God—prayers uttered by the king himself and intercessions on his behalf by the poet, royal oracles and portrayals
of the king's righteousness and piety. Sometimes one of these
elements will dominate an entire Psalm, as a royal oracle dominates Psalm 2. Sometimes they are mingled, it may be in liturgical fashion.

If we put together these several elements we get a har-
monious general picture—one of a divinely blessed, prosperous
and righteous king, who even in trouble is sure of divine help:
one to whom the prayer of his loyal subjects and the oracle of
his God proclaims whatsoever a royal heart may desire.

The vagueness of such portrayals—the absence of any royal
names (except those of David and Melchizedek), the omission
of definite political conditions—is significant and indicates that
the Psalmists were describing their ideal of a ruler rather than
an actual king. Indeed these Psalms could without difficulty
be transferred from one ruler to another.

It is further significant that these Royal Psalms are at the same time religious poems. This lies in the nature of the case; for the ancient state—more even than the modern—was one of the highest of human values for whose preservation man would pray. In Israel the state religion had two principles. The first, that the prince stands in a peculiarly near relation to Yahweh, receiving honor that approaches that of God Himself. The second, that Yahweh is *over* him, he depends on Yahweh for everything and his successes redound to Yahweh's glory, not his own.

Certain features of the Royal Psalms agree with what we learn of customs connected with the monarchy from the Biblical books outside the Psalter. The king is a priest; he is addressed and spoken of in extravagant terms; immortality is asked for him; his battles and victories are portrayed in the most exaggerated way as his personal accomplishments, nothing being said of the prowess of the army; and finally world dominion is ascribed to him.

When we compare this picture of Israel's king with what we find in the Royal Psalms, there is a remarkable likeness. The same forms, the same extravagance, the same ideas appear. This corresponds to the fact, which Gunkel establishes at some length, that the Israelitish monarchy itself was patterned after those of surrounding nations, especially the great empires of Assyria, Babylonia and Egypt, and that its royal court looked up to those as its high example. There can be no doubt therefore that the Royal Psalms of Israel imitated those of the world-peoples. Thus the Melchizedek of Psalm 110:4 is a foreign model of the Judahite princes. In Psalm 2 the depiction of subject peoples rebelling against the new king of Israel is a manifest copy of what took place so often in a change of rulers in an empire, while such a situation never existed in Israel. In the same way, the title "God" or "God's son," applied to the king, arose among the polytheistically-thinking world-peoples, not in Israel.

In spite however of all this imitation the Royal Psalms of Israel are no mere copies; they rise superior to the poetry of the same Type in other peoples. Their poetic greatness, the loftiness of their religious ideas, the way in which they subordinate the king to Yahweh, refusing him anything like worship, and finally their emphasis upon the idea of royal righteousness taken from the Prophets, all unite in making them unique.

The period of these Psalms is Pre-Exilic for they all emanate from the time of the first monarchy. To Gunkel's mind there is no ground for placing any of them in the Maccabean age.

A word should be said in closing as to the Messianic interpretation of the Royal Psalms. It has been the prevailing view in both synagogue and church that the majority of them refer to the Messiah about to come. Gunkel feels that Type-study, by considering these Psalms in their common features, has shown that they refer not to a future but to a reigning king. "This is seen first of all in those passages where the ruler is prayed for or where an oracle is announced to him. The Messiah, on the contrary, appears immediately in full possession of his glory. A like consideration applies to Psalm 2 where the ruler is not yet in actual possession of world dominion. It is true that the picture of an ideal king as painted in the Royal Psalms is very like that of the Messiah which floats before the Prophets. Some have endeavored to explain this remarkable similarity by holding that traits of the future king have been transferred to the present ruler (Ewald, Kessler, Kittel, Staerk). But it is much simpler to suppose that both circles of ideas have sprung from the same root. This is the ideal picture of a ruler, which the court-poets apply to their king and the Prophets see in the future. Only indeed it makes a very great difference whether the court-singer beholds this ideal in the present or the Prophet, standing far above him and turning away from the whole present, seeks it with glowing heart in the future."

Consider now the Author of the greatest Royal Psalm.

# The Author of Psalm 72

*He shall keep the simple folk by their right*

A young ruler has come to the throne of Judah, a legitimate scion of the royal house.[1] All the nation is rejoicing in high hopes. At the splendid feast which marks his accession our Psalmist steps forward amid the expectant silence of the new king and his whole court, perhaps also of a listening multitude of the common people, and striking full upon his tuneful lyre sings his song.

> 1. O Gód, gíve thy júdgments to the kíng     and thy ríghteousness to the kíng's són;
> 2. May he júdge[2] thy peóple in ríghtness     and thy poór in jústice.

It is with a prayer that he begins. That is characteristic of the Royal Psalms of Israel, which always subordinate the king to God. He can do nothing of himself, but only as God enables him. The first word therefore is *God*. And what better thing can a loyal subject do for his sovereign than to pray for him? Our Psalmist may be poor: some scholars think so because of his interest in the lowly. But does not God pay special heed to the prayers of the poor?

And his heart is with the common people. As he looks upon the face of this new and untried king his thought is of them

---

[1] Herkenne follows Christian and Jewish tradition in regarding this Psalm as spoken directly of the Messiah, not of any earthly king; though he admits that the Author may have drawn many of his images from the splendor of Solomon's reign. Oesterley (*Fresh Approach,* etc., p. 195) expresses uncertainty as to whether the Psalm is written of an earthly ruler or of the ideal Messiah, declaring that there is much to be said for either view. It is hard, he says, to interpret v. 17 of an earthly ruler. (Yet he seems to do so on p. 202.) König thinks that the Psalm was written concerning Solomon and not the future Messiah.

[2] The verbs following might equally well be translated by simple futures, as Mowinckel points out. "In reality," he says, "there is absolutely no distinction made here between blessing and promise. Such a distinction rests upon modern concept-forms and modes of thought." Both promises and blessings to the ancient Israelite were words of power which could have effect only if they came from a person divinely endowed with the capacity to pronounce them, such as a prophet. *Psalmenstudien* III, p. 93.

and what this accession may mean to them. So he prays first of all that the king may take them under the protection of his justice—nay of God's justice, for does not all right come from on high? And with justice may well-being mingle!

> 3. May the moúntains beár peáce to the peóple    and the
>    hílls ríghteousness.*

It is not quite clear what he means, for the Hebrew word *peace* is much wider than ours and usually includes the idea of prosperity. He is probably anticipating the petition he utters in v.16 for abundant harvests; may they clothe all the heights! Or he may be using a simile, as Gunkel thinks: may peace and righteousness sprout forth on the hills like the young grass after the rains! In either case he is holding fast to the thought of justice and in the next verse he goes on with it:

> 4. May he júdge the poór of the peóple,    may he hélp the
>    sóns of the neédy    and crúsh the oppréssor.

In those last words he strikes a note that is very characteristic of the Old Testament. Constantly its writers speak of the rich and powerful as grinding the faces of the poor, taking away their rights, even devouring them. Against these oppressors the poor can do nothing; the government must intervene if justice is to be had. One of the chief things expected of a king is that he champion the weak. In a very real sense he is not to be neutral, like an umpire whose function is to see that the game is played according to rule. If that were done the poor would have little chance for they are not strong enough to stand up to their opponents. No, the king, the government is to get into the contest, to fight on the weaker side. For God is fighting there also!

Now our Psalmist prays in the extravagant phrases handed down by custom for the enduring rule, the prosperity, justice, victories and world-wide dominion of the new king:

> 5. May he live ón* with the sún    and befóre the moón,
>    generátion on generátions;
> 6. May he come dówn as the raín upon mown gráss,    as
>    shówers that sprínkle* the eárth;
> 7. May ríghteousness* floúrish in his dáys    and abún-
>    dance of peáce till the moón be no móre;

8. And may he rúle from seá to seá     and from the Ríver
   to the énds of the eárth;
9. Befóre him may his ádversaries* bow dówn     and his
   énemies líck the dúst;
10. Let the kíngs of Társhish and the coástlands     rénder
    a présent;
    Let the kíngs of Shéba and Séba     bríng a gíft;
11. Let áll kíngs prostráte themselves before him,     let áll
    nátions sérve him.

We have seen how these court-poets, following the fashion
set by the minstrels in great imperial centers, do not hesitate
to ask for eternal life and world rule on behalf of their sov-
ereigns. Our Psalmist here paints a glowing picture of his
young king's reign, dashing on the colors with lavish hand.
With special delight he dwells upon the immense reaches of
his dominion: from one of earth's bounding oceans to the
other, from the Euphrates westward without limit. Up come
the subject kings, laden with tribute, from Tartessus in Spain,
from the Hellenic islands dotting the Mediterranean, from
Sheba in South Arabia, from Seba in Ethiopia. Overborne by
his prowess they do him homage—these proud commercial
peoples. And why? Because God thus rewards his care for the
lowly. So the Psalmist returns to his favorite theme:

12. For he will delíver the poór when he criés     and the
    lówly and hím who has no hélper;
13. He will have píty upon the poór and the neédy,     and
    the soúls of the poór he will hélp;
14. From oppréssion and víolence he will redeém their soúl,
    and précious shall their bloód be in his éyes.

Our Psalmist is enlarging upon his brief description of v.4.
One of the privileges of the poor was to cry to the king. They
had access to his presence and their appeal, "Help, O king" (II
Sam. 14:4; II Ki. 6:26) was regarded as binding the monarch
to listen to their case. He was indeed their powerful friend,
their *goel* or redeemer, sacredly obligated to obtain justice for
them. However the rich and influential might despise them,
holding their lives as of little account, to the king each was
valuable and the shedding of their blood no light matter. What
moved him was compassion. Like God, he was sorry for them,
he cared for their "souls," their poor selves so dear to them.

However far individual kings might fall below this high service
it remained still the ideal which Israel cherished in its heart
for its ruler; and our Psalmist is voicing it here.

He concludes with the thought of the new king's happiness—
a happiness that will rest upon the prayers of the poor!

> 15. And may he líve and may there be gíven him of the góld
>     of Shéba,
>     And may men práy for hím contínually,    all the dáy
>     may they bléss him;
> 16. May there bé an abundance of graín in the lánd    on the
>     tóp of the moúntains;
>     May his fruít rústle like Lébanon    and may they bloóm
>     from the cíty like the gráss of the eárth;
> 17. May his náme bé for éver    before the sún let his náme
>     endúre; *
>     And may all nátions bléss themselves in hím,    may all
>     fámilies of the eárth * call him háppy!

There he stops, for the last two verses appended to his
Psalm are no part of it, being the "Gloria" affixed to the entire
Second Book of Psalms.

The more we study Psalm 72 the more we are impressed with
its uniqueness in two important aspects.

First, it is the only one of the Royal Psalms to dwell at any
length upon the king's duty to befriend the poor. Gunkel does
indeed speak as if this feature characterised the Royal Psalms
in general but even a cursory glance at them will show that
almost all the expressions looking to such an ideal are confined to our Psalmist. We have already pointed out that the
only other Psalms in the Psalter which are colored through
and through with the passion for social justice are Psalms 82
and 146, and these are not Royal Psalms. True, we meet with
occasional utterances elsewhere which affirm God's care for
the poor but none of them is at all dominant in the Psalm that
contains it.

Second, our Psalmist is the only one of all the Psalmists to
bring out the idea of vocation. His king has a definite calling,
a work to do for God and man. Another Royal Psalm does
indeed give a ruler's declaration of policy (Ps. 101) and implies a sense of vocation; but our Psalmist is carried away by
his enthusiasm for the new ruler's calling. By fulfilling it truly

the king will obtain from God the reward of world dominion. Outside the Royal Psalms we meet Psalmists who feel constrained to testify concerning God's goodness to them, who are intent on persuading men to follow in His ways; but one gets the impression that this obligation does not constitute a life-work in their eyes. Perhaps it does. In the case of the Writers of Psalm 51 and Psalm 22 it may well be just that. But they do not speak as if such activity were to take their full time; it is rather something added to their daily employment, a voluntary use of leisure hours. It is not with them as with the Prophets, whom God summoned to dedicate their whole lives to His service.

It is because of these two qualities that our Psalmist was thought by both Jews and Christians to be describing the future Messiah. We have followed the modern view that he is speaking of a present ruler. For that reason we have translated the verbs prevailingly as jussives rather than as futures, making the Psalm a prayer instead of a prophecy. For our Psalmist claims no divinely given authority to declare what God will bring to pass; he contents himself with asking that his dream may come true. That is the interpretation given by the newer Jewish version of the Scriptures, and by several of the modern commentators. But we cannot deny that the Psalm possesses an atmosphere of exalted expectancy, a bold free power of vision, which makes the ringing futures of our American Revised Version seem almost convincing.

No, he did not intend to portray the Messiah to come; but he drew so nobly upon the common tradition which supplied both him and the Prophets with the picture of an ideal king that the only true parallels to his Psalm are to be found not in the Psalter but in the Book of Isaiah, where inspired Seers painted the same picture upon the vaster canvas of the Age to Be.

> For unto us a child is born,     unto us a son is given....
> And there shall come forth a shoot out of the stock of
>     Jesse....
> Behold, a king shall reign in righteousness,     and princes
>     shall rule in justice.... (Is. 9:6ff., 11:1ff., 32:1ff.)

We need not wonder then that the Psalm was held to be Messianic. And this fact suggests a question which is often raised today. If Jesus Himself so regarded it how far did He take over into His own conception of His Messiahship the program of social justice which it embodies? Weighty voices constantly assert that He had no such program; and certainly there is little evidence of it in His recorded teaching. He never quotes our Psalmist—indeed, no Book of the New Testament does quote him. But we know from the *Magnificat* that there lived in some circles of early Jewish Christians the burning hope of a divine social reconstruction connected with the Messiah:

> He hath showed strength with his arm;
> He hath scattered the proud in the imagination of their heart.
> He hath put down princes from their thrones,
> And hath exalted them of low degree.
> The hungry he hath filled with good things;
> And the rich he hath sent empty away. (Lk. 1:51ff.)

We know also that there survives in St. Luke's Gospel a form of the Beatitudes which looks in the same direction:

> Blessed are ye poor:     for yours is the kingdom of God.
> Blessed are ye that hunger now:     for ye shall be filled....
> But woe unto you that are rich!     for ye have received your consolation.
> Woe unto you that are full now!     for ye shall hunger....
>                                 (Lk. 6:21ff.)

We know again that Jesus' first action when He came into Jerusalem as its King was to purge the temple of its market, in which the poor were robbed by the great families. He was not allowed to show what His next step would be!

Perhaps none of these things point to a social program in Jesus' mind. Perhaps He believed that our Psalmist and the writers of the Isaiah passages and the other Old Testament utterances which held up the ideal of the ruler as shepherd of the people (e.g. Ezek. 34) were telling of something quite unrelated to His own Kingship.

Yet if the contrary be true then we are justified in thinking that He responded to the picture painted by our Psalmist and the Prophets, that He felt Himself one with them in spirit and aspiration, that when He was crucified as King of the Jews the title which was nailed above Him on the cross meant that He was on the side of the poor.

But apart from the possible influence of our Psalmist on the idea of the Messiah he has a contribution to make to the political thinking of our age. It is the Old Testament conception of the function and attitude of government. The men of the Old Testament from Moses down start with the conviction that the poor people, which means the majority of the people, cannot attain to well-being without the help of their rulers. The ruler then must be a shepherd; not in the sentimental modern sense of the word but in the very practical sense of a man in charge of sheep. It is his business to see that they get food and drink and are protected from their enemies. In other words the ruler must assume the economic responsibility for his people and his special care must be to prevent the rich and powerful from exploiting them. This appears plainly in Ezekiel 34 where good and bad "shepherds" are described. Many Americans may brand such a conception of government as "paternalism" and indeed it is, if by "paternalism" we mean that the ruler must look out for his people as the father looks out for his children.

Our Psalmist, who stands on common ground here with other Old Testament writers, has several things to say about government that may well challenge our thought.

One is, that the true attitude of the ruler should be one of pity. Anything like hardness is to be avoided. He is therefore not in the least afraid of letting tenderness and compassion dominate governmental measures for the poor.

Another characteristic of the true ruler is his sense of the value of the poor as individuals. Their blood will be precious, weighty in his eyes. He will save and redeem their *souls*, which means their "selves." In the Old Testament "soul" is not the immortal and spiritual part of a man but the man himself looked at as a center of desires, longings, feelings. It is usually spoken of with a real affection, with a very human sympathy. It is a term of warmth, of understanding and appreciation.

Again, our Psalmist knows that such a ruler will draw out the love of his people; and that ought to be the feeling of the governed for the government. They should regard it as their friend, not hate it or be indifferent to it. It in turn should be distinctly on their side against their exploiters; it is their "redeemer."

Finally, such a government need not fear poverty. It will see abundance of grain in the earth upon the top of the mountains. The reason is, that God will bless it for doing right by the poor. We perhaps would prefer to say that it will bring in prosperity because it is proceeding along fundamentally sound lines—in accord with God's purpose and the nature of things. The only economic policy which can hope to succeed is one that is built upon the broad base of universal well being.

# VII

# A PSALMIST WHO USED THE
# ANCIENT STORIES OF
# ISRAEL

EVERY READER of the Bible knows the unique beauty of
the ancient stories of Israel's early days as we find them
in the historical books beginning with Genesis and Exodus.
When these became current in their developed literary form
they furnished material which lent itself naturally to the purposes of the Psalmist. If a Hymn writer wished to celebrate
the glorious doings of God how could he do so better than by
recalling the mighty acts by which Israel had been freed from
Egypt and brought at last into the land of promise? The composer of a Lament, whose aim was to induce God to intervene
on behalf of His people, could find in these same mighty acts a
compelling reason why God should save Israel in the present.
A Wisdom Psalmist, undertaking to exhort and warn his contemporaries, might well draw from the ancient stories the admonition that Israel today should not repeat the rebellion of
the fathers who were overthrown in the wilderness.

Thus the several Types of Psalms made each its own use
of the early stories employing them at first only in passing
allusions which fitted easily into the forms of the Type. Later
however when the Types began to disintegrate certain Psalmists
(Pss. 78, 105, 106; cf. Deut. 32 and Is. 63:7 ff.) began to introduce such large blocks of narrative that these formed the *main
content* of the Psalm and gave rise to a new kind of composition. The forms of the original Type were still retained, whether

it were a Hymn, a Thanksgiving, a Lament or a Wisdom Psalm. But the preponderance in each case of the story element gave to such Psalms certain common features which mark them plainly as belonging to a distinct literary class, fairly recognizable from its material as well as from its style.

"They have a common form—the Narration—... (which) is limited to a circumscribed area of material, to *Yahweh's deeds towards Israel* from its immigration into Egypt to its entrance into Canaan." This material is handled with freedom, according to the several Psalmists' needs, but one trait distinguishes all: "The naturalness (*Naturwüchsamkeit*) and naivete of the old stories and their mutual independence in form and content has disappeared. On the contrary, the material is conceived as a unit and drawn under a prevailing religious point of view" enforcing the purpose of the Psalmist. Another characteristic of these stories is their extraordinary love of the miraculous; they tell exclusively of the marvels wrought by God in early days, such as the plagues, the crossing of the Red Sea, the leading of the fiery cloudy pillar, the water from the rock, the quails and similar features. All these traits show that the ancient stories had now become legends.

We must not suppose however that these legends ever constituted an *independent* Type of Psalm. On the contrary, they never stand independently but wherever they appear in the Psalms are always subordinated to the recognized Types.

"The place at which the legendary material fastened itself to the characteristic stamp that appears in the Psalms is the *exhortation,* as it is known preeminently from Deuteronomy. To admonish Israel to trust in Yahweh, to warn them against falling away from their God in sin and apostasy, these stories of the wilderness period were assembled telling of Yahweh's various miracles and of the sins of the wilderness generation, which Yahweh was compelled to visit with heavy punishment. Hence finally we get both applications of such material in the Psalms mentioned (i.e. for Hymns and for Laments). To this origin also we must ultimately ascribe the *didactic tendency,* of which likewise the legends in the Psalms show traces. The

Legend-class, which is the product of Deuteronomic exhortation, was in a later age yet further elaborated. A characteristic of the late form of the class is its increasing bulk and its close connection with the final revision of the Pentateuchal tradition. Such in its main features is the history of the Legends outside lyrical poetry."

It was in their late form, dependent on the written Pentateuch, that the legends found entrance into the Psalms and (as we have said) were used by the Psalmists to enforce their several purposes. Nor did these Psalmists stop with stories of the early period. Following the lead of the Deuteronomic editors of the books succeeding the Pentateuch they employed also narratives of the later times, as we shall see in the poem we are about to study.

# THE AUTHOR OF PSALM 106

## *We have sinned with our fathers*

Most of the Psalmists whom we have considered thus far have given utterance to some aspect of the life of the individual soul with God. But we have been reminded from time to time that the Psalter contains also Psalms which express the feelings of the nation or of a group within the nation. The Author of Psalm 44, for instance, voices a Lament of the People. There are also national Hymns, such as Psalm 105, and National Thanksgivings like Psalm 124. Psalm 72 and the other Royal Psalms may likewise be regarded as composed in the name of Israel. But of all the National Psalms that have come down to us the most poignant are those which declare the sin of Israel, such as Psalms 81, 78, and 106. The two latter use the ancient stories at great length. The Author of Psalm 78 speaks as a Wise Man drawing stern admonition from Israel's long history of rebellion and ingratitude. The man who wrote Psalm 106 [1] however utters what Gunkel calls a "General Confession" of his people's sins.

Like all his fellows this Psalmist throws little light upon himself and the situation in which he writes. From the prayer of verse 47, "Gather us from among the nations," scholars infer that many of the Jews of his time are scattered through heathen lands. This would point to the later Post-Exilic Period when the Diaspora had attained increasing size and importance. The fact that he makes free use of earlier writings and especially of the Pentateuch in its most developed form points also to a late date. Perhaps, as Gunkel thinks, he himself is a member of some expatriated Jewish community. It is plain that the

---

[1] Herkenne regards the Psalm as composite, the historical part (v.7c-43) being the work of an older poet which a redactor prepared for the use of his contemporaries by adding a beginning (v.4ff.) and a conclusion. Löhr (*Psalmenstudien*, p. 22) also holds that the Psalm is composite, the original part being v.7-46. "This core is also the part that properly has value in our Psalm—a poem, or better, the fragment of a poem—of the Type of spiritual, poetic treatments of Israel's history."

condition of his people is not a happy one. He says nothing indeed of their being persecuted or of any special disaster having overtaken them. But the mood of his Psalm is heavy, in spite of its opening burst of praise. The long doom incurred by Israel's sin still hangs over the nation and the thought of that sin has chief place in his mind.

In his Psalm he speaks for his people and he may have intended it to be used by them in worship, for it lends itself easily to a division among antiphonal voices. Kittel remarks that its very dependence on older words of scripture, its piecing of these together to make as it were a "mosaic," would render it a favorite in public worship since in its manifold borrowings the congregation would recognize familiar and beloved echoes. But of course the corporate character of the Psalm must not obscure for us the truth that after all it comes from the soul of the individual Psalmist. The opening verses, as Barnes rightly says, "forbid us to regard it as a simple piece of liturgy. Some one like Ezra felt in his own great heart all the emotions of this Psalm, before it was taken over by Levitical hands for Temple use. The cry of the individual soul is heard in the words, 'Remember me....O visit me (v.4).'"

His "General Confession" begins in a surprising way:

1. Give thánks unto Yahwéh, for he is goód,    for to etérnity is his mércy!
2. Whó can téll the mighty ácts of Yahwéh,    útter áll his praíse?
3. Bléssed are they who keép jústice,    who dó ríghteousness at all tímes!

This, one would think, is no Psalm of Penitence but a Hymn. Yet as he utters his beatitude on the happy righteous his thought turns sadly to himself. How different his own lot—for he is *not* righteous! (Gunkel). And so he passes to a prayer for deliverance such as marks a Lament:

4. Remémber me, Yahwéh, in the fávor to thy peóple; vísit me with thy salvátion,
5. That I may loók upon the goód of thy chósen ones, may rejoíce in the jóy of thy peóple, May glóry with thine inhéritance!

He is speaking of the great day to come when God will "turn the captivity" of Israel. May he be chosen to partake of its gladness! But even while he gazes upon that coming sunshine the dark cloud of the present shuts it away and he can think only of what now, as in the past, stands between Israel and Yahweh's salvation:

6. We have sínned with our fáthers,     have committed iníquity, have done évil!

7. Our fáthers in Égypt     understoód not thy wondrous wórks;
   They remémbered not the greátness of thy lovingkínd-ness,     but rebélled against the Most Hígh * at the Red Seá.

8. But he sáved them for his náme's sáke,     to make knówn his míght;

9. And he rebúked the Red Seá, and it dried úp,     and he made them to gó in the deéps as in the wílderness;

10. And he sáved them from the hánd of the háter,     and redeémed them from the hánd of the énemy;

11. And the wáters cóvered their ádversaries—     not óne of thém was léft!

12. And they had faíth in his wórds,     they sáng his praíse.

Thus, as is required in a General Confession, he goes back to the very beginning of the nation, setting in tragic contrast the "wondrous works" of Yahweh and the people's rebellion: a rebellion all the more unrelieved because it was met by God with undeserved kindness. In this sin of the remote past our Psalmist feels that he and his contemporaries have a share. It is not alone that his generation are still suffering from its *consequences;* they are burdened with its *guilt* (Kittel).

So he reviews one by one the succeeding sins of the people. First, their demand for flesh:

13. Quíckly they forgót his deéds,     they waíted not for his coúnsel;

14. But they lústed lúst in the wílderness,     and made tríal of Gód in the désert;

15. And he gáve thém their requést—     and sént wásting into their soúl!

Yes, for God cannot be resisted with impunity! Thus it proved in the rebellion of Dathan, Abiram and Korah:

16. And they were jeálous of Móses in the cámp,     of Aáron, the hóly one of Yahwéh;

17. The eárth ópened and swállowed Dáthan,    and clósed
    over the cómpany of Abíram;
18. And fíre búrned in their assémbly,    fláme set abláze
    the wícked.

Then came their defiance in worshipping the golden bull:

19. They máde a cálf in Hóreb,    and bowed dówn to a
    molten ímage;
20. And they chánged their glóry    for the líkeness of an óx
    eáting gráss!
21. They forgót Gód their Sávior,    who díd great thíngs in
    Égypt,
22. Márvels in the lánd of Hám,    feárful things at the Red
    Seá.
23. And he thoúght to wipe them oút,    had nót Móses his
    chósen
    Stoód in the breách befóre him    to turn awáy his wráth
    from destróying.

Persuaded by their cowardly spies they refused to invade
Canaan:

24. And they rejécted the desírable lánd,    they gave no
    faíth to his wórd;
25. And they grúmbled in their ténts,    they heárkened not
    to the voíce of Yahwéh.
26. And he swóre an oáth to thém    that he would make
    thém fáll in the wílderness,
27. And that he would scátter * their seéd among the nátions,
    and stréw them among the coúntries.

When finally they came into contact with agricultural civilization they fell a prey to its nature worship:

28. And they joíned themselves to the Báal of Péor    and
    áte the sácrifices to the deád.[1]
29. And they provóked him * by their dóings    and the
    plágue broke oút among them;
30. And Phínehas rose úp and wrought júdgment    and the
    plágue was chécked;
31. And it was réckoned to hím for ríghteousness,    to gen-
    erátion on generátion for éver.

Here for the second time our Psalmist draws a sharp contrast between an outstanding leader and the people. First
Moses, then Phinehas towered above the multitude, "blessed"
because they "kept justice and did righteousness at all times"
(v.3). But alas! the sin of the people finally involved even
Moses:

[1] This statement is not found in the Pentateuchal account and seems to
rest upon an independent tradition.

32. And they ángered him * at the wáters of Merî'bah,     and
    it went íll with Móses becaúse of them;

33. For they embíttered * his spírit,     and he spoke ráshly
    with his líps.

Then when Moses was dead and they had gained possession
of Canaan they fraternized with its corrupt population, taking
over the cruel rites of its nature religion:

34. They did not destróy the peóples,     as Yahwéh had
    bídden thém,

35. They míngled among the nátions,     and leárned their
    dóings,

36. And sérved their ídols,     and these becáme to thém a
    snáre;

37. And they sácrificed their sóns     and their daúghters to
    démons,

38. And they poured oút ínnocent bloód. . . . * and the lánd
    was profáned with their bloód,

39. And they became ancleán by their ácts     and played the
    hárlot by their deéds.

So the inevitable retribution followed, as it is repeatedly portrayed in the Book of Judges:

40. And Yahwéh's anger was kíndled at his peóple     and he
    abóminated his inhéritance;

41. And he gáve them into the hánd of the nátions     and
    their háters rúled óver them,

42. And their énemies oppréssed them     and they were
    brought lów únder their hánd.

43. Mány tímes he delívered them     but théy were rebél-
    lious in their coúnsel;
    And they were húmbled in their iníquity.

44. And he loóked upon theír distréss     when he heárd their
    crý,

45. And he remémbered for thém his cóvenant     and he re-
    pénted according to the greátness of his lovingkínd-
    ness;

46. And he máde thém to be pítied     bý all their cáptors,[1]

Thus the great confession closes upon the note not of Israel's
sin but of God's forgiving love. And because he is sure of this
love our Psalmist is bold to pass from penitence to prayer:

---

[1] This last clause does not seem to correspond to anything narrated in
the Book of Judges. Either it rests upon an independent tradition or it
carries the story down to the end of the Exile, when the lot of the captive
Jews was much ameliorated.

47. Sáve us, Yahwéh our Gód,        and gáther us from the
    nátions,
    To give thánks to the náme of thy hóliness,      to glóry
    in thy praíse.[1]

Now that we have reviewed his Psalm we may pause before
we conclude our study to frame some reflections upon this man's
religion. To begin with, we perceive that his outlook is far
removed from that of the Author of Psalm 44. A certain re-
semblance between the two men is indeed noticeable, in that
both look back upon the "mighty acts" of Yahweh towards the
fathers with gratitude and humility. It was not Israel's own
sword that possessed Canaan but Yahweh's "arm" (Ps. 44:4).
Both appeal to Yahweh's favor and put their trust in His
lovingkindness. But Psalm 44 is animated by the spirit of war.
Yahweh is called upon as the War-God to help Israel gore and
trample its enemies (v.6). Our Psalmist on the other hand is
quite removed from the atmosphere of war and displays no
rancor towards Israel's oppressors, past or present. But perhaps the chief difference is that Psalm 44 utters no word of
penitence. On the contrary, it declares that Israel have kept
faith with Yahweh; that it is their very faithfulness which is
exposing them to death (vv.18 ff.).[2]

Once more, our Psalmist expresses none of that resentment
towards the past which was felt in the time of Jeremiah and
Ezekiel, when men complained that they were suffering for the
faults of their ancestors: "The fathers have eaten sour grapes,
and the children's teeth are set on edge" (Jer. 31:29; Ezek.
18:2). Instead, he identifies himself and his contemporaries
with the men of old: "We have sinned with our fathers."

But the most amazing thing about him is his philosophy of
Israel's history. On looking back he sees two factors dominating
the successive stages of his nation's experience, giving unity to
them all: God's love and Israel's rebellion. This view of
course is not peculiar to him: it is derived from a great tradition. The Yahwist wove it into the early stories of the Exodus

---

[1] v. 48 is not a part of the Psalm, but the "Gloria" at the end of Book
IV of the Psalter.
[2] Verses numbered according to the Hebrew.

and the Wilderness Wandering, the Deuteronomists impressed it upon the final book of the Pentateuch and carried it down through Israel's history from the days of the Judges to the Exile. The Writing Prophets all shared it and in Jeremiah and Ezekiel it found expression in massive passages such as Jer. 2:4 ff. and Ezek. 23. After the Exile it became a commonplace when applied to the past and for purer souls colored the present. The Post-Exilic literature indeed contains no fewer than three such national confessions besides that of our Psalmist (Ezra 9:6 ff., Neh. 9:9 ff., Dan. 9:4 ff.); and these are rightly regarded as among the most beautiful and profound utterances of the late pre-Christian centuries.

We have used the word "amazing" to describe such an interpretation of Israel's history for the reason that it seems to be unique in the national and racial traditions of mankind. What other people have seen their whole past as a chain of sins? Among the nations of the present does any stand as a penitent before God? Nay, do the *religious people* in any nation regard its past and its present with repentance? Who can forget the ferocity with which in 1918 Christian people attacked Dr. Robert E. Speer when in a missionary address he acknowledged some of the wrongs that our country had done to weaker peoples? After 1929 Christian leaders here and there declared that the sufferings of the depression and the renewed danger of war were the result of human sin; [1] but this conviction apparently did not spread far and was not strong enough to make itself felt in the worship of the Church. The Episcopal Church, for example, never put into its Book of Common Prayer anything corresponding to the great national confessions of the Bible; and it probably does not stand alone in this.

Perhaps we do not need to make such confession. Perhaps our Psalmist and the other Old Testament exponents of the tradition of national penitence were too one-sided in their interpretation of the past. So Duhm maintains. "It is always a serious matter," he remarks contemptuously, "when history

---

[1] For instance, the Pastoral Letters of the House of Bishops of the Episcopal Church in 1933 and 1934.

falls into the hands of the preachers: that can root out 'stump and stalk' all historical meaning and sense of reality." Yet it is significant that Jesus, standing at the end of Israel's national history, read it in an even sterner light than did our Psalmist. Jerusalem, which had ever killed the prophets and stoned them that were sent unto her, was in His day refusing God's final Emissary. Her religious leaders were filling up the measure of their fathers, that upon their generation might come all the righteous blood shed upon the earth (Mt. 23:32 ff., Lk. 11:49 ff.).

But even if this gloomy view of Israel's history were correct, would it be true if applied to America's past and present? Certainly other factors than sin have combined to produce the miseries and forebodings of modern civilization. And over against our corporate sin we must in justice set the sterling qualities, the heroisms and devotions of the mass of our people, without which our common life could not go on.

Nevertheless the tradition which our Psalmist represents cannot be lightly set aside. There may be more truth in it than many of us like to think.

# VIII

# THE AUTHOR OF A PSALM LITURGY

ONE OF THE minor Types of Psalm is the Liturgy. In it portions belonging to different Types are rendered by antiphonal voices. We can call any Psalm a Liturgy if it combines elements belonging to different Types which are rendered by antiphonal voices to produce a unified effect. Such Liturgies follow regular patterns which study enables the investigator to recognize.

They arose from those occasions in public worship when an interchange of speakers took place. A layman, for example, might ask for instruction as to some requirement of the law and receive from a priest the needed *teaching* (Torah: Hag. 2:10 ff., Zech. 7:1 ff.). Again, he might seek guidance in a decision (I Sam. 23:2, 4, 10, 12, etc.) or an explanation of some trouble that had befallen him (II Sam. 21:1 ff.), obtaining the desired information through a priestly *oracle*. In view of the significance attached to both Torah and oracle it is quite understandable that just such questions and responses as contained them would come to be expressed in liturgical form.

Thus arose the Torah Liturgy, of which Psalm 24:3-6 is a good example. It contains the layman's question, the priest's reply and a concluding blessing. We shall study this pattern presently in the kindred Psalm 15.

The oracle was employed in connection with the Lament. When an individual however sought guidance in his perplexity or trouble the oracle would tend to be different in each case; and for that reason, even where these oracles originally existed, they have generally disappeared from the individual Laments that have come down to us. But in the case of Psalm 121 we can see what a Liturgy looks like that grew out of the Lament of an Individual. Here the layman cries for help, the priest reassures him, delivers to him an oracle of cheer (vv.5-6) and concludes with the blessing (vv.7-8). This Psalm may not indeed have been composed to be used as a Liturgy for it may be the creation of the Psalmist's free spirit employing liturgical forms, but in any case it exhibits the characteristic traits of such a Liturgy.

Liturgies that spring from National Laments are more frequent (e.g. Pss. 12, 60, 85), because national troubles and perplexities did not vary greatly from time to time. They show their origin plainly. The Lament is carried through to the prayer for help, then comes invariably the oracle of cheer. This may conclude the Psalm or a further prayer may be added or the certainty of being heard may be expressed. Here may be mentioned also the Royal Psalm 20, a Liturgy rendered when the king of Judah went out to battle.

But the Lament was not the only source of such Liturgies. Psalm 134 was written for the evening of a fast day, Psalms 132 and 24:7-10 for recurring festivals which celebrated the ark. Other Liturgies arose out of Thanksgivings (e.g. Pss. 66 and 118).

In view of the possibilities of effectiveness and variety which these Liturgies presented to public worship it is not surprising that the Prophets made use of them to bring home to the people in a familiar form the thoughts they desired to inculcate. The earliest examples of such use of Liturgies are Hosea 5:15-6:6 and 14.3-9, where the penitential utterance of the people is followed by Yahweh's answering oracle, and Micah 6:6-8, where the Prophet has laid hold of a Torah Liturgy.

But much more significant for the poetry of the Psalms is the way in which after the Exile the Psalmists began to introduce into their compositions the oracle of a Prophet. This was in imitation of the fashion in which the "former" Prophets (now held in high estimation) had interrupted the services of the temple to peal forth their message from God. Thus new liturgical forms of psalmody were created. We have already seen how in Psalm 95 a jubilant Hymn is broken into by a prophetic voice of warning, and the same thing occurs in Psalm 81. In Psalm 53, after a prophetic word of wrathful rebuke and warning (vv.1-6), the people turn to God with a prayer for deliverance (v.7). Psalm 82 gives a prophetic sentence of judgment against the heathen gods (vv. 1-7), which the people confirm with a prayer.

The encouraging side of prophecy also found expression in these Liturgies. The Author of Psalm 126 begins with a prophetic vision of deliverance (vv. 1-3) to which the congregation add their prayer for its consummation (vv. 4-6); and the same is true of Psalm 85, which concludes with an oracle declaring that God has heard the prayer (vv.9-14).[1]

After this brief survey of the varieties and origins of liturgical Psalms let us now consider the Author of a Torah Liturgy who has given us one of the great ethical utterances of the Old Testament.

[1] Verses numbered according to the Hebrew.

LORD, *who shall dwell in thy tabernacle?*

From our brief survey of the Liturgies of the Psalter we see that they cannot be as individual in their character as are Psalms which express the immediate feelings of their composer. What is written for the use of a congregation necessarily transcends the individual. But we must not forget the fact pointed out by Schmidt (see p. 12): however much the writer may merge himself in the assembly of the faithful, it is still he who speaks.

So it is with the man who composed the exquisite little service contained in Psalm 15. He seems to be picturing a company of pilgrims arriving at the gate of the temple. One question is in the minds of all:

> 1. Yahwéh, who may be a guést in thy tént?    who may
>    dwéll upon thy hóly híll?

It is the imagery of hospitality that he uses, the figure of the host and his home which Psalm 23 has employed so beautifully (Psalm 23:5-6). The first half-verse recalls the old nomadic life of the desert where the traveller approached longingly the black tent of the chief, sure of refreshment and protection. Only this is no human host of whom men crave a night's entertainment; it is the God of Israel whose tabernacle is their home and their refuge in the midst of the world, upon whose holy hill they would fain dwell "all the days of their life" (Pss. 27:4, 43:3, 84:11).

But who is worthy to dwell there? From within the voice of a priest returns the divine answer: [1]

> 2. He that wálks blámeless and doés ríght    and speáks
>    trúth in his heárt.

---

[1] Herkenne however maintains that there is no necessity of supposing different voices; question and answer are merely a rhetorical device. König expresses the same view. He also holds that the Psalmist may have been speaking of admission not to the temple, but to God's companionship.

Such are the requirements of God, summed up in a single verse, as now and again Prophets had summed them up (Hos. 6:6, Mic. 6:8). Although a priest is speaking we hear nothing of purification or sacrifice or any ceremonial demand. Even the spiritual duties of man to God, such as loyalty and consecration, are not expressly mentioned. No, it is the great ethical qualities that fit a man for divine companionship.

And now having sketched in bold outline the character of God's guest our Psalmist fills in the details, painting him, so to speak, from the outside:

> 3. He has no slánder upon his tóngue,
>    Doés not évil to his féllow,    and takes not úp a re-
>    proách against his neíghbor.

No need then of suspicion in dealing with him! He does not "foot it around" telling things about you (for that is the meaning of the Hebrew word). On the contrary, if he hears any story to your discredit he lets it drop (cf. Ecclus. 19:10). Have no fear that he is working against you: that he does not do.

Then he takes people for what they really are:

> 4. Despísed in his éyes is a bád man,    and the feárers
>    of Yahwéh he hónors.

No matter how successful a scoundrel may be, or how the crowd may go after him, he shows him the contempt he deserves. Those to whom he looks up are they who are in earnest about their religion, who treat their fellow men right. If they happen to be poor, it makes no difference to him.

Again, he keeps his oath:

> He sweárs to his own húrt and does not chánge.

Circumstances may indeed have altered since he made oath to you, so that to keep it is greatly to his disadvantage; but he will not come to you saying, "I am sorry, but of course I did not foresee...." He "does not change."

Finally, he is not out to make money:

> 5. His móney he does not gíve upon ínterest,    and a
>    bríbe against the ínnocent he does not táke.

When you go to him for a loan in your need he charges you nothing for it. Or if you are wrongfully accused and haled before him as judge, your well-to-do accuser will get nowhere by making him a nice present. That kind of thing "he does not take."

Here our Psalmist is touching upon two social wrongs which bore with special cruelty upon the poor in ancient Israel. The rates of interest exacted from a small borrower ran very high— almost if not fully as high as the legal rate of 42% per annum prevailing today in some of the states of our Union. The Israelitish legislators, unlike the Babylonian, had not gone along with commercial progress so far as to countenance such charges! The taking of *any* interest from a fellow Israelite was sternly forbidden (Exod. 22:25, Lev. 25:36, Deut. 23:19); but that did not trouble the money-lenders! The guest of God however "does not give his money upon interest."

The corruption of justice seems to have been very common. There existed no trained salaried judiciary with a high tradition of probity. The judges were the prominent men of the community, who received nothing or very little for their services and so were generally open to the temptation of a bribe. A poor litigant had little chance of winning his case, however good. And our Lord reminded His hearers that to open their prison doors might take their uttermost farthing (Mt. 5:26, Lk. 12:59). But before the judgment seat of the guest of God the poor man has the same chance as the rich!

The picture of the guest of God is painted; God's answer to the pilgrims' inquiry is complete. And now the priest concludes with a divine promise:

He that does these things shall not be moved for ever.

If there is one thing that man dreads it is to be "moved," to have the solid base of his life crumble beneath him, to feel himself slipping, tottering. All this is included in the Hebrew word. What he wants is security, feet firm upon a rock. And that, the blessing says, shall be his as long as he lives—if he be admitted to God's peace.

Thus the pilgrims pass through the temple gate.

What now can we say of the man who composed this little Liturgy? It is quite plain what he thinks to be the essence of religion. Doubtless one may charge him with one-sidedness. As we have seen, he says nothing of man's duty to God. Again, in portraying man's duty to man it is only in his first summing up that he speaks of positive virtues; the following details are all put negatively. Nor does he give any clearly marked place to the quality of lovingkindness which stands out so prominently in the summaries of Hosea and Micah.

Another criticism, voiced by several commentators, is that he says nothing of human weakness. After so vigorous an idealization of the guest of God one might expect the misgiving to arise: But who can fulfil it? Here, says Staerk, his Psalm falls below the purity and loftiness of evangelical religion. It ignores the "law of sin" in the natural man.

When however we look deeply we see that his omissions are more apparent than real. Certainly he believes that man must worship and love God. Even the ceremonial side of religion cannot be indifferent to him for is he not composing a Liturgy to be used by those about to enter the temple and participate in its sacrifices? As for his negations, who can read them without feeling that they have a most positive ring? There is nothing negative about the man whom he portrays! Nor is lovingkindness absent, though its name is not spoken. A warm humannness pervades his picture, a genuine interest in people and a desire to help which is nothing else than love. Neither would he deny man's inability to attain the ideal without divine help, any more than our Lord denied it when He said: "Every one that heareth these sayings of mine and doeth them, shall be likened unto a wise man, who built his house upon the rock" (Mt. 7:24, Lk. 6:47 f.). Indeed, this conclusion of the Sermon on the Mount may well contain an echo of his Psalm, especially its final promise.

No, his one-sidedness is not due to any poverty of religious life but to a desire to drive home a single great truth. The man whom God admits to His holy hill is the man of integrity, justice and truth—a truth that has nothing superficial about it for its seat is the heart. Our Psalmist is not describing what we call a "saint," a specially consecrated "man of God," a heroic leader sent on a great mission, but a plain everyday man whom one can trust because one knows that there are certain things that he will not do. In the very simplicity and modesty of its idea his Psalm possesses its peculiar strength.

Thus the study of our Thirty Psalmists, which began with the splendor of God set upon the heavens and man crowned with glory and honor, having traversed sunlit heights and dark valleys of man's life with God, comes to rest in the well-trodden paths of man's duty to man, whose fulfilment alone opens the gate to the divine presence.

As we close it may be well for us to consider again for a moment our Psalmist's word *"for ever."* We have often been at pains to remind ourselves that where it occurs in the Psalter it must (except in a few possible instances) be limited to man's earthly life; and we have also kept before us the fact that thus limited it introduces a massive element of uncertainty into the promises with which it is bound up. For again and again it happens that "he who does these things" *is* "moved"; his peace is broken and cannot be rebuilt. In real life Job's story does not always have a happy ending.

But looked at in their wider setting the promises of our Psalmist and his fellows regain the aspect of reliability. For through the Psalter we hear the heart-beat of a faith that transcends the life of the individual, a faith in God who is man's dwelling-place from generation to generation (Ps. 90:1). And this abiding God has created a universe in which righteousness is at home, in which nothing else than righteousness *is* at home. It is a fact then that "these things" cannot be "moved," however they may be obstructed or obscured by other things which are contrary to the will of God. And so in a deeper sense (quite apart from the accidents and calamities of earthly life) he who does them cannot be moved. It is this basic confidence that the Psalmists express. We are therefore not wrong when, reading their Psalms in the illumination of that immortality which Christ has brought to light, we catch the tones of eternity. "The world passeth away, and the lust thereof: but he that doeth the will of God abideth for ever." (I John 2:17.)

# SOME CONCLUDING REFLECTIONS

Now that we have brought our study of the Thirty Psalmists to a close, we may pause for a few thoughts upon their religion, especially as it applies to our own needs.

## The Religion of the Psalmists [1]

What we meet in the Psalter is a great company of individual Israelites, each of whom has uttered something about God and man. We cannot expect to find all these authors, in all their many moods and situations, thinking precisely the same thoughts about God. Moreover, in making our selection we have largely passed by some strains—nationalism, censoriousness, vindictiveness, self-complacency—which have ceased to have value or actually offend. And yet there are certain positive religious ideas and attitudes that run with surprising consistency throughout the entire book.

In the Psalter the individual soul deals in its own right with God. If the Prophets merged the individual into the nation, we may say that the Psalmists give tongue to the thoughts and experiences of the personal religious life. To them, God is intensely personal, a *Thou* with whom the *I* has intercourse. Psalms 22, 32, 73, and 116 are good examples.

The Psalmists regard Yahweh as the only God. Like the Prophets they were monotheists. Before Him "all the gods of the people are idols; but Yahweh made the heavens" (96:5). He shapes the course of history (75:7, 105, 106). Man cannot escape from Him (139:1-18).

To the Psalmists, Yahweh is a God of love. They have much

[1] With slight changes and additions, this section summarizes the last part of Fleming James's chapter "The Wise Men and the Psalmists," in *The Beginnings of Our Religion*, ed. by F. C. Grant (New York: Macmillan, 1934). Used by permission of the publisher. (Ed.)

to say of the divine wrath—as had the Prophets—but this is only a passing phase of His operations; He begins and ends in love (23:1f., 30:5, 73:25f., 91:1).

The Psalmists believe that Yahweh requires righteousness more than ritual. When they ask what God demands of men, they agree in the main with the Prophets (15:1f., 40:6ff., 51:17, 141:2, *cf.* I Sam. 15:22, Amos 5:21-24, Hos. 6:6, Isa. 1:11-17, Mic. 6:8, Jer. 7:4-15). Yet they have an abiding love of the temple worship that rises again and again to the height of passion (42:1, 43:3f., 84:10), and speak constantly of paying their vows (116:12-19) and of keeping His Law, which is perfect (19:7ff., 119:131, 147:19f.).

The Psalmists believed that both the good and the evil are adequately recompensed in this life. They were quite at one with the Wise Men, therefore, as to retribution. Psalm 1 strikes this note at the very beginning of the Psalter, and it continues to the end, though experience frequently contradicts the dogma (73:2f., 13f.). One effect of this view was that it led some Psalmists to exult in the contemplation of the fate about to overtake the wicked. But it must be remembered that these "Imprecatory Psalms" are not concerned so much for personal vengeance as for the carrying out of the principle of God's justice.

The Psalter pictures all men as the future worshippers of Yahweh. It saw, through eyes of faith, the day coming when all the ends of the earth would turn to Yahweh, and it invites all to share the God whom the Hebrew saints find so good (96:7-10, 97:1, 6, 100, 145:15-20, 150).

For the most part the Psalmists did not expect happiness after death. When a man dies, they thought, a sort of shadow of himself descends to Sheol—a vast cavern beneath the ground —where it continues a feeble, empty existence. In this domain of darkness there is no distinction of good and bad, no reward or punishment, but only forgetfulness (39:13). However, glimpses of a life after death are, perhaps, given in 16:10f., 17:15, and 49:15, and certainly by the writer of Ps. 73 (*cf.* v. 24).

## WHAT THE PSALMISTS CAN TEACH US

This company of saints, whose passionate outpourings to God we ourselves hear and repeat, can teach us much that is good and abiding.

For one thing, they are more *religious* than most of us. We may see more clearly in a number of respects than they; but when it comes to the life with God, they are miles beyond us. To them God is more real, more personal, more the center of everything. They know better how to pray. Their enthusiasm is more burning. They are the masters, we the pupils.

Their religious life is astonishingly well rounded. On the one hand they give utterance to the experience of the soul in its apartness. Yet on the other hand this individual religion finds its home in a *church*. They are not really solitary, however they may at times bewail their loneliness. They belong to a beloved community, and their highest joy is to take part in its common experience and worship. In fact, the religious fellowship they enjoy is something we might well try to build up in the Christian Church. Thus they supply a needed norm, drawing us away both from over-individualism and from a one-sided stressing of the Church to the minimizing of the individual.

Again, this individual and corporate religious life of the Psalmists is forced to sustain itself in a hostile environment. From the first Psalmist onward we hear continually of the "ungodly." These saints of the Psalter must struggle against a prevailing worldliness and unbelief. Here we meet them on familiar ground as our comrades in an eternal warfare.

Finally, they are like us in that they are not part of a new movement. How different their age from that of the New Testament, when a fresh world-conquering enterprise is afoot and the commonest disciple feels its power! In the Psalmists' day, Israel's religion is already old. Many apparently think that it is about played out. It has been in the world a long time, and has seemed to accomplish little. Their Post-Exilic period is a "day of small things" (Zech. 4:10). For all the Psalmists' extravagant utterances as to its magnitude, their

Israel comprises but a handful of people. And even in Israel, religion is not particularly effective. Yet these men prove that, in spite of its seeming decrepitude, Israel's religion can take hold of their lives and make them new; and thus remade they pour into the corporate worship of the Church a fresh enthusiasm which sweeps all before it. Nor do they ever doubt that the future of mankind belongs to their God.

The same thing is taking place, though in soberer fashion, in contemporary Christianity. When we incline to overlook it, the authors of these spiritual classics may help us to remember and take heart.

If [2] the Prophets showed us how to preach righteousness, it is the Psalmists of Israel who have taught us how to pray, to praise, and to meditate upon God. Their utterances passed over into the Christian Church so completely that for ages Christians have sung them as the melodies their own hearts would fain make; and today we often bind them in one volume with the New Testament as our best *Vade Mecum* for life's pilgrimage.

[2] *Ibid.*, p. 76.

# SELECTED BIBLIOGRAPHY[1]

1. Works that were chiefly used in the preparation of the original edition of this book.

Barnes, W. E., *The Psalms*, 2 vols. (Westminster Commentary), London, 1931.

Bertholet, A., *Die Psalmen (Die Heilige Schrift des Alten Testaments,* 4th ed.), Tübingen, 1923.

Davies, T. W., *Psalms 73–150* (New Century Bible), New York, 1906.

Davison, W. T., *Psalms 1–72* (New Century Bible), New York, n. d.

Duhm, B., *Die Psalmen,* Freiburg, 1899.

Gowen, H. H., *The Psalms,* Milwaukee, 1929.

Gunkel, H., *Die Psalmen,* Göttingen, 1926.

———, *Einleitung in die Psalmen,* Göttingen, 1933. Completed by Joachim Begrich after the author's death.

Herkenne, H., *Das Buch der Psalmen,* Bonn, 1936.

Kirkpatrick, A. F., *The Book of Psalms* (Cambridge Bible), Cambridge, 1902.

Kittel, R., *Die Psalmen,* 4th ed., Leipzig, 1922.

Leslie, E. A., *Psalms 1–72 (Abingdon Bible Commentary),* Cincinnati, 1929.

McFayden, J. E., *The Psalms in Modern Speech,* 2nd ed., London, n. d.

McNeile, A. H., *The Psalms (New Commentary on Holy Scripture,* ed. by Gore), New York, 1927.

Moffatt, J., *The Old Testament, A New Translation,* Vol. II, New York, 1925.

Schmidt, H., *Die Psalmen,* Tübingen, 1934.

Shelton, W. A., *Psalms 73–150 (Abingdon Bible Commentary),* Cincinnati, 1929.

Smith, J. M. P., *The Psalms Translated,* Chicago, 1926.

Staerk, W., *Lyrik (Psalmen, Hoheslied und Verwandtes* in *Die Schriften des Alten Testaments),* 2nd ed., Göttingen, 1920.

2. Other studies, old and new.

Baethgen, F., *Die Psalmen,* 3rd ed., Göttingen, 1904.

Barth, C., *Die Errettung vom Tode in den individuellen Klage- und Dankliedern des Alten Testaments,* Basel, 1947.

[1] See Editor's Foreword.

Briggs, C. A., *The Book of Psalms*, 2 vols. (International Critical Commentary), New York, 1906.

Crim, K. R., *The Royal Psalms*, Richmond, 1962.

Gunkel, H., *The Religion of the Psalms* (in *What Remains of the Old Testament*, trans. by A. K. Dallas), New York, 1928.

——, *Ausgewählte Psalmen*, Göttingen, 1917.

Hempel, J., "Psalms, Book of" (in *The Interpreter's Dictionary of the Bible*), New York, 1962.

Johnson, A. R., *Sacral Kingship in Ancient Israel*, Cardiff, 1955.

——, "The Psalms" (in *The Old Testament and Modern Study*, ed. by H. H. Rowley), London, 1951.

Kalt, E. (ed.), *Herder's Commentary on the Psalms*, Westminster, 1961.

Kissane, E. J., *The Book of Psalms*, Vol. I, Westminster, 1953ff.

König, E., *Die Psalmen*, Gütersloh, 1927.

Kraus, H. J., *Gottesdienst in Israel*, Munich, 1954.

——, *Psalmen*, 2 vols. (*Biblischer Kommentar*), Neukirchen, 1958ff.

Lamb, J. A., *The Psalms in Christian Worship*, London, 1962.

Lamparter, Helmut, *Das Buch der Psalmen*, 2 vols. (*Die Botschaft des Alten Testaments*) Stuttgart, 1959–61.

Leslie, E. A., *The Psalms*, Nashville, 1949.

Löhr, M., *Psalmenstudien*, Berlin, 1922.

Mowinckel, S., "Psalm Criticism between 1900 and 1935" (in *Vetus Testamentum* 5, 1953), pp. 13–33.

——, *Psalmenstudien I–VI*, Kristiana, 1921–24.

——, *The Psalms in Israel's Worship*, 2 vols. (trans. by D. R. Ap-Thomas), Oxford, 1962. See especially the extensive bibliography.

Oesterley, W. O. E., *A Fresh Approach to the Psalms*, New York, 1937.

——, *The Psalms*, 2 vols., London, 1939.

Paterson, J., *The Praises of Israel*, New York, 1950.

Peters, J. P., *The Psalms as Liturgies*, New York, 1922.

Ringgren, H., *The Faith of the Psalmists*, Philadelphia, 1963.

Scott, R. B. Y., *The Psalms as Christian Praise*, London, 1959.

Simpson, D. C. (ed.), *The Psalmists*, Oxford, 1926.

Snaith, N. H., *Hymns of the Temple*, London, 1951.

Taylor, C. L., *Let the Psalms Speak*, Greenwich, 1961.

Terrien, S. L., *The Psalms and Their Meaning for Today*, New York, 1952.

Weiser, A., *The Psalms* (The Old Testament Library), Philadelphia, 1962.

Westermann, C., *Das Loben Gottes in den Psalmen*, Göttingen, 1954.

Widengren, G., *The Accadian and Hebrew Psalms of Lamentation*, Stockholm, 1937.

# CROSS-REFERENCES
## TO GUNKEL'S *EINLEITUNG*

Among the chief values of this book is its extensive and accurate presentation in English of the substance of Gunkel's Type-study. In the original edition of *Thirty Psalmists*, Dr. James made it absolutely clear (see especially p. 247) that he had conducted no independent research in this field of *Gattungsforschung*, but was content to use and pass on the results of Gunkel's work, as given in his monumental *Einleitung in die Psalmen.*

In the following table, cross-references are given from this revised edition of *Thirty Psalmists* to the pertinent sections of the *Einleitung,* from which the material was drawn.

| *James* | *Gunkel-Begrich* |
|---|---|
| pp. xxiff. | pp. 1-31 |
| 15ff. | 32ff. |
| 61f. | 80ff. |
| 78ff. | 94ff. |
| 85ff. | 117ff. |
| 97ff. | 172ff. |
| 141f. | 254ff. |
| 163ff. | 265ff. |
| 187ff. | 381ff. |
| 213ff. | 140ff. |
| 225ff. | 323ff. |
| 236ff. | 404ff. |

# INDEX OF PSALMS STUDIED IN THIS BOOK